The Bunker

Dedications & Acknowledgements

Zach for drawing the front cover
Ana for the Spanish translation
Mom for proofreading
Jessica for the back cover

The Bunker

By Alexander Bellissimo

September 30, 2031
Health Report Log-04
Doctor Linda Marie
Subject: The first death

    "This is Doctor Marie reporting that our oldest citizen, Harry Jenkins, has passed away today due to cardiac arrest. Unfortunately, this marks our first death, only a week into being down here. It was hardly surprising, given his advanced age and history of heart problems. First a case of liver failure, and now this? I know the whole 'lottery' thing is bullshit, but whoever's in charge of it isn't even screening for health? I'm starting to think maybe it *was* randomly selected. Ahem, anyways. Officially, Barry Eldren is now our oldest living citizen. On the lighter side, Mary and Billy Lovell have just informed me that they are a few months pregnant. That's all I have to report for now."

End of log.

President Alan Berkoff

Vice President Eustace Toaden

Chief Researcher Dr. William Harrack

Chief Physician Dr. Linda Marie

Head of Security James House

Security Force (20):

Roy Bant - Joshua Black - Robert Cansky - Winston Castor - Peter Corrad - Lucille Desin - Jonathan Dinlum - Richard Farkass - Jacob Faunt - Aranai Fielding - Kate Finn - John House - Barney Keeling - Roberta Kisk - Jane McVellion - Joseph Nine - Scott Samona - Catherine Vilner - Gordon Yackit - Zachary Zyz

Citizens (90):

Bing Abbot - Ann Akai - Rose Anderson - Jacob Ardune - Robert Beaner - Sarah Barnes - Cherry Beau - Dylan Beecut - Margaret Belcher - Andrew Bigelow - Alfonzo Bogardanzi - Daniel Butler - Marino Cantopus - Booker Cooper - John Dash - Jet Dashel - Mark DeFrana - Samuel Dunkard - Barry Eldren - Jeremy Finickle - Candice Finnell - Haiten Fish - Henry Flagelmeier - Maxwell Geck - Dr. Phillip Genson - Marta Girasol - Casey Goodwill - Chandler Haal - Ernest Handler - Garrison Hartford - Alfred Hatton - John Heegan - Mario Henderson - Nancy House - William House - Conrad Jackman - Vincent Jax - ~~Harry Jenkins~~

[DECEASED] - Leyna Kase - Martin Kievan - Wanda Lamon - King Liardi - William Lovell - Mary Lovell - Geoffrey Lowell - River Maple - Oliver Markus - Delegan McHarvan - Diana Mint - Gilbert Nose - Mickey November - Conor O'Reilly - Patrick Peaskill - Jim Penn - Jonathan Peterson - Angel Puer - Richard Reel - Captain Rex - Doug Roberts - Hank Rockell - Dishtowel Sacks - Jillian Sampson - Nadia Schwartz - Argus Scott - Jeremiah Shoostand - Robert Simpson - Howard Skittering - Jaime Slewdjack - Toby Smalls - Harold Smidt - Janet Smith - Nicolas Smithson - Meegan Spoon - Sean Tilling - Gary Tills - Barnaby Tob - Colin Vacett - Tia Valentine - Amelia Vanisha - Anthony Weitson - Hannah Welt - Dean Wentell - Theodore Weston - Andrew Wicker - Peach Williamson - Dell Willis - Percy Winkle - Denger Woof - Laney Youth - Johnson Zip

Bunker Layout

The bunker was built into a remote Nevada mountain range, a spot that was very unlikely to attract attention in the event of diplomatic failure. Although the entire bunker was reinforced with steel, the designers had made a distinct choice to replace much of the removed rock along the ceiling, walls, and ground, even sculpting all materials and features out of it, barring a few exceptions. The overhead lights, powered by a self-sustaining generator in an adjacent cavern, cast powerful light across the entire bunker, illuminating everything in their blue-white glow. However, being set twenty meters above all else gave them a distant feel that left everything seeming to be in a perpetual state of dusk. This was not helped by the fact that all of the rock that lined the entirety of the bunker was of a dark grey color. A loudspeaker system was set up throughout the bunker.

As for the buildings themselves, many seemed to have been built into the ground itself, many buildings melding seamlessly with it. Most of the bunker was occupied by 4 rows of small houses, consisting of only a living/bedroom hybrid, and a bathroom. Every other house faced the same way, and each had a single glass window in the front. Next to the door of each house was a number and the name of the current resident of the house. There were disposal hatches in every house that led to a gigantic, industrial incinerator that was adjacent to the main bunker. The hatches opened from the top, and didn't open further than forty five degrees, and automatically snapped shut when not being held open. In each living room/bedroom combo, there was a single bed off to the side which had been built into the wall. Next to the bed, there was a desk with a standard lamp built into the back wall. Right next to the desk was the garbage chute. There was a grey, metal chair in front of the desk. There were a total of one hundred and twenty houses, despite the bunker only having one hundred fifteen residents. The rows of houses extended all the way to the very back of the bunker. Houses were distributed on basis of last name, leaving some with a long walk each day. Each house was roughly three and a half meters tall.

A large area in front of the rows of houses was the common and dining area. It was filled with numerous tables and benches, most of which were also built into the ground, as were the houses. There were automated food dispensers evenly spaced throughout the tables. The dispensers also handed out metal forks, spoons, and knives, as well as large plastic trays. On the other side of each dispenser was a receptacle for the utensils and trays that automatically washed them and redistributed them.

On the other side of the dining area from was the security station, a large building meant for housing the security force, as well as many of the supplies for the bunker. The supplies were stashed in multiple large storage rooms. The storage room contained everything from mundane folding chairs to highly experimental military supplies provided by the bunker's benefactor. There were also twenty five holdings cells in the back, as well as an interrogation room. The front area of the security station was fashioned like a locker room, with short rows of lockers and benches in between them. The station was one of the only buildings not sculpted from rock, but instead was made of steel, even having a chainlink fence wrapping around it, only letting those by with the proper password.

In the back of the security station, there was an elevator, which could only be unlocked with a second password. It led straight up to the rather fascinating structure built into the ceiling above the station. Dubbed the "High Rise," the building had seemingly been sculpted into the ceiling. While it appeared to be made from the same as most of the other buildings in the bunker, it was shaped like the base of a cone on one side, and was flat on the other side. On the cone shaped side, there were large windows looking out in every direct across the bunker. The exception to the field of view was behind the elevator and security station, but the only thing in that direction was the massive door to the bunker. The common and housing areas were fully exposed for the viewing pleasure of anyone in the High Rise. Additionally, in stark contrast to the rest of the bunker, with it's greys and virtually nothing else, the High Rise was furnished with exquisite decor, almost all of which was bright and vibrant. Many red and gold armchairs were in no shortage, as well as large rugs with abstract patterns covering the floor. On one of these carpets, surrounded by some of the armchairs and a bright red sofa, was a glass table with elaborately welded metal legs. While the windows took up most of the walls inside the High Rise, the walls on the side of the elevator were made with a classic wood panelling, stopping halfway to the ceiling and being replaced with an almost tacky green wallpaper. A large, wooden conference table was also set up closer to the windows than the glass table, and had six official looking swivel chairs surrounding it. There were also a few large terminals built into the wall, controlling many functions of the bunker, including the public address system and meal distribution, if it was not set to automatic.

Back down on the ground, two more metal buildings flanked the security station, though neither was surrounded by the same fence. To the left of the station was Dr. Harrack's laboratory, where all of his scientific supplies, and usually himself, were kept. To the right was Dr. Marie's office, open to anyone seeking medical attention. Both buildings were nearly identical, mirror images of each other, with the only differences being the furnishings in both. They each had a main, public room that led directly in and out of the office, and an equally large, private, back room that only Harrack and Dr. Marie were allowed to enter, in their respective offices, unless they saw fit. Each building was about five meters tall.

Harrack's front room appeared to be a normal lobby, with nothing but a receptionist-like desk, and a few chairs shoved into the corner. In the backroom, every inch of the walls were covered in shelves or cabinets stacked with multitudes of various jars, vials, and flasks. In the center of the room was a large table, not dissimilar to an operating table. However, there were leather straps at both ends of the table. Next to the table was a tall, wheeled shelf, stacked to the brim with sealed glass jars, all containing an identical white powder. Dr. Marie's front room contained a bed off in the corner, similar to one in a pediatrician's office. In the back room of her office, there was a terminal in the far wall, built into a long, sleek desk. There was a shelf filled with papers and files jutting out above the desk. In the center of the room was another operating table, missing the straps that Harrack's table had. There were shelves of various medicines lining the walls.

Off to the left of the High Rise was by far the largest singular building in the entire bunker. The benefactor's mansion measured ten meters tall. Aside from being built out of the same rock, it looked like a standard mansion. While most of the contents of the benefactor's mansion were a secret to the general public, the one thing that was known was that there was a garden in the back. The garden was using advanced artificial lighting and synthesized fertilizer. This experimental fertilizer was developed by Harrack. This was in addition to Harrack's own experiments to create nutrient-rich sustenance, directly for consumption by people. The mansion could also only be unlocked and entered with the express permission of the benefactor, and measures had been installed to make sure no unauthorized entrance would take place. The words "Winkle Enterprises," along with the infamous fireworks logo, took up most of the outside of the third floor of the building.

There was also a bar off to the left of the houses. It was about the size of three of the regular houses and had large, glass doors. Inside the building was a standard bar in the main area, and a large stage complete with red velvet curtains at the far end.

September 23, 2031

President Alan Berkoff and Vice President Eustace Toaden watched the parade of people enter the bunker. The twenty foot tall steel door was more than capable of withstanding a nuclear blast. The people entering moved slow, solemnly shuffling as if they were being led to an executioner's block. The president and vice president, along with Chief Researcher Doctor William Harrack, Chief Physician Doctor Linda Marie, and Chief of Security James House, stood together in the High Rise. They, along with the benefactor, where the only ones with access to the High Rise.

"They seem sad, don't they? I wonder why that is," VP Toaden asked. Alan nodded absent-mindedly, hardly processing his inferior's comment. The two leaders seemed to be almost opposites in appearance. Toaden was short and pudgy, was mostly bald with not one, but two large moles on his face. One on the center of his left cheek, the other on the right side of his nose.

He wore thick, large glasses, reminiscent of the 1970's, and suitably matching the wood panelling and green wallpaper.

Alan Berkoff, on the other hand, was tall and slender, with nearly jet black hair that had a natural shine to it. As Alan watched the mindless shuffling of the masses, Dr. William Harrack approached from behind him, stopping next to his old friend to gaze out the window with him.

"So many people. So much potential. Just imagine the-" Alan cleared his throat, interrupting Dr. Harrack. Harrack, confused for a moment, glanced at Alan, who was already looking at the chief physician as she was listening to them with a furrowed brow.

"I do hope you realize those are actual people down there. I've heard about your unauthorized human experiments in the past," Dr. Linda Marie said sternly.

"The door hasn't even closed, and you're already talking about experiments. We still have the rest of our lives down here, so don't rush," Alan said, never removing the window from view. His mind was preoccupied. Someone was missing...

Before Alan could finish the thought, he elevator door behind them opened, and the whole group turned around. The man was dressed in a white suit with a golden tie. He was remarkably made up, and seemed quite out of place, even for the exclusive High Rise. He surveyed the room for a quiet moment before the chief of security approached him.

"Excuse me, but how did you manage to get in here?" James House asked.

"Let him pass, Jim. I'm sure you know who Percy Winkle is, correct?" Alan stated.

"James. And my apologies, Mr. Winkle," James said, stepping to the side. Percy turned to Alan, Toaden, and Dr. Harrack. He approached the small group and cleared his throat.

"Right, well, I should return to my lab and make sure I have everything I'll need," Dr. Harrack said, heading for the elevator. As Harrack left the room, Percy cleared his throat again.

Dr. Marie and James both took the hint and excused themselves, though neither seemed particularly willing to leave. Still, they both had important business to attend to.

"I'm surprised you came in person," Alan said to Percy.

"Well, without my funding, this project would still be in the development stage. You know how the government is. I'm here to make sure that my money was not wasted. Besides, if nuclear war really is around the corner, then I don't want to be caught in the middle of it," Percy responded.

"I can assure you I will do everything in my power to have complete control over the situation," Alan promised, saluting the man. Percy gave him a cursory glance, dismissed the gesture.

"I can only hope," Percy said, pulling one of the swivel chairs up to the window, sitting down and looking out. As he watched the citizens bring their belongings into their new houses, Toaden pulled Alan off to the side, away from Percy.

"I don't think it's a good idea to have him up here," Toaden whispered to Alan.

"Relax. He funded this bunker and I've known him for a while. He contributed to my campaign. I trust him. Besides, if he causes any trouble we can just have him detained. Or executed," Alan said with a laugh. Toaden gave him a suspicious glance.

"We shouldn't even joke about abusing our power. Our responsibility is to the American people," Toaden said. Alan covered his disgust with more laughter, almost starting to sound maniacal.

*   *   *

Within a few hours, all of the citizens had moved into their new homes and were trying their best to settle into the new home. Many were also sitting in the dining area. Despite all the citizens were now in the bunker, the door remained open. It had been decided that these people deserved one final full meal, before they started on the multiple centuries' worth of food stored in Percy's mansion, along with his garden and Harrack's nutrient experiments. Trays of turkey, and chicken, and roast beef, dozens of different kinds of fish, as well as many sides including almost every kind of steamed vegetable and potatoes.

DT Sacks sat at one of the tables, while patiently waiting for the announcement to begin eating, he thought about how he had gotten to this point in his life. His mind eventually drifted to how he, likely with everyone else, would die here. DT wasn't particularly bothered by this thought, though. After all, he had no reason left to live, himself. He sighed and wished that someone else had been selected in his place. But that's just how the lottery went.

As he continued to let his mind drift in absent thought, he remembered when he was much younger. He had come from a very wealthy family. Neither of his parents had any siblings, and DT was the only child they ever had. DT had been a rebellious child, which was most likely due to his parents trying to micromanage his life.

When they had both suddenly died in a car accident when he was eighteen, he was curious as to the extent of his new freedom, after properly mourning, of course. After legally changing his name to Dishtowel Sacks, just to see if he could, he realized he could do anything he wanted. He began participating in dangerous and stupid stunts, burning through money like it was nothing. Despite his parents being of considerable wealth, it didn't take long for DT to piss away most of his inheritance. Once the money was gone, he was abandoned by all of his supposed friends. All alone in the world, with nothing left, he entered a state of depression. This depression had persisted until the day he had received the letter stating he had been randomly selected by the government to help America march forth, even in the event of nuclear winter. Now, miles below a mountain, he pondered his reasons for living.

While he was letting these thoughts bounce around in his head, two men sat down directly across from him, pulling him back into reality.

"Huh? What are you doing?" DT asked, as though he was in a daze.

"We're sorry to bother you, but we just wanted to sit down to eat," one of the men stated.

"Yeah, and we noticed you had plenty of room at your table. Besides, if we're all gonna spend the rest of our lives down here, we might as well get to know each other!" the second man gleefully exclaimed. DT looked at him. He was rather short, barely above five feet tall. He had dirty blonde hair and bright blue eyes. "My name is Toby, by the way. Toby Smalls." He reached his hand out. DT took it and limply moved his arm. Toby didn't seem to notice his weak handshake, though.

"I'm Howard Skittering," the first man said, also reaching his hand out. DT gave it the same limp shake, but Howard put in the same amount of enthusiasm.

Toby took a small bite out of a turkey sandwich. DT didn't remember hearing the announcement for food to be served. "What's your name?"

"Just, uh, call me DT," DT said, offering a weak smile.

DT got up and returned with food a few moments later. A fourth man was now sitting at the table.

"Oh, hi," the new man said.

"Hi," DT said, sitting down.

"I'm Tony Weitson. What's your name?" the man said.

"Just call me DT," DT said, beginning to eat his food.

"Nice to meet you," Tony said, too busy with his food to offer a handshake to DT. DT didn't mind.

The four men then all sat together, eating and passing idle conversation.

*   *   *

Meanwhile, only a few tables away, James, Nancy, John, and Bill House sat together, eating lunch themselves. James and John were wearing their security uniforms with Nancy and Bill in their casual clothes.

"Enjoying the security force so far?" Nancy asked John with a chuckle.

"I mean, nothing has really happened yet, but yeah. I guess so," John answered. He turned to James. "Thanks for getting me on the security force."

"Anything for my little brother," James said, playfully ruffling John's hair.

"You do realize Bill is the little one here, right?" John responded, smacking away James' hand.

Bill just pouted and grumbled.

"Oh, quiet. Can't we just have fun without acting like idiots?" Nancy said sternly. John and James quieted down respectfully.

"Well, we *are* here to celebrate the House siblings!" James said, raising his glass for a toast. John also raised his and Nancy rolled her eyes.

"Doesn't feel like we have much to celebrate," Bill grumbled.

"Well, your brother is head of security down here. It's a good enough reason to celebrate with my family to me," Nancy said, raising her glass. Bill sighed and begrudgingly raised his glass.

*　　*　　*

That night, shortly after dinner, John Dash stood in front of the bunker door, now closed. All he could think about was how he was trapped in this underground prison. As he thought about it, he was suddenly aware that another figure had stepped up next to him. He turned to the figure.

"*¿Es bastante abrumador, verdad?*" she asked. Dash looked at her.

"I'm sorry?" he asked.

"Oh, my bad," the woman said. "I was just saying it's a lot to process. Do you think there's ever a chance that we could leave?"

"As soon as all those politicians settle their differences and decide not to nuke each other, yeah. We'll get out."

She sighed. "And what if they don't?"

"Supposedly, this bunker will keep us safe. Though, honestly, I'd rather take my chances out there than in here."

"Really? Why?"

"Because of this 'President' Berkoff. I'm sure you've heard of him. Retired from politics due to a career-ruining scandal. If it weren't for him, we might not even need this bunker in the first place," Dash answered.

"How did he even get in here in the first place?"

"Percy Winkle."

"Well, the explains the massive Winkle Enterprises building down here. What's the connection?"

"Winkle was Berkoff's biggest contributor before Berkoff disgraced himself and this country. He only got off because of Winkle's influence. And then Winkle offered to help with the bunker, he did so on the condition Berkoff be in charge. Obviously, the government didn't immediately agree, but many negotiations later the figured out some sort of compromise. I don't know the exact details, though."

"That must've been after I got fired."

"Fired from what?"

"I used to be an architect working on this bunker. But then I got fired not too long into work on the project." She sighed again. "Not to worry you, but someone should know. This place has a ton of structural flaws. At least it did when I was working on it. I'm sure they managed to fix them, but still..."

"I'm sure."

"Name's Marta Girasol. *Mucho gusto*," she held her hand out to him.

"John Dash." He shook her hand.

"How do you know so much about Winkle and Berkoff?"

"I'll explain it some other time. I know someone who was behind of a lot of the closed doors that happened to get this bunker built," Dash said.

"*Ya veo*," Marta said thoughtfully.

"I should be heading to bed. Our new lives start tomorrow, after all," Dash said. Marta nodded in agreement, and the two walked back to their houses.

September 24, 2031

As Alan stood alone in the High Rise, staring out into the bunker, he noticed Toaden down below. He was taking a survey with James and two other members of the security force. The door opened behind Alan and Harrack stepped in. Alan glanced over his shoulder to look at him, then returned his attention to the window.

"Was there something you wanted, Will?" Alan asked.

"I was just coming up here to follow up about what you said yesterday. I know you told me to hold off on my experiments, but I am not a fan of wasting time," Harrack said bluntly. Alan let out a frustrated sigh.

"For a leading scientist, you sure are an idiot," Alan snapped impatiently. Harrack frowned, otherwise seeming unfazed. "It's far too early. Wait a few weeks, I'll see what my agent discovers. We'll find someone who won't be missed, don't worry. Then you can start your experiments. Until then, why don't you focus on that nutrient research you promised the government?"

"I can have that done before the week is over. It's not that difficult, you know. I just don't want to waste too much time in between that and my advanced experiments."

Alan leered at him. Harrack sighed, defeated, then turned to leave. As he reached the door and pressed the button, he suddenly stopped. "Agent?"

"Don't worry about it. You have more important business, after all, don't you?"

Harrack wanted to ask more, but agreed he had better things to do and left.

*   *   *

"... and that's how we got the truck on the roof," Tony Weitson finished his story. Howard Skittering laughed, but Toby Smalls just gave Tony a mildly concerned stare. They were just finishing lunch.

"Are you sure it was a good idea to drink *that* much alcohol?" Toby asked.

Before Tony could answer, DT Sacks sat down at the table with a wrapped up sandwich.

"Hey, you missed a great story," Howard said.

"Oh," DT said softly.

"It's okay, I have plenty more," Tony said. As Tony continued talking about his drunken exploits, Howard's entertainment, Toby's concern, and DT's indifference only seemed to grow.

*   *   *

Meanwhile, at the same time, Marta Girasol had managed to find John Dash sitting by his lonesome. Sitting down next to him, she began eating.

"Hey. I didn't see you at breakfast. I was almost starting to think you were a dream," Marta said with a smile.

"I sleep late," Dash lied. He had never gone to sleep at all, instead choosing to listen to old recordings he brought down with him. He preferred those to actual people. He had very little

15

social interaction growing up, being homeschooled and surrounded by only his mother and her colleagues, distinguished scientists of multiple different disciplines. This included his mother, herself.

While this proved great for his education, his mother had only ever taught him science, psychology, and other hard skills, it had also left his social growth stagnant, and he often represented a human machine. While he normally didn't care much for human company, he didn't mind the company of Marta. She appeared smart and nice enough, and was likely to be able to hold an intellectual conversation. She certainly didn't seem to mind his company, regardless. As the two talked, Dash considered his earlier stance of admonishing his mother for getting him into the bunker in the first place.

*   *   *

John Dash was not the only one who had missed breakfast. Jim Penn had spent the entire morning curled up in pain in his bed. During lunch, he decided to go see Dr. Linda Marie.

She was almost startled when the soft chime went off, indicative of someone entering the building. As she emerged from the back room, she saw Jim Penn waiting patiently.

"How can I help you?" Dr. Marie asked kindly. She smiled warmly at him. He attempted to smile back, but was interrupted by an escaping groan.

"My stomach is in a lot of pain. I can't eat, and I threw up two times last night," Jim Penn answered painfully.

"Alright, I'll take a look. Please sit on the bed," Dr. Marie said, turning away to sit down at a computer. Jim Penn hopped onto the patient bed, glancing nervously at the operating table, which took up the center of the room.

Dr. Marie noticed his discomfort. "Don't worry, i seriously doubt we'll need to use that thing anytime soon," she lightly chuckled. After running a few simple tests, she was relatively confident in her findings. "It's a stomach bug. You'll to feel crummy for a week or two, but it'll pass. I would give you antibiotics, but we need to save as much medicine as we can. I'm sure you understand, Mr. Penn."

"Please, call me Jim," Jim Penn said. He then thanked Dr. Marie, and took his leave from her office. He didn't feel any better, but he knew there wasn't anything else to be done. On his way out, he practically bumped right into a petite woman. She was under five foot, and had shimmering golden hair that was almost silver. She was standing outside the medical office, and quickly walked away. "Huh, weird." Jim Penn then headed back to his house.

*   *   *

John Dash and Marta Girasol were idly chatting during dinner when Toby Smalls sat down at their table. They stopped talking and turned their attention to him. They were soon joined by DT Sacks, Tony Weitson, and Howard Skittering.

"Mind if we sit here?" Toby asked.

"No, of course not," Marta said gleefully, before Dash had a chance to object.

"Thank you. My name's Toby. This is Howard, DT, and Tony."

Marta then introduced herself and Dash. Dash and DT stayed quiet as the other four idly chatted.

"I'd just like to get to know everyone. After all, we're all that we're ever gonna have," Toby said with a smile, only a hint of sorrow escaping at the sentiment.

"Well, it's more than I had on the outside world," DT said depressingly, before letting out a depressing sigh.

"Could ya lighten up a bit?" Howard snarked.

"Hey, just so long as they got booze, I don't see anything in my life changing," Tony said, raising a glass of water. The others gave him a short stare, then continued.

"Well, I can't say I don't miss my family. But I'm looking forward to seeing where this chapter in my life takes me!" Toby said, keeping his smile.

"Yeah, it was pretty hard to leave my family behind," Marta agreed. "What about you guys? Miss your families?"

"Eh, I was never really too close with my family. I can't say I *don't* miss 'em, but I wouldn't have passed up my chance to not die to stay with them. Even if I'm not really a fan of confined spaces," Howard said.

"Can barely remember my parents," Tony said, gently swaying back and forth. He let out a short burp.

"Are you drunk?" Dash asked with faint apprehension.

Tony burped again and smiled. "Only as drunk as five beers can get ya!" He then proceeded to fall of the seat onto the floor. Howard got up to help him, but got his leg caught on the table and fell on the ground, himself.

"Should we get him to the doctor, or..?" Marta asked, unsure.

"This is why I avoid people," Dash muttered under his breath.

DT sighed, stood up, walked over to Tony, and pulled him up, slinging Tony's arm over his shoulder. "I'll take him to the doctor. See you guys later?"

"Um, alright then?" Howard said. DT nodded, leaving to take Tony to Dr. Marie's office.

*　　　*　　　*

After dropping Tony off at Dr. Marie's office, DT went to the bar. Despite his rebellious streak, he had never really gotten into alcohol. The taste usually disgusted him, but he figured a drink or two couldn't hurt. Only a few other people were in the bar. Al Bogardanzi and King Liardi were in the middle of a heated poker game off to the side, and Dylan Beecut was looking even more sloshed than Tony. DT ordered a drink as Toby walked into the bar. As his drink was served, Toby sat down next to him.

"Thanks for helping Tony," Toby said.

"He needs a lot more help than I can give him." DT took a sip from his glass. He instantly regretted this choice and decided not to take another sip. "What are you doing here? You don't seem like the type to drink.

"I don't. I just wanted to thank you."

"Why? It was just the right thing to do. I don't need a thanks. And even if I did, you're not the one who owes it to me," DT stated. Toby was about to say something else, but a sudden flurry of spontaneous Italian broke out at the poker game. The yelling continued until King stormed out of the bar. Al swiped all of the cards onto the floor and stormed out after King.

"Great. Another idiot's mess to clean up," remarked the bartender, Mickey November.

Dylan Deecut piped up. "Wonder what's got them so... *hic* ... worked up?"

DT was about to say something, but Dylan suddenly collapsed off of the bar stool, drooling on the floor and faintly snoring. DT sighed. "I guess I should get going soon. It's a little late." DT considered his beer glass, before pushing it back towards Mickey.

"You sure? You might miss the show," Mickey said.

"Show?" Toby asked.

Mickey indicated to a stage set into the back of the bar. The curtains were closed. However, as he said that, the curtains opened and a beautiful, young woman in an elegant, purple dress stepped onto the stage and started singing a slow song. The words were smooth, flowing like a stream.

"That's a beautiful voice," Toby said in awe.

"Never heard of Tia Valentine? She released her debut album last year. Topped out the charts. The only bit of talent in this whole damn bunker," Mickey said, emptying out and cleaning DT's glass. DT and Toby sat back and watched the show.

As Tia sang, Bill House entered the bar and sat at a table. He was shortly followed by Marta Girasol and John Dash, who took a seat by the entrance. As Bill was gulping down a drink, Mickey went over to Marta and Dash.

"How come you didn't order anything?" Marta asked Dash after Mickey had left.

"I don't drink," Dash said. Marta shrugged and drank her beer, enjoying Tia's show with everyone else. At one point Toby turned around and spotted them. Marta gave him a polite wave. Toby smiled and walked over to their table.

"Where's Howard?" he asked, sitting down. Marta shrugged again.

"Said he was going back to his house for a bit."

Standing outside the bar, gazing in through the fancy glass doors, stood a short figure with flowing gold hair. Meanwhile, Howard was curled up in the bed in his house, trying to slow his hyperventilation.

*　　*　　*

Dr. Marie finished examining Tony Weitson. He rolled off the table, not sticking the landing and falling on his face. Dr. Marie sighed and helped him to his feet.

"Thanks," he groaned.

"When was the last time you saw a doctor?" Dr. Marie asked.

"Oh, it's been a while. Maybe about five years," Tony answered. Dr. Marie sighed then gave him a few pills and a glass of water. "What's this?"

"Advil," Dr. Marie said. He swallowed the pills, leaving a little water left in the cup. "Your liver is failing." Tony choked and coughed, then turned to look at Dr. Marie. He then let out a defeated laugh and finished off his water. "It's advanced. You probably don't have much time left. I doubt longer than a month. There's not really anything I can do for you down here. We can't do a transplant."

Tony continued laughing. "You know, I was gonna turn down the offer. Refuse to show up, let someone else take my place. But then I decided maybe this would be best for me. I figured if I was isolated from it, I could quit cold turkey. I had no fucking clue there'd be a goddamn bar down here. And old habits die hard, y'know?" He paused, then sighed and looked at Dr. Marie, tears forming in his eyes. "I'm an awful person, aren't I?"

"No. You couldn't have known," Dr. Marie said, trying to comfort him.

"But I could've. I could've just seen a doctor…" The tears began flowing freely from his eyes. Dr. Marie attempted to comfort him further, but he simply pushed past her, walking out of the office. He never noticed the small figure with long, golden hair.

September 25, 2031

It wasn't until lunch the next day that Tony told his new-found friends about what Dr. Marie had told him. Breakfast had been rather quiet and uneventful, much to Dash's relief.

"The doctor, she…" Tony choked up, but let out a wavering sigh and continued. "I'm dying." He waited until the shocked expressions wore away before adding. "As good as dead."

"*Siento escuchar eso. Mis condolencias,*" Marta said.

"Wow, that sucks," Howard said.

"Yeah," Tony replied, apparently not bothered by the comment.

"What's causing it?" DT asked.

"Liver failure. Got less than a month, she said," Tony answered, sighing again. The tears were clearly welling up in his eyes.

"Well, I guess we could try to make the most of the time you have left," Toby suggested.

"Just let me die with a little dignity. I'll just lock myself in my house until it's over," Tony said, hanging his head. DT gently placed his hand on Tony's shoulder.

"Is that really how you want to go?" Toby asked sadly.

"It's his choice. Let him do what he wants," Howard said.

"*Oh, vamos!* You can't just mope around, feeling sorry for yourself!" Marta said.

"I guess you're not wrong..." Tony sighed. "But what can I do?" Lunch was just ending, and the crowd was beginning to clear out of the dining area.

"Well, let's meet up for dinner, then we can think of fun things to do!" Toby said.

"Fine. Not that there's anything to actually do down here," Tony said. He stood up, and without looking back, disappeared into the crowd heading back for their houses.

"I'd say trying to make him happy is a waste of time, but it's not like we have anything better to do," Howard said callously. Marta shot him a nasty glare. He stopped eating to return her stare. "What? Am I wrong?"

"Doesn't matter. It's the good thing to do," Marta replied resolutely.

"Wouldn't you want to spend the end of your life being happy?" Toby asked sincerely.

Dash stood up. "I don't know why you all are arguing. Just let him do as he wants. It's his life." With that, he walked away. DT sighed.

"If it makes you feel better, I think it's very noble how you're trying to help him. Even if he doesn't take the help," DT said, also getting up from the table and walking away. Toby gave a somber smile at the disappearing figure.

"Honestly," Howard said, finishing off his sandwich.

*   *   *

President Alan Berkoff watched as the lunch crowd emptied out of the dining area. He sighed and turned away from the window. Sitting in one of the big armchairs was a young woman, with familiar long, golden hair. He sat down in the chair next to hers, and she silently handed him a file.

"Thank you, Robbie," he said. She didn't react. "I know this kinda busy work is below your skill grade, but I just wanna get Will off my back so he stops bothering me." Angel tilted her head to the side ever so slightly. Alan took notice. "No, I don't want you to take him out. He still has plenty of use. And I *guess* he's a friend." Angel straightened out her head. "Trust me, I know."

It had recently dawned on him that there was unlikely to be any sort of excitement down here. He looked at the glass table, of which two stacks of detailed, personal files of every citizen of the bunker rested. One was much taller than the other. He looked back at Angel. He sighed. "I, uh, hope you don't mind your... 'accommodations.' I just like to have you close, in case I need you for something." Angel glanced over her shoulder, at the wood paneling in the corner of the room. She turned back to him and gave him a shrug. He puffed out a laugh. The orderly conduct of the citizens might make the bunker a rather boring place, but if it hadn't been for boredom, he likely never would've discovered the secret compartment built into the wall.

Without anything else to do, Alan walked over to the files on the table. Taking the top one from the much larger pile he skimmed through it, then placed it on the smaller pile in disappointment. He randomly selected one file from the middle. The front had been stamped with large, blue letters reading SECURITY FORCE. He opened it up, reading it aloud. "Jonathan Dinlum has a nervous disposition, and while appearing timid and mild, is quite capable of handling a firearm. He also has a very clear sense of morality and blah blah blah." Alan closed the file and put it on the other pile.

He then thumbed through each of the files, stopping at one to pull it out. The file had the name "Angel Puer" written on the front. "Hey, it's you," Alan said, showing the file to Angel, laughing slightly. She didn't share his sense of humor. Placing that file on the smaller pile, without even bothering to open it, he continued looking through the files. Then, as if playing a game of jenga, he gently tugged the bottom file out of the pile. Angel turned her head away to avoid looking at the upcoming catastrophe. However, it didn't happen, and Alan successfully pulled the file out.

"Zachary Zyz was a soldier... yada yada... honorably discharged... whatever." He frustrated tossed the file onto the smaller stack, steadily growing bigger. "Aren't any of these people interesting at all?" Alan slumped back in his chair, with a sigh of defeat. Angel stood up and walked over to the pile, thumbing through, herself. She didn't get very far down the pile, before sliding a file out of the stack. She opened it up and looked through it, then handed it to Alan. "What is it?" he asked curiously, sitting upright and taking the file.

"No, it can't... It's too common a name. But..." Alan said to himself, looking at the file. Almost the entire file was blank, with only a single sheet of paper, with only one sentence on it. "John Dash is the son of Dr. Barbara Dash," Alan read. He looked up from the paper and stared right at Angel, who was undeniably thinking the same thing. "Doc-tor Bar-bara Dash," he said again, slowly, enunciating every syllable, as if it were the first time he was ever reading the words.

*　　*　　*

Down below, James House patrolled the security station, checking up on every member of the security force. He made sure that they stood at attention, before making sure their uniforms were well kept, their weapons were clean, and they responded to their superior officer. He didn't have trouble with most. But there were always a few troublemakers.

"McVellion. Is there a particular reason you're not standing at attention?" James asked. Jane McVellion, sitting on the locker room-style benches, turned to look up at him. Her face was twisted into a snarl.

"I already know what I need to do. My clothes and gun are clean," she stated. James sighed.

"There's a reason I'm doing things this way. I have to make sure we don't get lazy or start slacking off in the event of an emergency. I'm trying to keep you on your guard so you're always ready to protect," James said, trying to be sympathetic.

Jane grabbed her gun, then pointed it at the floor and stared down the barrel. "Don't worry. I'm always ready to shoot."

"The job is more than *just* shooting, Jane," James said in an exasperated tone. Jane looked back up at him. Before she could say anything else, a second female officer stepped up.

"I'm sure she can handle herself. She looks more than capable. And I don't think I've ever seen her without her gun, so I doubt you have to worry about her being unprepared," she said. James sighed again. Then looked back down at Jane.

"I hope you're right, Vilner," he said.

"You can call me Cat," she said, offering up a smile.

"I'll stick to being professional, Vilner," James said, then proceeded on to finish up the routine. Cat sat down next to Jane. Jane ignored her and went back to looking at her gun.

"You're welcome," Cat said. Jane grunted.

"I don't owe you anything."

"Didn't say you did."

At that moment, another office came over. Wearing an overconfident smile, he sat down next to Jane.

"That guy's a real dick, huh?" the officer said.

"What do you want, Rick?" Cat asked.

"Please. It's Officer Farkass. Flattery will get you nowhere."

"You say that like you've gotten somewhere," Cat retorted back. Even Jane momentarily stopped frowning to smile slightly. Rick didn't seem phased.

"Well, I will. One day, I'll replace that tight wad as chief of security." Jane looked up from her gun to give him a stare of disbelief and annoyance. Rick smirked at her. Without taking her eyes off him, Jane fired her gun. The bullet slammed into the tile floor, centimeters away from Rick's foot. Rick jumped at and shrieked. James and all of the other officers came running.

"What the hell is going on?" James yelled.

"She tried to shoot me!" Rick yelled back, pointing at Jane.

"If I wanted to shoot him, his brain would be all over the walls," Jane said, without even looking up.

"Do *not* do that again!" James said sternly, getting in Jane's face. Jane simply glared at him silently. The two locked stares until after a few palpably tense moments, James stood up straight and cleared his throat. "Alright, everyone back to your positions," James said. The small crowd dispersed, as did he.

"Well, *I* thought he deserved it," Cat said once everyone had gone. Jane didn't acknowledge the comment.

*   *   *

That night, at dinner, DT Sacks, John Dash, Toby Smalls, and Marta Girasol once again sat together. They were idly passing the time - much to Dash's annoyance - waiting for Tony Weitson to arrive. Howard Skittering was also missing, but everyone was just thinking of Tony.

"I hope he's okay," Toby said, the concern ripe in his voice.

"*Estoy segura de que esta bien.* Just give him a few minutes," Marta said reassuringly.

After a few seconds of awkward silence, DT piped up. "So, uh, do you guys watch any sports?"

"Nah. I prefer sitcoms and comedies," Toby replied happily.

"I'm more into programming and that sorta stuff, even if I could never quite get into it, myself," Marta said.

"I enjoy a game of baseball every now and then," Dash said.

"So, coding huh? I enjoy a bit of VR every now and then," DT said.

"VR is pretty cool," Marta said.

"Yeah," DT said. The silence soon became awkward.

"I once met a professor who was heavily involved in developing virtual reality technologies," Dash said flatly, breaking the silence.

"*¿De veras?* How?" Marta asked.

"My mother has a lot of connections. I can't really go into full detail, but she partnered up with him to run some tests and experiments with VR," Dash explained.

"Is your mother also a programmer?" DT asked.

"No, she's a psychologist," Dash answered flatly.

"Oh," DT said. Dash turned away and stared into the crowd.

"Well, I think that all sounds really cool. I'll have to try VR one day!" Toby said happily. The silence fell again, and no one could really think what else to say. By now, people were finishing their dinners and heading home for the night, and they had begun to assume Tony had decided to just stay in his house. However, as they prepared to leave, Tony finally arrived.

"Getting anything to eat?" Marta asked.

Tony shook his head. "Not hungry. Now what exactly did you wanna do?"

The group exchanged glances. "We didn't really think about it too much. We figured you'd choose what we could do.

We'd just help make it happen," Toby said and offered a weak smile.

Tony gave them a very agitated glare. "And I already told you what *I* want to do is just sit in my house until I die."

"We were just trying to help," Toby said, visibly hurt. Tony sighed and sat down.

"Well, I suppose I wouldn't mind spending *some* of my time around you guys." Tony said. Toby smiled. "So now what?"

"Well, we were just talking about VR and coding," DT said.

"That's... pretty cool, I guess," Tony said. He then added hesitantly, "I've never really done any VR."

"It's okay, neither have I," Toby said, smiling.

"So what are your interests? Besides alcohol," Dash asked. Marta then glared angrily at him. Dash seemed oblivious.

"Oh, I didn't really do much. I wasn't really into anything really. I'd watch a football game every now and then. That's about it," Tony replied, not acknowledging Dash's comment.

"I'm more of a baseball fan, myself," Dash replied. Marta's glare loosened up a bit.

"I volunteered at a retirement home. Oh, also at an animal shelter," Toby gleefully said. The others turned to him.

"That's nice. You a cat person or a dog person?" DT asked, after a pause.

"Oh, dog person, definitely," Toby replied. "What about you guys?"

"Dogs, definitely. Grew up with them. There was always a german shepherd or two around my house when I was a kid," Tony said.

"I kinda like em both the same. I've had both, and I couldn't really choose one over the other," Marta said.

"I prefer cats. Much less maintenance. Plus they respect your personal space a lot more," Dash said.

"Yeah, cats are pretty cool," DT agreed. The conversation continued on, switching between topics as they arose, and they continued talking long after the main lights were shut off and the auxiliary lights had snapped on.

September 28, 2031

Alan Berkoff and Angel Puer were relaxing in the High Rise when the light above the elevator blinked on with a ding, indicating that someone was coming up. Alan and Angel exchanged a quick glance, before Angel stood up and walked over to the corner of the room. Inserting her fingers in between two slats of wood, she pulled open a small door to a hidden compartment. Crouching down, she ducked inside of the compartment, silently pulling the door closed. It seamlessly blended in with the rest of the wall. The elevator doors opened, and Dr. William Harrack stepped out. Alan gave him a smile.

"Will, good to see you again. You've been holed up in your lab for a few days. I was beginning to think one of your experiments finally caught up with you," Alan said happily. Harrack was not impressed.

"Inventory took longer than expected. Some idiots over at Winkle Enterprises must be really terrible at their jobs. I have jars upon jars of nothing but white phosphorus, and nowhere to put it aside from a wheeled shelf in the middle of my lab. What the hell do I even need that much white phosphorus for?" Harrack paused a moment. "What the hell do *they* need that much white phosphorus for?"

"You say that like you don't have plenty of other, highly dangerous substances of your own," Alan snarked.

"Yes, but mine are experimental. We already know fully well what white phosphorus does." Harrack regained his composure and cleared his throat. "Regardless, that is not why I came up here."

"Then why are you here?" Alan asked curiously.

"I was wondering if your 'agent' has found any suitable subjects for my experiments," Harrack asked, sitting down in a chair next to Alan.

"Before I answer that, I do have a request," Alan said, smiling. Harrack sighed.

"Fine. What is it?" Harrack asked.

"You use this first line of... 'subjects,' as you put it, to create a deadly poison," Alan said. "I mean, unless you already have some, then don't worry about it."

"No, Winkle Enterprises didn't permit any known toxins with no other purposes," Harrack said. "What do you want a poison for, anyways?"

"Oh, just for self defense. If someone attacks me or something, I can just stab them with a needle," Alan replied. Harrack have him a suspicious look.

"That's specific. Why not just carry around a gun for self defense?" Harrack asked.

"Who says I don't? Besides, multiple methods of self defense are not a bad thing, are they?" Alan said, still smiling. Harrack kept his suspicious look, but sighed.

"Fine. I'll make your poison. Now tell me about what you found."

"Well, we've managed to find three suitable people. The first is in advanced stages of liver failure. He's already dead, anyways. There's also an alcoholic. Spends every night in the bar, getting drunk off his ass., and the third is just recovering from a stomach virus. He's been cooped up in his house since day one," Alan concluded.

"We'll start with him. Have your agent gather him up at once," Harrack ordered. Alan frowned.

"Neither me nor my agent are your personal errand runners. Be glad I had h- my agent do any of this *at all*," Alan said sternly.

"Alright, fine. But I still need someone to gather him up, I can't do it myself," Harrack said.

"Well, I think I might have an idea on who could help you with that," Alan said, turning to look at the two stacks of files on the table. The stack that was originally taller now only had a handful of files remaining, while the other one was now much taller. Off to the side of both stacks was an open file. The paper it was open to showed a woman with short brown hair, stopping a few inches above her neck. She had a vicious smile on her face, and big letters next to the picture stated clearly, "Jane McVellion."

*   *   *

Breakfast was quite often disorganized, as most people tend to wake up at different times, and are still rather tired. Due to this, people usually met up at lunchtime. DT Sacks, John Dash, Marta Girasol, Toby Smalls, and Tony Weitson were no exception to this rule. As they got their food, they found an empty table, sitting down. Howard Skittering sat alone at a nearby table.

"How are you feeling today?" DT asked, biting into his food.

"I'm doing a little better. The doctor's been giving me some painkillers. Not many, though. Rationing, and all that," Tony groaned. "I just wish I wasn't always so tired."

"Well, we're here to support you," Toby said, smiling warmly. Tony looked down at his food, then pushed it away.

"I'm sorry, I'm not really in the mood right now. I'm gonna go get some rest. Maybe I'll catch you at dinner," Tony said, standing up and walking away. As he walked away, the others watched with sympathetic frowns.

"I wish we could help him better," Toby said.

"Well, sometimes there's not really anything you can do," DT said. Before anyone else could say another word, Howard Skittering swooped in, sitting down in Tony's empty seat.

"Where've you been?" Marta asked, mid-bite.

"I've been... occupied," Howard answered. He indicated the direction Tony had disappeared to. "What's with him?" The others stared incredulously.

"He's dying," Marta said, in a tone of slight disbelief.

"That tends to make some people depressed," DT added.

"Oh," Howard said. He then stayed silent. No one else said anything until they all dispersed a few minutes later.

*   *   *

Just as Jim Penn had finally fallen asleep, a sudden knock came at his door. Groaning and dragging himself out of bed, he moseyed over to the door, opening it just a crack. "Who-" he didn't even get a word out before the door was forced open and he was thrown back. He stumbled back, and just as he regained his footing, something hard struck him square in the face, causing him to fall back. As he fell, he smacked his head on the table behind him, and collapsed on the floor, motionless. The intruder then walked through the doorway, into the house. She stooped down and yanked Jim Penn's body into the center of the room. She then lifted the man up, and slung him over her shoulder. Walking out of the house, she stopped to close the door. She then headed back to Harrack's office in the cover of darkness. The auxiliary lights were incredibly dim, and only a few few shades brighter than pitch darkness. Still, she stuck close to the lines of houses in case she needed to duck in between them.

"Thank you very much, Ms. McVellion" Dr. Harrack said gleefully as Jane dumped Jim Penn's limp body onto a metallic, adjustable table in the back room in his lab. "I see Alan was not wrong about you. Though, I am curious. What did he see in your file that made him think you'd agree to this?" Harrack said, strapping Jim Penn's arms and legs down with restraints that were built into the table.

"Don't know, don't care," Jane paused for a moment. "Just felt nice to cause some pain, again. Wish I could've done more, though."

He gently examined Jim Penn's face, and dabbed at the blood running out of his nose. "Ah, I see," Harrack said as he typed on his computer. He then walked over to his shelves and cabinets, preparing the chemicals he would need. He looked over his shoulder at Jane. "Thank you for your help. You may go, now."

"Let me up to see Berkoff."

At that moment, Jim Penn started to stir. Before Harrack could do anything, a gentle ding went off, signifying the opening of the door. "I don't have time for any of this," Harrack groaned in frustration. "Wait here," he said to Jane. He then quickly stormed out of the back room and into the waiting area. Tony Weitson was waiting patiently in the middle of the room.

"Good, you're here," Tony said.

"What do you want?" Harrack snapped. Tony took a defensive step back, but quickly regained his composure.

"Well..." Tony hesitated. "I was hoping you would have something that would kill me." It took only a few minutes for Tony to fully explain his situation.

"Well, it would take almost no effort to simply stop your heart, but would this benefit me in any way? Why should I waste my resources on you?" Dr. Harrack questioned.

"I'm in a lot of pain, and the painkillers only do so much. I'm not doing anything but wasting air," Tony said pitifully. Harrack sighed impatiently.

"This bunker is outfitted with a state of the art ventilation and filtration system. It can continue pumping breathable air, even if the outside is full of with radiation," Harrack explained. Tony was about to plead again, but Harrack held up his hand to stop him. "I do apologize, but I am in the middle of a very important experiment that I need to get back to. Come back later, and maybe we can reach an arrangement." Tony considered saying something else, but nodded in agreement and left.

Jim Penn was finally regaining consciousness. He was naturally groggy at first, and there was a splitting pain both in his face and head. He tried to wipe the wet spot under his nose, but quickly realized his hand was restrained. This sobered him up quite quickly, and he began panicking and fighting against the restraints, to no avail. He began to scream for help, but Dr. Harrack walked into the back room before he could get more than a single scream out.

"I was hoping to be here when you woke up, but I had to quickly take care of something, first. Save your voice, though. This place was built to be completely soundproof," Harrack said. His words didn't stop Jim Penn from screaming, though. Harrack sighed, and injected Jim Penn with mild tranquilizers. Jim Penn relaxed into a dazed state of mind, remaining fully conscious. Harrack walked over to the arranged chemicals he had set up for this experiment, and picked one up.

*   *   *

Alan Berkoff stood alone in the High Rise. He was taking a light nap, while Angel continued reading through her own file. She was curious to see what was written. When the light above the elevator dinged on, she looked up. Placing the file gently back on the desk, she returned to her little corner. Alan stirred awake as the elevator door opened, and Jane McVellion stepped out.

"What is it?" Alan said sleepily.

"I did your dirty work. And as fun as it was, I'd still like to be repaid," Jane said.

"I'm afraid I don't really have much to offer you," Alan said with a cocky half-smile. Jane twisted her lips into a gruesome smile.

"Well, I'm sure the vice president, and everyone else, would just *love* to hear about what you had me do for you and

Dr. Harrack," Jane said, her evil smirk growing. Alan's smile disappeared, and he stood up. Fully erecting his spine, he was much taller than her, but that didn't seem to phase her.

"I will not sit here while you threaten me. Besides, this was hardly a difficult task, and I don't just give out rewards. You want them, you have to earn them," Alan said, dismissing her and turning away. Jane drew her weapon. Angel, peeking out from her corner, now slowly crept up behind Jane.

"I didn't do this for nothing!" Jane almost yelled, aiming her gun at the back of Alan's head. Alan stopped and turned around to make a snarky comment, but paused as he spotted her gun. When he saw Angel behind her, his smirk returned.

"Y'know, you really should be a little calmer." Jane stared him down as Angel slowly rose to her feet behind Jane. At that moment, Alan started thinking. "On second thought, maybe your anger isn't quite so bad."

Jane lowered her gun slightly, clearly confused. "What the hell are you talking about?"

"You're willing to pull a gun on your president. And what was that you mentioned about enjoying the, as you put it, 'dirty work?' I might be able to get you more of that type of work, *and* a mutually beneficial reward," Alan said, rapidly running plans through his head.

"Alright, what's this reward?" Jane asked. She holstered her weapon

"I can't promise anything, so I won't get your hopes up for now. But I will get in contact with you if and when I am ready for you. You can leave now," Alan said, turning his back.

"You really think I'm going to leave with just that?" Jane snarled.

"It's your only real option right now. Trust me, you don't want to cross me."

"And you don't want to cross *me!*" Jane growled. Alan just laughed. Jane considered shooting him in the head, but decided to wait and see what would happen.

"Don't tell anyone about our agreement. Or you *will* live to regret it," Alan added before the doors opened with a ding. Jane bared her teeth at him before turning around to face the completely empty room, the elevator suddenly dinged. Within a few moments of both parties being surprised, the door opened and VP Eustace Toaden walked in. While he was wiping his glasses on his shirt as he walked in, he quickly finished and looked up, right as he stepped directly in front of Jane, startling him.

"You do not have permission to be up here!" Toaden said sternly, clearly upset.

"It's okay, Eustace. She has my permission," Alan said, stepping in.

"You should *not* go around, granting these sorts of permissions to anyone! I can see why you were sent into forced retirement," Toaden said, stepping around Jane. Alan gritted his teeth.

"Yes, well, down here, *I* am the president! And I will *not* have my second in command question me," Alan growled. Toaden glanced over his shoulder. He looked at Alan with a tired look, then turned to Jane.

"She should leave. This is a private matter."

Alan sighed and turned to Jane. "I'll get back to you," he said to her. Jane let out a grunt and turned to the elevator. She pressed the button and stepped inside. Moments later, the elevator doors closed and sent her down. Alan turned back to Toaden.

"Did you really think they'd actually let you be president after all the national embarrassment you went through?" Toaden said, sitting down at the conference table. Alan sulked over and sat down across from him.

"The hell are you talking about?" Alan asked.

"I'm sure you only know you're down here because of your friend Percy Winkle. Well, one of his conditions for funding the bunker was that you be placed in charge. We could never quite figure out why, but we just assumed it was because he didn't want his investment in you to be wasted. But, because *you* got us into this mess in the first place, they were very much against it. However, they were desperate for the money and materials, so they agreed to install you as a figurehead. All the title and privileges, with none of the power. We decided not to tell you so you wouldn't make an issue out of it," Toaden explained. Alan was practically seething over with rage. However, he managed to keep his cool temper and calmed himself.

"I'm not a child," he responded. "And I would've prefered to just not have been given the title than given a fake title."

"Well, I do apologize. I thought it was a rather immature way to handle the situation, myself. But there was much more at stake and we didn't have time to waste quarreling over you with Winkle," Toaden sighed. "Really, I am quite sorry," Toaden said sincerely. Alan's mind once again rushed, formulating a plan.

"Am I at least still on the Council?" he asked.

Toaden nodded. "Well, I suppose you do have *some* responsibilities to do along with the title." Alan smiled and stood up.

"Well, don't you worry. I swear to make the most of my limited power," Alan said, his smile growing. Toaden gave him a suspicious glare, but remained silent.

*　　*　　*

Tony sat alone at one of the tables in the dining area and looked up at the bunker's ceiling. He was studying the patterns the lights had been arranged in. The main lights blanketed the ceiling. In between every third main light was a smaller auxiliary light. Those came on during the later hours to simulate nighttime. Although it was automatic, the lights could also manually be adjusted by the monitors in the High Rise.

It was apparently midnight and the entire bunker was mostly asleep by now. The aux lights reminded Tony of moonlight, and he smiled at the thought of the moon. The realization of just how many things he would never see again suddenly hit him like a freight train. The moon, the sun, clouds, birds, trees, grass, the list was endless.

"What am I even doing here?" Tony asked himself, on the verge of tears. "I could've been spending my last days relaxing on the beach, not giving a damn about sunburns. I could start overheating, to the point where I'd buy an ice cream. I wouldn't even care if it melted, just so long as I could see the sun again."

As tears flowed freely from his eyes, Tony tried to recall his every experience. Everything he's ever felt, smelled, tasted, touched, seen. He thought about the german shepherds he had grown up with, Buddy and Luna. The big goofs. He remembered the very first bee sting he received, and how much it had hurt at the time. Funny, that pain seemed so insignificant now. He remembered his dad losing his job, and the bank foreclosing on their house because they couldn't keep up with the payments. And how everything only went downhill from there. He didn't even realize he had all of this stored in his memory. How many things he hadn't thought about in years, were suddenly flowing back, filling his thoughts like a tidal wave.

He suddenly remembered the last job interview he had ever gone to, right down to the color of his interviewer's tie. They decided to hire him. It was nothing more than a standard office job, something to pay the bills and keep him out of debt. He remembered how his father had also passed of liver disease, and how he had taken up drinking shortly after, upon realizing that he was never gonna have enough money stored away to travel the world.

"Why am I here?" Tony repeated to himself. "I never should've come. Even if we are nuked, I would've died before they struck." Tony's crying intensified. "It's better if I die sooner rather than later, anyways. I mean what's the point of surviving down here if there's nothing left up there?" Tony wiped the tears from his eyes. "I don't even get to feel a breeze again before I die."

A sudden movement in the darkness startled him. Tony jolted up, and silenced himself. He forced himself to stay motionless as he scanned the area, or as well as his tear-filled eyes could see. An apparition suddenly appeared, and approached, getting ever closer and closer. Tony felt his muscles tense up, then right as the figure was on top of him...

"Howard?" Tony asked, relaxing significantly. The figure, who was indeed Howard Skittering, nodded.

"Sorry to disturb you. I didn't think I'd find anyone out here." Howard's voice and was low and tired. He was clearly in need to sleep, Tony observed. But, then, so was Tony. Howard sat down next to Tony, and sighed. The two sat in silence for a moment, before Howard turned to Tony. "I'm sorry for being such an insensitive dick. I've just been... going through a lot, myself." Howard paused. "N-nothing compared to you, though!" he suddenly stammered out. Tony sighed.

"It's okay. I know I'm not the only one with problems. Besides, all of my problems will end soon enough," Tony said, even letting out a small, depressed laugh.

Howard let out a similarly depressed laugh. "Well..." he said, rubbing the back of his neck. "I shouldn't complain about my issues in front of you." Tony offered a smile. Not that it could be seen in the darkness.

"It's fine. I don't mind."

"Well... alright." Howard took a deep breath. "This entire place just feels like one big tomb. Sorry, I'm being insensitive, again."

"It's fine. Continue."

"I've always been a bit of a claustrophobic, but... this place makes me feel worse than anything else I've ever encountered. It's taking all of my self control not to just... snap. And I'm not sure I can last too long down here."

"Well, I'm sure you can," Tony said, the tears finally drying up. Howard sighed again, more in relief this time.

"Thanks. I'm sure I'll be fine just so long as everything remains nice and calm."

October 1, 2031

A few days later, while Tony was rapidly deteriorating, there was someone else who was doing much worse.

"Interesting," Harrack said thoughtfully to himself as he inspected Jim Penn's leg. The skin had turned a grey color, and the veins just below it were a pure black. Jim Penn was barely conscious from the agony, but managed to faintly stay awake, though not lucid. Even through the haze, his leg still managed to feel like the skin was rotting off the bone. As he lazily swung his head from side to side, he barely noticed Harrack preparing the next batch of chemicals. As he finished up, he filled a syringe with the mysterious liquid and approached Jim Penn.

"I was hoping for something a little more subtle," Harrack directly at Jim Penn. Jim Penn let out a slight gurgle in response. "And a little more fatal," Harrack added flatly. He injected the syringe into Jim Penn's left arm. Harrack waited patiently, as no change was immediately evident in Jim Penn's drowsy form. After a few moments of silence, Jim Penn began violently seizing. As his body spasmed he vomited, causing Harrack to quickly step back in alarm. Harrack still, however, took care not to bump into the metal, wheeled shelf filled with rows and rows of large glass jars, each sealed and filled to the brim with a white powder. But the seizure ended quickly, and Jim Penn's body relaxed completely, becoming limp and lifeless.

Harrack waited a few moments, to make sure the seizures and vomiting didn't started up again. After it was clear they wouldn't, Harrack checked Jim Penn's pulse. He undid the restraints on Jim Penn's arms and legs, then grabbed a patented type of concealer. Harrack then meticulously began to cover up

Jim Penn's leg. It wouldn't be perfect, but Harrack's office also doubled as the bunker's morgue, and he was the one who was in charge of examining the bodies. Though he was not permitted to do an autopsy, that was Dr. Phillip Genson, the bunker's surgeon. But Dr. Genson would only be brought in if Harrack deemed an autopsy necessary. Harrack began painstakingly cleaning the vomit up. After that was clean, Harrack then ran a few extra tests to determine the exact biological process that had caused this reaction.

Once he was finished, Harrack left his office, locking the door behind him. Walking to the security station, he entered the password to get in. Most of the security force was still in there, with only a few out on patrol. Only a few glanced up as he passed, the majority minded their own business. Once in the back, he entered the password to the elevator and stepped inside. The doors closed and he flew up. The doors opened and he found Alan sitting alone in the High Rise. He informed Alan about the results of his test. As Harrack finished his report, Alan smiled and Harrack expressed his desire to repeat the experiment to be absolutely sure of the results. The two departed the High Rise to find Jane McVellion, who would return Jim Penn to his house until the smell bothered the neighbors.

*   *   *

Rose Anderson and Casey Goodwill were sitting at one of the tables near the security station. As they idly ate their breakfast, they occasionally glanced at the station, or up at the High Rise. Both were frail, older women in their mid forties, and, as such, were two of the first earliest risers in the bunker. One of the only other early risers, a security officer, was standing outside of the station, apparently surveying the nearly deserted area.

"Why do you think he's just standing there?" Rose asked. Casey happened to be glancing up at the High Rise at that particular moment.

"I'm more interested in what they do up there," responded Casey. Rose looked between her and the High Rise.

Zachary Zyz had also noticed Rose Anderson as she watched him. He the two were usually up early. He had seen them often at this hour. Ten years serving the military had trained him to wake up early. Even though he had no reason to wake up that early everyday, habits were hard to break. This experience is also why he had the position of keeping the chief of security in check, should he start to abuse his power. However, Zyz didn't worry about James House. James ran the security force in a comfortably familiar way. Zyz considered asking if James had ever served. For the most part, Zyz used the early hours to think. Currently, he was thinking about how Alan Berkoff had weaseled his way into the top position of the bunker. He knew it had something to do with Percy Winkle's interference, but that was the extent of his knowledge.

As he thought about the bunker's leadership, James House walked out of the security station. Yawning, he gave Zyz a curious glance, then exited through the gate. Within minutes, VP Eustace Toaden and Dr. Linda Marie had also appeared, and the group sat down at an isolated table. Rose Anderson also noticed the sudden, unofficial conference. She poked Casey Goodwill and pointed at them.

"I believe Berkoff is up to something. I can't be certain, though," Toaden said, while keeping his voice down. Even though they had made sure there was no one without earshot, Toaden was still nervous.

"I wouldn't be surprised. Should we get Dr. Harrack in on this?" James House asked.

"I wouldn't do that. I don't trust him," Dr. Marie said.

"I agree. He was already friends with Berkoff, so they could easily be working together," Toaden said. The conversation stopped as the three brainstormed what they could do. Finally, James sighed and slammed his hands down on the table.

"Well, there's one quick and easy way to settle this," he said, standing up. "Let's just talk to him." Dr. Marie and Toaden exchanged a quick glance of worry.

"That's probably not a good idea," Dr. Marie said. James looked at her.

"Why not?" James asked impatiently. "If the 'president' is really up to something, I want to know. *Now.*"

"We don't know what Berkoff is up to. Or even *if* he's up to something! I mean, we all know about Berkoff's scandal, so it's almost guaranteed he's plotting something. And that goes for Dr. Harrack, as well. But we don't know *what* they're plotting. They could be up to anything! And who knows what they'd do if they found out we were onto them. We should lay low and try to figure out what's happening, before we make any decisions," Dr. Marie cautioned. He looked to James. "And sit down." James looked agitated, but sat down, anyway.

"While I agree with Dr. Marie, we shouldn't worry about too much danger. He may be a terrible politician, but down here he's harmless. He might be a disgrace, but he's smart enough not to do anything rash. But we definitely need to find out more before acting," Toaden concurred. James sighed and nodded in agreement. "We should probably finish this up before people start coming for breakfast." The three all stood up, nearly at the same time.

"I'll get back to my office. I told one of my patients to come in today for a checkup. I should be there in case he shows up early," Dr. Marie said, and excused herself. James and Toaden exchanged a look before James shrugged and walked away. Toaden sighed and also departed.

"What do you think they were talking about?" Casey Goodwill asked as she and Rose Anderson watched the three of disappear.

"I have no idea, but if the security chief's reaction was anything, it can't be anything good," Rose said.

"Now what was that all about?" Zachary Zyz said to himself.

*   *   *

Shortly before lunch, Dr. William Harrack met Alan Berkoff in the High Rise. Harrack informed Berkoff that he had created a batch of his poison, and was off to run a second test. If it was successful, Harrack would hand over the poison, along with syringes, to Alan. Alan thanked him and Harrack turned to leave. Before Harrack could press the elevator door button, Alan suddenly asked him if he knew about the Dash-Fickward experiment.

"Only as much as everybody else. Why do you ask?"

Before Alan could answer, The elevator dinged. "I was just wondering if you had heard more about it than what had been publicly released. Thought you might've had connections in the scientific community, or something," Alan said before the doors opened.

"None in psychology," Harrack said. The door opened and James House stepped out. He seemed very unhappy. Harrack darted into the elevator as the doors closed and disappeared along with it. Alan greeted James with a smile. James returned a menacing frown.

"Hello, Chief House," Alan said genially.

"Let's skip the formalities," James said, aggressively walking up to Alan. "I know you're up to something. You and Dr. Harrack. I *was* going to try and ignore it, but as I was downstairs, one of my officers, Jane McVellion, demanded I take her up here to see you. When I told her that she wasn't authorized to come up here, she continued to demand I take her up here, anyways. Said she had to talk to you. Now, I don't know what you and the scientist are up to, and maybe it's none of my business, but as soon as you involve my officers, it *becomes* my business. Now tell me what you're up to, and how my Officer McVellion is involved."

Alan maintained his pleasant smile throughout, however it became less genuine with each passing word from James. "Now, Chief House, I can assure you that my intentions are pure, but there is a reason for the secrecy. I am very sorry for deceiving you. But if you would like to know about what is going on, then give me some time to organize everything so I can give you a clear presentation. I will send you for when I have everything ready. It should not take long."

James' anger had simmered down considerably. "Alright, fine. But don't think I'm forgetting about this. And you better have a *damn* convincing argument." After finishing the final sentence, James lingered for just a moment more, then turned and proceeded to exit the High Rise. As soon as he was gone, Alan's smile twisted into a much more malicious one.

*   *   *

"Oh, come on! Just one more drink? Please?" Dylan Beecut said, hiccuping. He sat pitifully on the ground, in front of the doors to the bar.

"Sorry. Bar's closed for lunch," Mickey November said, locking the bar doors. He pocketed the keys and began walking away.

"Oh, come on! I won't tell anyone!" Dylan pleaded from the floor. "Please?!" He could barely stand and his speech was slurred almost beyond recognition.

"Sorry, them's the rules. Besides, you could benefit from a little time sober. Go home, Beecut," Mickey said as he walked away, leaving the pathetic mess blubbering on the ground. As Dylan wobbled to his feet, he turned and pulled on the door handle. After he was finally convinced they truly were locked, gave up and began stumbling home.

As he tried to remember his way home, an task of which he had incredible difficulty with, he walked down a narrow alley between two houses. Leaning on the house for support, he tripped and fell when he reached the end of the alley. He decided it was probably just best to stay on the ground. While he was laying there, a shadow suddenly appeared over him. He stirred and looked up at what had suddenly blocked out the lights. Even through his blurred vision, he could still make out a white lab coat, though that was it.

"D-doc?" Dylan sputtered out. The doctor then bent down, reaching towards Dylan. Dylan felt a vague but surprising prick in his neck. "Ow. What the he-" Suddenly, he started spasming, and began vomiting all over the ground. Before he even had time to think about what was happening, he was dead.

*   *   *

DT Sacks, John Dash, and Toby Smalls sat together at their usual table. Tony Weitson, Marta Girasol, and Howard Skittering were all not with them.

"Where's the group?" Toby asked, looking around.

"Marta told me she usually sleeps late," Dash offered.

"This late? I mean, I usually miss breakfast, too, but I'm up by lunch," DT added. Dash just gave him a clueless look.

"I imagine Tony is either alone, or at the doctor's again. He's hasn't been good lately," Dash said.

"Yeah, that sounds about right," he said. A man and a woman walked up to their table.

"Would any of you happen to know where the chief of security is?" the woman asked.

"No. Sorry," DT replied.

"Try checking the security station," Dash said. The woman gave him an annoyed look.

"Come on, Bill," she said, practically dragging the younger man away. The three at the table watched with mild curiosity as they walked away. Once the two stopped at another table with two older women, they turned back to their own conversation.

"What about Howard? I know he's kinda not nice, but still," Toby asked.

"You could always pay him a visit," Dash said, taking a small sip of water.

"And we should probably check on Tony, just to make sure he's alright," DT said. He looked at Dash. Dash sighed and put down his cup.

"Sure," Dash said. "Can we finish eating first?" Only a few minutes later, the three stood up from their table and walked back towards the houses.

*   *   *

"Yeah, I saw him a little before breakfast. He seemed upset," Rose Anderson said as the two strangers questioned her and Casey Goodwill about James House.

"He was with the vice president and the doctor," Casey added.

"Which doctor?" the woman asked.

"The lady one. I think she's the *actual* doctor," Casey answered.

"I'm pretty sure that scientists count as real doctors," Rose retorted.

"I mean, they definitely have the schooling, and the title. But I wouldn't go to them for a sore throat," Casey responded.

"Well, there are different kinds of doctors. You don't go to the same doctor for every issue, do you?" Rose said.

"Well, no. But who visits the science type of doctors for any personal issue?" Casey said.

"Medicine is a type of science," Rose said. As two debated, the two figures turned away and left.

"Nancy, you *know* he's fine, right?" Bill said, a bit angrily.

"I know he's fine, but I'd just like to spend more time with him. We never let anything get in way of family time, but now we hardly ever see him," Nancy House answered.

"He has a lot of responsibilities as the chief of security. I'm sure he doesn't want to miss family dinners, but he doesn't have much free time," Bill House responded. Nancy sighed and stopped.

"I guess you're right. He's fine. I just miss seeing him," Nancy said.

"I know. Now can we get lunch?" Bill asked.

*   *   *

"I just wish I could run a few more tests," Dr. Harrack stated as he handed Alan a small case of five vials and two syringes.

"But it works well so far?" Alan asked, taking the case. Harrack nodded.

"It should prove quite fatal. If messy," Harrack said. Alan smiled. "Please just try to only use it if necessary." Alancocked his head to the side.

"Of course. It's not like I'm just gonna go around killing everyone I disagree with," Alan said, his smile unnaturally wide. "Now what do you mean by messy?"

"It's very quick acting, but it also causes violent seizures and significant vomiting," Harrack informed him.

"I see. Well, I'm sure I can find some way around that," Alan said confidently, his smile growing on his lips. Harrack furrowed his brow.

"I thought you just said you'd only use it if necessary," Harrack snapped.

"You mean like how you had to murder innocent civilians to make this formula?" Alan asked.

"That was scientific research!" Harrack defended. "If I didn't do that, I couldn't fully test the chemical! It's not my fault

Winkle Enterprises refused to include those sorts of toxins in my supplies. And you said you would use this for self defense. And right now, I can definitely think of more than a few reasons some would attack you."

"You murdered people, plain and simple," Alan said. "And don't pretend this isn't the exact sort of thing you've already done. Many times."

"I'm done. I'm not manufacturing anymore concoctions for you. When your murder plans inevitably backfire, I don't want to go down with you. I'm sticking to my own projects, and *only* my projects," Harrack said, clearly frustrated and angry. Harrack turned his back to Alan and marched to the elevator. A few moments, he had left the High Rise.

Alan smiled to himself once he was alone. "Clearly, you haven't known me long enough, Dr. Harrack. You underestimate me," Alan said to himself. As he stood alone in the High Rise, began laughing uncontrollably.

*   *   *

DT Sacks and John Dash stood in front of Tony Weitson's house. Neither moved and DT kept awkwardly glancing between Dash and the door, while Dash kept his stare on the door.

"So... should we knock and wait, or knock and go in, or should we just go in?" DT asked. Dash slowly turned to look at him.

"It doesn't matter to me," Dash replied.

"Let's just knock and go in, and hope he doesn't mind," DT said, then knocked on the door. He waited a few seconds and then opened the door, walking inside. The lights were off, leaving the entire house nearly pitch black. It took a minute their eyes to adjust to the dark. The house appeared to be empty, and DT began poking around, looking for any signs of Tony. Dash just stood in the doorway, silently scanning the room. As his eyes rested on the bed, he spotted a person-shaped lump under the covers.

As DT continued looking around, Dash went over and slowly peeled the blanket back. Tony stirred and groaned, then looked up at Dash. After a moment, he sat up.

"What are you doing in my house?" he asked sleepily.

"We just wanted to check up on you. Make sure you were okay, and all," DT said. Tony swung his legs off the bed and turned on the lamp on his desk. Sitting on the bed for a minute, he stood up and wobbled on his feet. He almost fell, but Dash caught him and helped him stay upright until he regained his balance.

"I'm fine," Tony said crankily, pulling away from Dash.

"You sure?" DT asked.

"Yes," Tony snapped, walking over to the small bathroom in his house. He stared into the mirror for a few seconds and sighed. He then turned around to look at Dash and DT.

"Why are you still in my house?" Tony snapped. He turned back to the mirror, and Dash and DT slowly headed to the door. "I'll meet you guys at the usual table," he added softly, right as they were stepping out. The two paused for a brief second, then proceeded out.

*   *   *

The two returned to find Toby and Marta at their table. As they sat down, Toby spoke up.

"How's Tony?" Toby asked.

"Not great," DT said.

"Oh," Toby said.

"What about Howard?" DT asked.

"He wasn't at his house. I didn't know where else to look for him," Toby said.

"Did you try to bar?" Marta asked.

"No," Toby answered.

"That'd be a good place to check," Marta added, and took a bite of her food.

"So what's today's conversation topic?" DT asked.

"Jobs. Careers. Before we got locked down here, I mean," Marta asked in between bites.

"Aside from the animal shelter, I didn't really have a job," Toby said.

"I was, uh, in between jobs at the time," DT said.

"Well, what was your last job, then?" Marta pressed. DT nervously rubbed the back of his neck.

"I don't remember," he responded feebly. Marta narrowed her eyes and stopped chewing.

"*No te acuerdas?* Did you forget where you worked?"

"Um..." DT was at a loss for words. The silence became awkward as Marta stared intently at DT. After a few moments, Toby placed his hand lightly on Marta's arm.

"Maybe he doesn't wanna talk about it," Toby said gently. Marta relaxed slightly and went back to eating.

"Oh. I'm sorry," Marta said, going back to her food. DT sighed.

"It's okay. I never actually held a job. My parents had a lot of money, so I was able to live off that," he admitted nervously.

"That must be nice," Toby said pleasantly.

"Yeah, it was," DT said sadly. Marta's expression changed to a more empathetic one.

"Sorry to push," she apologized.

"It's fine," DT said. Silence descended once more.

"I actually worked for my mother," Dash said. Everyone else turned to him. "I was basically a stock boy in her lab. Helped organize files, and other menial tasks."

Lunch was just coming to a close, and people began to stand up and head out, with the exception of the two older women who never seemed to leave. Marta was the last to finish her meal, and once she was done the group also stood up and left with the rest of the crowd.

*   *   *

Tony Weitson had begun walking to lunch, despite still feeling a little fatigued and off balance. While walking through the alley in between two houses, he suddenly stopped and clutched his stomach. His vision blurred and distorted, and the world began spinning all around him. As he tried to adjust his body to brace himself against the spinning, he instead lost his balance.

He grasped for the side of one of the houses, but it was too late, and Tony fell to the ground. He couldn't force himself up, and looked all around, unable to really see anything around him. Despite his distorted vision, he did manage to distinctly see a figure in white running towards him. As Tony's vision worsened, he began to rapidly lose consciousness. The last thing he saw before passing out was a hand reaching towards him.

*   *   *

After separating from lunch, DT Sacks and John Dash both returned to their homes. Toby Smalls went looking for Howard Skittering once more, and Marta Girasol decided to go for a walk around, and ended up getting lost in her thoughts.

Dash was in his house, reading a book he had brought. His house was packed with them. He hadn't planned on meeting people he enjoyed the company of, so he had brought enough books to last the rest of his life. Still, he was sure that he would have more than enough time to finish his books.

As he was reading, there was a swift knock on his door. Dash looked up from the book, and the knocking got more intense. He sighed, putting his book down and getting up. He walked over to the door and opened it, unsure what to expect.

*   *   *

Toby Smalls led Dash into Dr. Marie's office. Marta Girasol and DT Sacks were already there. They were both facing away from the door, standing over the bed in the room. Toby and Dash slowly approached, and as they got closer, Dash saw it was Tony who was laying on the bed. He was unconscious, but groaning softly.

"How is he?" Toby asked anxiously. Dr. Marie sighed.

"Not doing great. He's worsening quicker than I thought," Dr. Marie replied.

"Well, is there anything we can do?" Toby asked, his anxiety growing.

"I'm afraid not," Dr. Marie said, sitting down at her computer.

"What happened?" Dash asked.

"I was going to check on another patient of mine, who was late for an appointment. While I was walking there, I saw Mr. Weitson collapse," Dr. Marie started.

"I heard the doc calling for help, and so did someone else. The three of us carried him back here," Marta finished.

"I see," Dash said.

"I... have to go," Toby said suddenly, and promptly walked out of the office.

"I guess he doesn't know how to deal with death," Marta said after a few moments of silence.

"Who does?" DT said. Nobody replied. Dr. Marie looked at her monitors.

"His liver is beginning to enter complete failure," she stated numbly. She rested her forehead in her hands. "It's amazing he's still as good as he is. But how didn't I see this sooner?"

"We all make mistakes," DT said.

"No one could've guessed this would happen," Marta said.

"Yes, but this is my *job*," Dr. Marie said.

Before anyone could respond, Tony stirred. Everyone turned their attention to him as he woke up. Groaning, he tried to prop himself on his elbows. Unfortunately, he was too weak and lost his balance, his elbows slipping out from under him and causing him to fall back on the bed. As he tried lift himself up again, Dr. Marie rushed over and gently tried to keep him on the bed. He ignored her and tried again. After a few moments of struggling, he finally managed to get himself into a sitting position. Swinging his legs off of the bed, he looked around the room. Dash tried to keep a straight face, but it was constantly interrupted by pained twitches.

"What's going on here?" Tony winced. His voice was hoarse and he was clearly dehydrated. Dr. Marie handed him some water, which he begrudgingly accepted and slowly drank. Letting out a refreshed sigh, he quickly entered a coughing fit. It was over in another minute.

"You collapsed. The doctor found you laying in the street, and we carried you back here," Marta said. Tony pushed himself off the table.

"Please, you should really lay back down! You're in no condition to go anywhere," Dr. Marie said, trying in vain to get him to lay back down. He just pushed past her. It took him a moment to get his balance back, but he eventually stabilized himself.

"I'm fine," Tony said. Then he coughed. "Just let me go back to my house." He began to collapse, but caught himself on the edge of the table. DT reached out and caught him, helping him back onto his feet again.

"I can't let you leave. I already made one mistake with you, I won't make another," Dr. Marie said. Tony looked at her with a frown. "Please. You need some rest. You're just putting unnecessary strain on yourself," Dr. Marie said to him. Tony gave her an unhappy look, then wordlessly pushed his way through the small crowd, exiting the office. Dr. Marie sighed.

 *   *   *

James House had sent all of the officers on patrol. This had left the security station completely empty. This allowed him to pace back and forth in front of the elevator without question. Alan Berkoff had informed him that he was ready to tell James what he had been up to lately. But James sensed something fishy, and was debating with himself whether he should go up and confront the president. VP Toaden had said the president was harmless, but James had a bad feeling in his gut.

Finally, sighing, in defeat, he dropped down onto one of the benches. He stared down at his feet. Zachary Zyz silently appeared from the door of the security station. He and his partner, Lucy Desin, were both supposed to be out to patrol. Zyz stepped towards James, but before Zyz could get a word out, James sensed his presence and quickly turned his head towards him. James stood up.

"Didn't I order you to go out on patrol? What are you doing back here?" James snapped angrily. Zyz reflexively stepped back.

"You know it's my job to keep an eye on the chief of security, right? Well, sending every officer out on patrol for no apparent reason is a little suspicious. It's not even like there's anything actually happening that would warrant that," Zyz explained. James's anger dissipated, and he sighed.

"True," James said. "My apologizes. I just needed to be alone to think." He paused. "Didn't the vice president hand pick you to watch over the security chief?"

"Yes, he did. But why did you stay in the security station instead of going back to your house or up to the High Rise?" Zyz asked.

"I didn't want to run into my younger siblings. I'm sure at least one of them are home right now. And the High Rise is what I'm thinking about," James answered.

"What?" Zyz asked.

"Sorry, that didn't come out right. Just don't worry about it," James said. After waiting a moment for a response from Zyz that didn't come, James asked, "What do you think of President Berkoff?" Zyz debated whether or not to share his true thoughts for a few moments. Coming to a decision, he sighed.

"I don't believe President Berkoff is competent enough to run this bunker," Zyz said frankly. James nodded slowly, processing Zyz's answer. James then stood up and walked over to his locker. Opening it up, he pulled out some paper and a pen. He then closed and locked it.

"You served in the military, right?" James asked as he pressed the papers against the wall, and began scribbling furiously. Zyz tilted his head

"Yes. Why?" Zyz responded.

"I need an ally I can trust. Berkoff is up to something, but I have no idea what. Since I'm too busy with keeping the security force running, I need someone who can look into it for me," James finished writing on one piece of paper and folded it over twice. He switched over to the other paper and began writing on the second page. "I hope I can trust you."

"Why me?" Zyz asked.

"Never mind that, now," James said, finishing writing on the second piece of paper. He handed the first piece of paper to Zyz. "If anything happens to me, give this to Toaden or Dr. Marie. Or both, if you can." Zyz cautiously took the paper.

"What are you planning on doing?" Zyz asked. James looked up at him.

"I'm going to confront the president." James folded the second piece of paper and handed it to Zyz. "And make sure this one gets to my siblings. If anything happens, at least." Zyz nodded and took the paper.

"What do you think Berkoff is going to do?" Zyz asked with significant curiosity.

James sighed and let out a pathetic laugh, looking away from Zyz. "If I'm being honest, I don't think he'll do anything.

I'm probably just overreacting and worrying about nothing. I just have a bad feeling about this, y'know?"

"If you're worried, you don't have to go to Berkoff," Zyz stated.

"I know. But I *need* to settle this, if only for myself. Just to see what he's really up to," James said. His expression turned more serious as he looked back at Zyz. "But... just in case... there's one more thing I need to ask of you."

"Yes?"

"If anything *does* happen to me, make sure to look after John. Make sure nothing happens to him. Or my other siblings, of course, but John could easily get swept up into the middle of all this. And I just want my family to be safe."

"I'll look after them, if needed. Though I'm sure it won't be," Zyz said offering a slight smile. James smiled back and faced the elevator, with renewed resolve. Zyz watched as James pressed the button to call the elevator down. Without looking back, James stepped into the elevator as the doors opened. James was still facing the opposite wall as the doors closed. Zyz then stuffed the two pages into his vest.

*   *   *

Alan Berkoff was starting to get impatient as he waited for James House to arrive. However, despite taking longer than expected, the elevator did eventually ding. Within a few moments, James was stepping into the High Rise.

"James! How pleasant," Alan said with genuine enthusiasm. He quickly trotted over to James and vigorously shook his hand. James yanked his hand away, giving the president a suspicious glare.

"You said you were ready to show me what you've been doing?" James said, unable to keep the distrust out of his voice. Alan seemed not to notice the inflection in his voice, and continued smiling enthusiastically.

"Ah, yes. But, first, come with me to the window. I want to show you something," Alan said, leading James away. James cautiously followed, looking around the room. He saw nothing that looked like it would be part of any sort of presentation. In fact, the only noticeable thing in the room, aside from the furniture, was the tall stack of personal files on the glass table.

"What do you want to show me?" James asked.

"Just... look out at the people down below for a minute," Alan said.

"I don't know what you're getting at, but alright..." James said. The two stood side by side, looking out of the window at the bunker below. As they stood there in silence, James suddenly felt something pinch his neck. Before he even had time to touch the spot, something was suddenly forced over his head and tighten over his face. He quickly recognized it was a plastic bag, maybe nothing more than a grocery bag. This was all his mind could comprehend before his body started shaking. He then vomited, which quickly filled up the bag in front of him. He didn't even time to be completely disgusted before he collapsed.

Angel Puer supported his body and laid him down gently on the ground, her one hand still holding the vomit-filled bag against his face, the other hand still holding the syringe. Alan was standing over the both of them, his enthusiastic smile ever-present.

October 2, 2031

The Council, which was normally composed of President, Vice President, Chief Researcher, Chief Physician, Chief of Security, with Percy Winkle as an unofficial sixth member, had assembled for the first time. The Council only met for matters of extreme importance, such as when a member of the Council needed to be replaced. All five living members of the Council sat at the far side of the large conference table. Standing in front of the Council was Jane McVellion.

"Personally, I believe Officer McVellion will make a perfect replacement for the chief of security. In the short time I've known her, she's proven herself to take her responsibilities quite seriously. She doesn't fool around and is even dead serious most of the time. She, uh..." Alan paused to think. His confident exterior wavered slightly. Then it returned as his face brightened up. "I know she can get the job done, and handle any situations thrown her way," he concluded confidently. Toaden looked at every person in the room, stopping on Alan.

"That's a rather short argument. And a lot of trust you're putting into this officer. Especially considering you barely seem to know much about her, yourself," Toaden said. "Is that all you have to say on her behalf?" Alan nodded. Toaden turned to Jane. "Do you have anything to say on your own account?"

"The dude's dead. You need a replacement, and I don't see anyone else here."

"Elegantly put," Toaden said sarcastically, turning to the rest of the Council. "Now it's just time to vote."

"What do you mean, *vote*?" Jane asked impatiently, taking a step forward. She began tapping her foot.

"In order to replace a Council member, dead or alive, at least three of the remaining Council members need to approve of the replacement. I believe we already know President Berkoff's stance." Toaden explained. "I vote no. This is far too early to make a decision on this matter."

"I also vote no," Dr. Marie added. All eyes turned to Harrack. He sighed.

"I abstain," Harrack said. He looked very tired.

"And why is that, Dr. Harrack?" Alan asked, cocking his head to the side.

"I am not comfortable making a decision on this matter," Harrack stated. "And with the sudden death of Chief House, I don't think we should rush to find a new chief yet."

Alan smiled and stared directly into Harrack's eyes. "*What* exactly was it that killed Mr. House, doctor?" Alan said slowly, putting significant emphasis on the "what."

Harrack swallowed. "So far, all signs point to natural causes."

"That's bullshit. James House was a healthy individual, without any medical issues to speak of!" Dr. Marie durst out.

"Sometimes, these things just happen," Harrack said feebly.

"I think we both know they don't," Dr. Marie snapped back.

"Dr. Marie, now is hardly the time to bring this up," Toaden snapped.

"No, no. It's perfectly alright," Alan said in a relaxed tone. He looked at Dr. Marie. "Do you have any proof to backup your claims?"

"I have his medical record," Dr. Marie said.

"And that proves what, exactly?" Alan said, his smile growing.

"It proves that James House was incredibly unlikely to die of 'natural causes.'"

"I agree it was unlikely, but is it impossible?" Alan said, leaning forward.

"Well... no, not technically, but-"

"But it proves nothing," Alan said, cutting Dr. Marie off.

"It's just too much of a coincidence," Dr. Marie said, thoroughly convinced.

"Maybe, but coincidences are hardly facts. And it certainly doesn't prove anything," Alan said. The corners of his lips curled into a devilish smirk. "I know it's tough to believe, Dr. Marie, but it's the truth." Dr. Marie stared at him, analyzing his face. But she had nothing else to say, and sighed in defeat. Everyone turned back to Harrack. "Well, Dr. Harrack? Do you still abstain?"

Harrack looked at Alan, whose smile was still attached upon his face. "No. I vote for Officer McVellion as the new chief."

"Thank you very much, Dr. Harrack," Alan said. Dr. Marie let out an agitated sigh.

"Are we done yet? Am I chief now?" Jane had a frustrated tone.

"No. There needs to be three votes yes for someone on the Council to be replaced. You only have two," Toaden said, his own patience short.

"So I suppose now I have to vote," Percy said. Everyone reacted with mild surprise.

"You shouldn't even have a vote," Dr. Marie stated with clear frustration.

"This is *my* bunker, so I should have a say in who represents it to the citizens. And you need a tiebreaker." Percy leaned forward. "I've listened to both sides state their cases." He turned to Jane. "Officer McVellion, President Berkoff speaks highly of you. But I'd prefer to hear you speak for yourself." Alan's smile began fading. Percy cleared his throat. "Do you understand what the responsibilities of security chief are?"

"Yeah," Jane responded. Percy waited for her to continue. When she didn't, he elaborated.

"Can you tell me what they are?"

"Tell the other officers what to do, and keep idiots from screwing shit up."

Percy wore a completely neutral expression. "And what would you do if another officer didn't do what you tell them to do?"

"I'd *make* him do what I said," Jane said. Alan's smile had completely disappeared. Percy considered her words for a minute.

"And what would you do if, as you say, 'an idiot screwed something up?'"

"I'd punish him, and make an example out of him so that others knew to stay in their place."

"I see…" Percy said thoughtfully, leaning forward. "When I asked you what the responsibilities of the security chief were, your answer missed the most important duty. As a chief of security, you and your fellow officers job is to make the citizens here feel secure. Can you tell me how you would do that?"

"I…" Jane paused to think. "I would…" Jane was unable to produce any more words. Alan also leaned forward.

"I'm sure you would do that by making the officers' presence known and swiftly apprehend anyone who would disturb the peace, right Officer McVellion?" Alan said.

"Yeah," Jane said.

"Thank you, President Berkoff. I'm sure you would make a great security chief, but you're not the one who's being interviewed. So please refrain from distracting Officer McVellion," Percy said. Alan slumped back in his seat, now frowning deeply. Dr. Marie snickered slightly.

"Officer McVellion," Percy said in a blunt tone. "Do you believe you would be able to keep the peace and make citizens feel safe, especially in the wake of the recent string of sudden deaths?"

"Uh," Jane seemed not to register the question. Before she had the chance to say anything else, Percy leaned back in his seat.

"I don't know what kind of joke this is, Alan, but it's not a very funny one. This woman is clearly not qualified to lead the security force, and, quite frankly, I'm amazed she got on it to begin with. I imagine she must have some skill that would cause her to be placed on it, but that doesn't make her a preferable choice to lead it. My vote is a definite no. Now can we stop wasting our time here and return to our responsibilities?"

With the last word, Percy stood up from his seat. The other four sitting down also stood up. As Percy, Toaden, Harrack, and Dr. Marie headed for the elevator, Alan just stood there scowling. The other four walked around Jane, then headed into the elevator. As the doors to it closed, Alan and Jane exchanged a glare.

October 2, 2031
Medical Report Log-05
Doctor Linda Marie
Subject: Suspicious Deaths & Politics

"This is unbelievable. James House's body wasn't even warm, and the president tried to replace him! On top of that, Dr. Harrack refused to bring in Dr. Genson to do an autopsy on Mr. House. Harrack just cremated the body, claiming he died from 'natural causes.' Bullshit. James House was healthy. But President Berkoff railroaded me, and I couldn't prove that Dr. Harrack was hiding something. Those two must be working together. This isn't the first time Harrack has done this, either. There were three deaths yesterday, a patient of mine, named Jim Penn, and an alcoholic named Dylan Beecut, both of which died under mysterious circumstances. Harrack said Beecut had died from alcohol poisoning and that Penn had died from viral infection. But Mr. Penn was recovering the last time I saw him. He should be alive and walking around right now. But he isn't. Something is definitely going on here. I don't know what, but I know that Berkoff and Harrack are definitely involved. And where does Jane McVellion fit into all this? At least Berkoff's plan to replace James House failed.

"Dr. Harrack's decision to vote with President Berkoff weren't a surprise, but what did surprise me was Percy Winkle. I know that he's a close personal friend of the president, so I assumed he would vote with Berkoff. But he instead questioned McVellion. All of his questions were surprisingly smart. I was not expecting that from him, but I was pleasantly surprised. I didn't trust him at first, but I'm starting to think Percy Winkle is not all that bad after all. I don't think this will stop whatever Berkoff is planning, but at least it'll slow him down. Hopefully that will give the rest of us enough time to figure out what he *is* planning. Well, that's all there is to report for now."

End of log.

President Alan Berkoff

Vice President Eustace Toaden

Chief Researcher Dr. William Harrack

Chief Physician Dr. Linda Marie

Head of Security ~~James House~~ [DECEASED]

Security Force (20):

Roy Bant - Joshua Black - Robert Cansky - Winston Castor - Peter Corrad - Lucille Desin - Jonathan Dinlum - Richard Farkass - Jacob Faunt - Aranai Fielding - Kate Finn - John House - Barney Keeling - Roberta Kisk - Jane McVellion - Joseph Nine - Scott Samona - Catherine Vilner - Gordon Yackit - Zachary Zyz

Citizens (90):

Bing Abbot - Ann Akai - Rose Anderson - Jacob Ardune - Robert Beaner - Sarah Barnes - Cherry Beau - ~~Dylan Beecut~~ [DECEASED] - Margaret Belcher - Andrew Bigelow - Alfonzo Bogardanzi - Daniel Butler - Marino Cantopus - Booker Cooper - John Dash - Jet Dashel - Mark DeFrana - Samuel Dunkard - Barry Eldren - Jeremy Finickle - Candice Finnell - Haiten Fish - Henry Flagelmeier - Maxwell Geck - Dr. Phillip Genson - Marta Girasol - Casey Goodwill - Chandler Haal - Ernest Handler - Garrison Hartford - Alfred Hatton - John Heegan - Mario Henderson - Nancy House - William House - Conrad Jackman - Vincent Jax - ~~Harry Jenkins~~ [DECEASED] - Leyna Kase - Martin Kievan - Wanda Lamon - King Liardi - William Lovell - Mary Lovell - Geoffrey Lowell - River Maple - Oliver Markus - Delegan McHarvan - Diana Mint - Gilbert Nose - Mickey November - Conor O'Reilly - Patrick Peaskill - ~~Jim Penn~~ [DECEASED] - Jonathan Peterson - Angel Puer - Richard Reel - Captain Rex - Doug Roberts - Hank Rockell - Dishtowel Sacks - Jillian Sampson - Nadia Schwartz - Argus Scott - Jeremiah Shoostand - Robert Simpson - Howard Skittering - Jaime Slewdjack - Toby Smalls - Harold Smidt - Janet Smith - Nicolas Smithson - Meegan Spoon - Sean Tilling - Gary Tills - Barnaby Tob - Colin Vacett - Tia Valentine - Amelia Vanisha - Anthony Weitson - Hannah Welt - Dean Wentell - Theodore Weston - Andrew Wicker - Peach Williamson - Dell Willis - Percy Winkle - Denger Woof - Laney Youth - Johnson Zip

Shortly after finishing her report, Dr. Marie decided to go out for a walk to soothe her nerves. As she walked out of her office, she practically walked into a man wearing a security officer uniform. He had just been about to enter her office, but the two quickly stopped inches from each other. After an awkward moment, she stepped back, entering her office and inviting him in. The man graciously nodded and stepped inside.

"Sorry to bother you, but there's something of vital importance you should see," the man stated.

"What are you talking about? Who are you?" Dr. Marie asked, shaking her head with confusion. She looked at his uniform, and grumbled. "Don't tell me you're here to tell me why *you* should be the next chief of security. I really don't have the time or the patience to deal with that right now."

"My name is Zachary Zyz, and I can assure you that is not at all why I'm here," the man said, and removed a folded piece of paper from his vest and handed it to her. Dr. Marie took the paper, eying him suspiciously. She carefully unfolded it, and began to read it over. then read it over a second time, just to make sure she had read it right. When she was certain she had, she looked up from it.

"I have to show this to Toaden!" she said, running out the door, shoving the letter into her lab coat pocket. Zyz walked out the door, following at a slower pace. A familiar, golden haired woman also stepped out from around the corner of Dr. Marie's office, and began following them at a safe distance.

*   *   *

Rose Anderson and Casey Goodwill watched as the two female security officers set up a medium sized folding table outside of the fence surrounding the security station. Breakfast had just ended, and an announcement had been made that the security force was looking to recruit more officers, or at least one to fill in the now-empty position on the force. Once the table was set up, the two officers also set up two folding chairs, and Rose and Casey watched the officers sit down. The two waited patiently as the breakfast crowd cleared out, leaving very few people still around. After about ten minutes, one officer turned to the other.

"I don't think we've formally met yet," she said, smiling nicely. The other officer looked at her and smiled back.

"No, we probably haven't," she said.

"I'm Lucy Desin," the first officer said.

"Cat Vilner," said the second, and the two shook hands. They continued to sit in silence for a few more minutes while nothing happened.

"So how did you end up on the security force?" Lucy asked.

"Oh, well, I don't really know. I kinda tried to become a cop, but I never quite made it. Still went through most of the training, though. The only other thing I can think of is that I've been *told* I'm excellent at diffusing tense situations. My parents always said I should become a politician," Cat said, and laughed.

"That's cool!" Lucy said sweetly. "Yeah, my father used to always take me out to go shooting. Turned me into a 'crack shot,' as he would say. I never killed anything, though. I could never bring myself to do it."

"Ever had any official training?" Cat asked.

"In what?" Lucy returned.

"Marksmanship," Cat clarified.

"Oh, no. But I have won more than one shooting competition, if that counts," Lucy said. They both suddenly heard the sound of someone clearing their throat. Lucy and Cat turned their attention away from each other to notice a short line of only two people standing in front of them. The first of the two, likely the one who had cleared his throat, stood at about 4 foot seven inches.

"Can we help you?" Cat asked.

"My name is Garrison Hartford, and I would like to apply to the security force," he stated professionally. Cat and Lucy exchanged a nervous look. They turned back to Garrison.

"While we appreciate your for your interest, we don't really have any uniforms that would fit you," Cat said, giving an awkward yet apologetic smile. Garrison sighed and nodded.

"I understand," he said simply, then turned away.

"Wait!" Lucy said suddenly. Garrison turned back to face her. "I mean, you probably don't *need* an official uniform. We could always use undercover, or - how do you say it? - 'plain-clothes' officers."

"Well, we'd need to clear it with the new chief, but I don't see why not," Cat said. "Now, what is your experience with firearms?"

"I only got into them a few years ago, however I've been practicing with multiple types of firearms, including automatic and semiautomatic, regularly since then. I even built up a collection of guns, but as I'm sure you can guess, they aren't allowed here, so I had to give them away to friends," Garrison explained. Cat nodded respectfully.

"Please fill this out. Thank you," she said as she slid a paper form and pen across the table to him. Garrison took the pen and paper and stepped off to the end of the table, and began filling out the form. The second applicant, young man stepped up to the table. He had curly, ginger hair and was quite thin. Cat and Lucy once again exchanged another look.

"Um... exactly how old are you?" Cat asked.

"I'm eighteen. Why? Does that matter?" he asked, tilting his head. His short, ginger hair fluffed up slightly.

"Just making sure you're even old enough to own a gun," Cat said.

"Well, the army recruits people my age, so I guess I am," he responded.

"Right, well... I suppose I should ask what your name is," Cat said.

"Jaime Slewdjack," he said.

"And what experience do you have with firearms?"

"Well, my pa has been teaching me to shoot since I was little. I've just always been around guns, and I know how to use them," Jaime said.

"I see. Alright, here's the application. Please fill it out and return it to us once you're finished," Cat said, sliding him the pen and paper. He took them, and stepped to the side to finish filling it out. While he was, Garrison handed his form in.

"Thank you. We'll get back to you soon," Lucy said with a smile. Garrison nodded pleasantly and walked away. A minute or two later, Jaime did the same.

"I think that's all we're gonna get," Cat said.

"If I didn't have to go out on patrol soon, I'd say we should stay a little longer," Lucy responded.

"You still go on patrol? Even though we don't have a chief?"

"Well, my partner used to be in the military. So he's sticking to Chief House's patrol schedule," Lucy said.

"Your partner is Officer Zyz, right? Isn't he supposed to be second in command, or something like that?" Cat asked.

"Yeah, something like that," Lucy said. "By the way, who's your partner?"

"Oh, Officer McVellion. She usually just does her own thing, though. Sometimes she'll just disappear and leave me all alone. I don't really mind it too much, though. Alone time never really bothered me."

"Yeah, alone time is nice sometimes," Lucy said. Cat looked down at the two applications in her hands.

"What do you think we should do with the applications?"

"I say we just hold onto these until a new chief is selected. Like I think we're supposed to," Lucy said with a shrug. The two then stood up and folded up the chairs and tables and brought them back inside. It would still be some time before lunch started.

*   *   *

Candice Finnell was once a professional athlete, who had spent most of her life training for the Olympic track and field competitions. Upon being selected for residence inside of the bunker, she had decided that it was probably a better option than risking being evaporated in an instant. However, since they would likely open up the bunker once more if international tensions had been relieved, at least to the point of relative safety, she decided to keep up with her training. And old habits were hard to get out of.

Her routine included jogging from her house all the way through to the back row of houses, and then continuing to jog along the entire perimeter of the bunker. She had just started and was still jogging through the rows of houses. Entering the "T" section, she spotted something interesting in the corner of her eye. As she slowed to a stop, she saw in one of the alleyways a figure lying on the ground. At least that's what she thought she saw. It was pretty dark in between the houses. She squinted and took a few steps forward, but before she could get much closer, something suddenly hit the back of her head and knocked her down.

As she landed, her face smashed into the hard rock on the ground. She felt her nose break on impact. Before she could even move, she was kicked hard the right side of her ribs. She coughed once, and another, harder, kick rolled her onto her left side. As she tried to look up at her attacker, a third kick hit the center of her chest, knocking all of the air out of her lungs.

She gasped for air and yet another kick connected with her face, knocking her teeth in. She coughed out some blood and loose teeth as blood also freely ran from her nose. She began to cry, and risked looking up again. Jane McVellion stood over her, holding a baton. Jane struck Candice on her right side. Candice coughed out a gurgled cry for help. Crying much harder, she desperately reached one arm out and attempted to crawl away. It was then that the baton struck her head for the first time, disorienting her. When the second strike on her head came down, she nearly blacked out. The third did knock her out. The fourth, fifth, sixth, seventh, eighth, and ninth times made sure she stayed out.

Jane was long gone by the time anyone found the body. The figure in the alleyway had managed to crawl out into the light. As he tried to force himself to stand up, the most Tony Weitson could manage was to crawl on his hands and knees. Still, as he trudged back along the route Candice had taken to get where she was, he was eventually found, sooner than she was.

*   *   *

Less than an hour later, DT Sacks, John Dash, Toby Smalls, Marta Girasol, and even Howard Skittering were all gathered around the bed in Dr. Linda Marie's office. Tony Weitson was laying there, breathing hoarsely. A young, thin man with curly hair stood off to the side, near the entrance. He was shifting his legs awkwardly. Marta looked at the young man.

"What are you doing here?" she asked, light tears in her eyes.

"Mr. Slewdjack, here, was the one who found Mr. Weitson on the ground," Dr. Marie explained as she hooked Tony up to a respirator and heart monitor. "I happened to be nearby, looking for… anyways, Mr. Slewdjack found me and told me about Mr. Weitson, and I dropped what I was doing to bring him back here immediately."

"Oh. *Gracias*," Marta said, then turned her attention back to Tony. Jaime nervously muttered a thanks, but no one was paying attention. After another few seconds of awkwardly standing there, he excused himself from the office, and slipped away without anyone noticing. Tony's breathing had become slow and labored. Everyone stood silently around his motionless body, unsure what to do. A few brief moments of silence seemed to stretch on forever. As time seemed to stand completely still, they were suddenly brought back to reality by Toby spontaneously breaking into tears. Sobbing uncontrollably, he bolted out of the room, disappearing.

"Should someone go make sure he's okay?" DT asked.

"Let him be for now. If he doesn't cool off on his own, he can always be comforted later," Dash said. They stood there for another painfully silent ten minutes. After that time, Tony began violently coughing and everyone tensed up fearfully. He coughed for a few moments, then his body relaxed. The respirator stopped moving, and the heartbeat monitor let out a steady, constant tone.

Dr. Marie shut off the heartbeat monitor. She gently and respectfully pulled a white blanket over Tony Weitson's body. She turned to the small crowd still gathered in her office.

"You're welcome to stay here, if you need. But I have some business I need to attend to," Dr. Marie said, slowly leaving the room.

*　　*　　*

Dr. William Harrack stared down at the body on his crematorium. It was bloody and broken. He quickly identified the body as that of one Candice Finnell. Harrack was flipping through her file. After skimming through it, he stamped a large [DECEASED] at the end of the file, then closed it and put it back on his desk. Harrack heard the ding signifying that someone had entered his office. He sighed and walked out of the back room. He was genuinely, but not pleasantly, surprised to see Dr. Linda Marie standing in his office. "What?" He asked curtly.

"I just figured I'd let you know that someone has just passed away. I have something else to attend to, but I figured I'd at least give you a head's up," she said unhappily.

"I appreciate your warning," Harrack stated neutrally. Dr. Marie glared at him once over.

"Before I go, I heard some citizens talking about a young lady who had died. I'm sure her body would have reached you by now," she said.

"Yes. Her body is in the back, actually. A Miss Candice Finnell. Fantastic record. It's a shame her life was cut short in this way," Harrack said. Then, after a minute, he added, "She had much potential." Dr. Marie eyed him suspiciously.

"What happened to her?" she asked cautiously.

"Murder, unfortunately. I'm not at liberty to divulge any more than that," Harrack said, then turned away and walked back towards his back room. Dr. Marie silently glared at his back as he disappeared into his back room. In another minute, she heard the crematory fire up, and she decided now was a good time to leave.

*   *   *

"At the rate people are dying, we won't last two years down here," Vice President Eustace Toaden said to President Alan Berkoff as the two stared at the latest census report. Alan, with his hand on his chin, nodded slowly.

"Did you do the exact math?" he finally said. Toaden looked at him with slight disbelief.

"You *can't* be serious," Toaden said impatiently, completely in disbelief. Alan acted as if he didn't notice Toaden's tone, and looked at him with indifference.

"Well, *I* think it's important to know *exactly* how long we've got," Alan answered, almost indignantly. Toaden sighed and walked away from him, leaving the report on the conference table. Alan picked up the report and stared at it. The elevator dinged, and within a few moments, it opened and Dr. Marie walked in. She briefly scanned the room, ignoring Alan and resting her eyes on Toaden.

"Vice President Toaden," she said formally. "I need to speak with you." She looked at Alan. "Alone." Toaden nodded quickly, almost knowingly, and the two were soon walking back towards the elevator. As they were about to press the button, however, Alan interrupted them.

"Is there something that I should be aware of?" he asked passively, almost with disinterest. Dr. Marie paused and thought for a moment, before turning around and looking at him, wearing a polite smile.

"I wouldn't want to disrupt your important presidential duties," Dr. Marie said politely, barely concealing her condescending tone. Alan smiled politely back and nodded, before turning away with indifference. As he turned away, Dr. Marie quickly pressed the button and the doors opened. She and Toaden stepped inside, and the doors closed.

"What is it?" Toaden asked as the elevator moved down.

"I can prove that President Berkoff had something to do with Chief House's death!" she said.

"Really?" Toaden said, surprised. "How?"

Before Dr. Marie could answer, the elevator stopped and the doors opened, revealing Jane McVellion standing right right in front of it. Jane immediately glared at both of the elevator's occupants, not even trying to hide her anger.

"Officer McVellion," Toaden greeted her formally and attempted to walk directly towards her. Jane didn't step out of the way and Toaden stopped as the two were inches away. "Please step out of the way." She ignored him and stayed exactly where she was. There was a moment of tense, awkward silence and nobody moved. Dr. Marie finally cleared her throat and took a step forward. She looked at Jane, who continued to glare. Dr. Marie took another step, this time around Jane. Toaden, eying Jane annoyedly, followed suit. Dr. Marie looked away from the agitated Jane as they were shoulder to shoulder. As Jane continued to do nothing but glare, Dr. Marie started walking away. Her pace picked up with each step, and she could feel Toaden right behind her. Dr. Marie breathed a slight sigh of relief. However, she did not make it to the exit uninterrupted.

"Where are you going?" Dr. Marie and Toaden stopped in their tracks. Jane's tone was unpleasant, to say the least. Dr. Marie sighed heavily and slowly turned back around.

"I may not know why you think you're entitled to question us, but your job is to keep peace and order down here, not to question us. Just because the president thinks you should be the next chief of security does not mean you have privileges that go along with the position. Now get back to work," Toaden said firmly. Dr. Marie froze in surprise. She hadn't expected Toaden to speak up. But she was glad he did.

Jane's face twisted into a furious expression. She let out a low growl, but then seemingly calmed herself down slightly. "Fine. I was just asking." Jane turned away from them, and sat down on the bench, picking up a large rifle that had been left there. Dr. Marie hurried away and exited the building, and Toaden quickly followed. Once they were out of the security station, Dr. Marie increased her speed, then glanced over her shoulder at Toaden.

"Come on, we should get back to my off-" Dr. Marie was suddenly cut off as she walked into something with enough force to knock the air out of her. She stumbled back. Once she realized that the something was a some*one*, she mouthed out a quick apology and continued on at the same pace, without even looking at the person. Toaden followed at a similar speed. The woman Dr. Marie had bumped into brushed some long, golden hair out of her face.

"I wonder what Berkoff sees in McVellion," Toaden said as they entered Dr. Marie's office. He waited until Dr. Marie had finished locking the door. "Now, what was it that you wanted to tell me?"

*   *   *

Lunch would begin shortly, and Jaime Slewdjack sat alone. People were just beginning to gather. Jaime was letting his mind drift, and was lost in thought. As such, he didn't notice Toby Smalls approach him and sit down. Jaime snapped out of his thoughts and looked at Toby.

"Thanks for, uh, finding Tony," Toby said.

"Don't mention it," Jaime said hesitantly. The two sat in awkward silence, the tears still fresh in Toby's eyes. "I'm, uh, sorry for your loss."

"Thanks," Toby sniffled. He smiled at Jaime, anyways.

"Were you close?" Jaime asked.

"Well, I'd like to think so," Toby said, his smile growing a little bigger.

"Were you friends outside of the bunker? I know we were all randomly selected, and all," Jaime said, rubbing the back of his head.

"No, we met down here," Toby replied. His sobbing was subsiding.

"Oh," Jaime said. He thought for a moment. "I didn't know you could get that close to someone in such a short period of time." Toby's smile widened a little more.

"Well, I like to think that people are naturally friends until they're given a reason not to be. At least that's what I believe," Toby explained.

"Ah," Jaime said.

"What about you? Made any friends since you've been down here?" Toby asked.

"No, not really," Jaime said nervously. "I'm not really great with people."

"Oh, that's okay. I know a lot of people aren't," Toby said.

"What about all the others?" Jaime asked.

"Others?"

"The others who were with you when your friend... passed," Jaime elaborated.

"Hmm... well, I met all of them down here, too. But I'd like to think they're all also my friends!" Toby said with a little happiness.

"That's nice," Jaime said. He paused. "Tell me about them."

"Oh," Toby said. "There's Howard. He spends a lot of time alone, but I think he's pretty cool. He's kinda rude sometimes, though. There's also DT. He's quiet a lot. Doesn't smile much. But he seems nice enough. Marta's also pretty nice, but she can be tough at times. She speaks Spanish, too, which is cool. Even if I don't know what she's saying most of the time. John's also quiet a lot, but when he does talk, it's usually pretty interesting."

"That's cool," Jaime said, leaning forward. "What about your friend who just passed. What was his name? Watson, Whiteman, something like that?"

"Weitson. But his first name is... was Tony," Toby said. His smile held a hint of sadness as he continued on. "He was drunk when we met him. But then he found out he was sick, and he spent a lot of time sad and grumpy. But he also had some really cool stories! When we first met him, he talked about the adventures he and his friend used to go on! Like the time they all got drunk and snuck into a fancy golf course for rich people. They almost got caught, but managed to get away."

Jaime let out a light laugh. "Well, that sounds very exciting."

"Yeah, I know!" Toby said gleefully. The lunch crowd then began filing into the dining area. Toby and Jaime were soon joined by Dash and DT. Toby introduced them to Jaime.

"Where's Howard and Marta?" Toby asked.

"They both said they needed some time alone, and went back to their homes. At least, that's where I'm assuming they went," DT answered.

"Oh," Toby said, a little disappointed. But he perked right back up. "Well, I'm sure we'll see them later!"

"I'm certain," Dash said flatly. DT turned to Jaime.

"So, uh... tell us a little about yourself?" DT said uncertainly.

"Oh, well," Jaime said, pausing to think. "Not much to say, really. Nothing special about me."

"Oh, come on! Everyone's got something special about them!" Toby said.

"Well..." Jaime was stumped. "I guess I'm the youngest person here? At least from what I've seen."

"Yeah, I've noticed a surprising lack of kids. It's... kinda weird," DT said. "Wonder why there aren't any down here."

"They're harder to evaluate," Dash said, taking a sip of his drink. Everyone turned to him with confused expressions.

"Evaluate? What do you mean by that?" DT asked. Dash finished taking his drink and set the cup down.

"The lottery," he stated. The others waited for him to continue. He didn't.

"What *about* the lottery?" DT asked.

"When evaluating potential candidates to be sent in here, they excluded children," Dash continued. The other three were now leaning intently towards him.

"Why not?" Jaime asked. "And how do you even know all this?"

"They based the lottery off of tax information and what the US census could supply. Plus they didn't want unattended children roaming freely, as there weren't quite enough room for full families." Dash paused. "And I know this because my mother... well, it doesn't matter too much. We're all down here already, so this won't change anything." The others continued to press for information, but Dash kept his lips closed.

Meanwhile, Howard Skittering had locked himself inside of his house. He slowly rocked back and forth on his bed, muttering slightly and crying softly. Tears were streaming down his face. As his cries turned into panicked hyperventilation, he suddenly felt that he could no longer stay in this house.

*   *   *

"I can prove President Berkoff had something to do with the death of Chief House," Dr. Marie quickly said. Toaden didn't immediately react. After a moment of processing the information, Toaden cleared his throat.

"How?" was all Toaden said.

"I have a letter, written by James House himself!" Dr. Marie said confidently, smiling victoriously.

"Can I see it?" Toaden asked, raising an eyebrow. Dr. Marie nodded and reached into her pocket. In a single instant, her smile disappeared and her face took on a panicked look. She violently dug around in her pocket, then began searching every other pocket on her person, each second her movements growing more desperate. Toaden sighed.

"I had it!" Dr. Marie practically yelled.

"Look," Toaden started. "I'm sure you did. You're not the type who seems like they would just make something like this up. At least, I didn't think you were. But without any actual proof, we can't *do* anything. So I'm sorry, but there's nothing we can do. If you find that letter, come get me. Otherwise... I think we'll just have to let this go."

Before Dr. Marie had a chance to respond, Toaden had unlocked the door and walked out of her office, leaving utterly infuriated and confused.

*   *   *

Alan was alone in the High Rise, sitting across one of the many chairs. His back against one arm and his legs dangling over the other, reading through Jane McVellion's file. Then the elevators beeped. He didn't pay it much mind and when the doors opened a few minutes later, he looked up.

"Ah, Robbie!" He said happily as Angel Puer walked into the room. She leisurely walked over to him. When she reached him, she dropped a folded piece of paper in his lap. "What's this?" he asked, straightening his body and sitting up. Angel backed up as he opened the letter and read it.

"Huh. House was smarter than I gave him credit for. I didn't think he'd leave behind a 'just in case' note." He looked up at Angel. "Where did you find this?" She didn't respond. Alan stood up. "Well, no matter. It's here now, and we'll make sure no one ever sees it." Alan smiled viciously and reached into his back pocket. His smile then disappeared and was replaced with a neutral expression. He looked up at Angel.

"You wouldn't happen to have a lighter, would you?" he asked. She raised her shoulders slightly, then let them drop back down. "Ugh, fine." Alan then began ripping the paper up, into smaller and smaller pieces. Finally, when he had hands full of what looked like confetti, he walked over to one of the smaller carpets in the room, lifted it up, and tossed all the small pieces of paper underneath.

"*There*," he said in a satisfied tone. He then went back over to his chair and sat down once more. As he went back to Jane's file, Angel walked to the wood-panelled wall, to the left of the elevator, where the secret compartment she hid in was. She began to feel all around the wall. Alan looked up from the file. "What are you doing, Robbie?" he asked. She ignored him and continued searching the wall. He shrugged and returned his attention to his chosen reading material. Angel continued examining the wall. As she reached the spot directly to the left of the elevator, she stopped. Alan looked up with only mild interest. As he watched, she pushed in on the wall, which caused a small section to swing open, like a little door. Inside was a nine digit keypad. Alan suddenly perked up.

"Well, *that's* interesting!" he said. The two stared at the keypad. "Wonder what it does," he speculated. After a minute or two, Angel closed the door and continued her search along the wall. Alan, now much more interested, placed the file on the table and stood up. He walked over to her and stood behind her as she continued her search to the right of the elevator. It wasn't long before she found another loose piece of wall. As she pressed it in, a little drawer slid open. It was filled with official-looking manuels. Angel pulled the drawer out further and started digging through it. Alan walked around to the other side of the drawer and also began looking through it.

It wasn't long before Alan pulled out a spiral bound book. Angel stopped going through the drawer and looked up at him. He opened up the book, and began reading. "Congratulations! You have just been elected president of the bunker! I'm sure you are very happy, but be careful of the responsiblah," Alan said, and began slowly flipping through the pages. Finally he stopped and let out a satisfied, "Ah! As president, here's what you can and can't do." Alan shifted the book to one hand and began running his finger through it. Finally he looked up and Angel and smiled devilishly. "Let's see what Eustace thinks of this."

*   *   *

Zachary Zyz and Lucy Desin were patrolling through the residential area. Given the general calmness of the bunker, Zyz was able to be preoccupied with his thoughts. James House had been right to be wary of President Berkoff. Zyz had already handed the letter James wrote over the Dr. Marie. She could do more than he could. He still had the letter James had meant for his siblings. However, at that moment, Zyz was more concerned with what to do about John House. Zyz wasn't overly worried, but he hadn't been overly worried about James, either. However, there was very little Zyz could do from his current position, and he simply hoped that John House would be able to take care of himself.

The lunch crowd was just making their ways back to their houses. As the two security officers were walking down to the back of the residential area, something suddenly grabbed Zyz's shoulder. He spun around, his hand on his weapon. Dr. Marie looked up at him with an incredibly unhappy expression. Zyz removed his hand from his weapon. Lucy looked between the two of them in confusion. Dr. Marie glanced nervously at Lucy, then turned back to Zyz.

"Can we talk in private?" she asked. Zyz looked at Lucy.

"Um... I can go on ahead. Just try not to take too long, okay?" Lucy said. She walked slowly, turning and looking at them as she left. After a moment, she finally turned away from them and picked up speed.

"James's letter went missing," Dr. Marie said.

"What happened?" Zyz asked, shocked.

"When I went to show the letter to the vice president, it was just... gone," Dr. Marie said.

"So you lost it?" Zyz asked.

"No!" Dr. Marie yelled, offended.

"Then what happened to it?" Zyz asked, crossing his arms.

"Aren't we supposed to be on the same side here?!" Dr. Marie sighed. "I don't know where it went, okay!? Look, did James leave any other letters?" she asked desperately.

"Only one other letter meants for his siblings," Zyz answered.

"Can I see it?" Dr. Marie said. Zyz just frowned at her. "I just want to see if it indicts Berkoff. If it doesn't, I'll give it right back." Zyz sighed and pulled the letter out of his vest and handed it to her. She snatched it out of his hand and began furiously reading the document. After a minute, she sighed and handed it back to Zyz. He folded it back up and placed it in his vest.

"There has got to be some way for me to prove that Berkoff killed Chief House," Dr. Marie said finally.

"As much as I'd like to help you figure that out, there's nothing more I can offer you. I need to get back to patrol now," Zyz said. He turned his back on Dr. Marie, walking at a brisk pace to catch up with Lucy. After walking a few steps, he stopped and turned around. "I hope you find that letter. I really do." Then he was gone. With nothing left to say, Dr. Marie sighed heavily and trudged away.

*　　*　　*

The rest of the day passed without any noteworthy incident. After almost everybody else had gone to sleep, John Dash once again found himself wandering over to the vault door. The lights had long since been shut off for the night. As he walked through the barely-illuminated darkness, he nearly bumped something standing in the darkness. As he tried to get his bearings, what he had nearly bumped into shifted.

"*Lo siento,*" Dash heard a familiar voice say.

"It's alright," he responded.

"John?" the familiar voice asked. It took Dash a few seconds to register the voice.

"Marta?" he asked, surprised. "What are you doing here?"

"Probably the same reason you're here," Marta replied.

"I'm just going for a walk," Dash answered. As Dash's eyes better adjusted to the darkness, he could see Marta's outline. She turned away from him to face the door. He remembered how he had met her the first night in almost the exact same situation.

"It's funny how quickly things can change, isn't it?" she asked suddenly.

"Yes, it is," was all Dash could think to say.

"It's only been a little over a week, and... well... I've made the friends that I'll have for the rest of my life. Lost one, too," she said, the sadness evident in her voice. Dash was unsure how to respond.

"I'm sure the situation outside will improve, and this door will open, and we can leave," he stated in his most comforting voice, which was not very comforting. Marta sighed.

"What if it doesn't? What if we really all do end up as the last of humanity? And *don't* say anything about repopulation!"

Even Dash smiled at that one. "I wasn't going to. Besides, I don't think that's what they had in mind when they sent us down here," Dash replied knowingly.

"Why do you think we're down here, then?" she asked.

"Most likely just so America can say it's citizens survived longer than any other country," Dash said.

"But brag to who, if everyone else is dead?"

Dash smiled in the darkness. "If you have to ask that, then you don't really know much about America."

"Well, I was born in Puerto Rico, and we always had our own set of issues to worry about," Marta replied.

"In that case, I can assure you that the US government sending us down here just so we survive *slightly* longer than everyone else is *far* from one of the worst plans the government has had. If you don't believe me, I'd be happy to tell you some of the CIA's plans to assassinate Castro," Dash said with a slight laugh. Marta also let out a laugh. "Or MK Ultra, for something more serious."

"Even so, I'd still expect them to have *some* common sense," Marta replied, still laughing.

"Well, as my mother always says, 'Common sense becomes more and more of an oxymoron everyday,'" Dash said.

"Oxymoron?" Marta asked, turning to him.

"It basically means two words put together that are opposites or each other," Dash explained. "Popular examples are 'jumbo shrimp' or 'a fine mess.'"

"Oh, I get it," Marta said, turning back to the massive steel structure. They stood still for a moment longer.

"How long did you live in Puerto Rico?" Dash asked.

"More than half of my life, actually," Marta said. "I moved out when I was nineteen."

"So were you there when those devastating hurricanes hit a while back?" Dash asked.

"Yeah, it was really bad. A lot of people ended up suffering pretty bad. There was a lot of property damage, and a lot dead. A lot of trees fell," Marta said. She sighed. "After they hit, I got out as soon as I could. I had to leave most of my family behind. I still think about them, sometimes." Dash stayed silent. "Anyways, that's enough thinking about the past. I think I'm gonna head home and go to bed."

With that, the two separated, Marta heading home and Dash lingering for another moment.

October 3, 2031

At breakfast, Marta Girasol was introduced to Jaime Slewdjack. Shortly after, President Alan Berkoff held a private meeting with Jane McVellion to fill her in on his current plan. Less than an hour before lunch, the Council called again to meet. Jane McVellion once more stood before the same people as last time.

"Alan, why have you dragged us all back here?" Percy asked, irritated. "We already voted on this matter. Officer McVellion is not going to be the new chief of security, unless Vice President Toaden or Dr. Marie have changed their minds." He looked at Toaden and Dr. Marie.

"I haven't," Dr. Marie said casually.

"Nor have I," Toaden said more officially.

"Don't worry, I didn't think any of you would change your minds," Alan started, smiling. "I've assembled the Council for a *different* reason."

"So then why are we here?" Percy asked again.

"And why is Officer McVellion here?" Toaden added. Alan's smile widened.

"*Wellllllllllll,*" he said, drawing out the word for as long as possible. "As the president, my powers and responsibilities are *quite* expansive. I might not be able to veto your votes against Officer McVellion, but I do have the power to grant temporary Council positions, for as long as the position remains open. As such, I grant Officer McVellion the title of Interim Chief of Security until the Council can vote upon a permanent one," Alan said. Jane's face twisted into a vicious smile. Worried looks crossed the faces of the Council members. Alan looked at Toaden. "Isn't that right, vice president?" Toaden was at a loss for words.

"Y-you c-can't!" Toaden stammered out pathetically.

"Yes. He can," Percy said bitterly. "The rules and politics we have down here are very clear about what the president can and can't do. I don't know why you think he can't, but I can assure you he can." Percy sighed. "Alan, you're really starting to make me regret giving you this position."

"So I wasn't just given the position as an appeasement?" Alan asked, ignoring Percy's last comment. Percy tilted his head to the side.

"No, you're *really* the president. I don't know where you would get that idea from, but I can assure you that you really are the president. Why would you think you aren't actually the president, anyways?" Percy answered. Alan smiled innocently at Toaden.

"No reason," he said cheerfully. Toaden frowned angrily and his face quickly turned a bright red. Percy leaned forward in his chair.

"But, as the owner of this entire bunker, I technically outrank the president," Percy continued. The smiles on both Alan and Jane's faces faded.

"So you could keep Officer McVellion from being chief, even temporarily?" Dr. Marie asked, also leaning forward.

"Yes," Percy said. Alan's smile turned into a frown, and Jane bared her teeth. "However, I won't." The entire room was then sent into a surprised silence.

"Why not?! You voted against her becoming the security chief, but you would let her be the temporary chief?" Dr. Marie snapped after a few minutes of stillness.

"As much as I disapprove of this woman becoming the chief of security, the fact remains that we still need one. I don't know if you've noticed, but most of our security officers have been slacking off since Chief House died. I've only seen a few actually doing their jobs. And I know we don't really have a need for the security force at this time, or hopefully any time. But in case we do, I don't want the officers being unprepared and caught off guard. And until the Council can officially agree on a new one, we need someone to at least keep them on their feet. And while I am certain Officer McVellion would make a horrible leader, she at least seems capable of keeping all the officers in line," Percy explained. He sighed. "Is there anything else, Alan?"

"Nope!" Alan said, the smile once again returning to his face.

"In that case, I think we can adjourn this meeting," Percy said, and stood up. Alan and Jane smiled at each other. Harrack sighed and also stood up. Dr. Marie slumped back in her chair. She looked to Toaden.

"Now what?" she asked. Toaden just gave her a sympathetic glance and said nothing.

*   *   *

Almost every security officer was sitting around in the station. As the elevator opened up into the security station, barely anyone even turned to see who was stepping out.

"Attention!" the president yelled as he walked out of the elevator. Most of the officers sprung up to attention. A few others lazily got to their feet. "Thank you all for taking time out of your *busy* schedules to actually stand up," Alan continued. He cleared his throat. "Despite how *vigilant* you've all been without a proper chief to order you around, we upstairs have decided that you need a chief, just in case." Alan paused.

"Since it could be awhile before we are able to agree on selecting a permanent chief, we have selected an interim chief, instead. I'm sure you're all familiar with Officer McVellion." Jane stepped forward. "Despite the word 'interim,' she is very much your chief right now. Show her the same respect you would show any chief of security, and do as she says. That is all." With the last word, Alan returned to the elevator, ascending to the High Rise only a few minutes later.

"Listen up!" Jane shouted, her deep voice reaching every inch of the station. "The president's gonna tell the whole bunker about me in a few minutes. He also wants to cancel lunch, for whatever reason. We just gotta keep the people from getting too smart. If anyone speaks up, smack 'em down. Here's my rule for handling the masses, and feel free to apply this to everything, not just this one thing. There is no such thing as 'too much force.' Be as forceful and rough as you need to be. If they get hurt, it's their fault for making you have to get rough with them. Anyways, get ready."

As the officers began suiting up into their kevlar vests, and equipping their pistols, rifles, and batons, Johnny Dinlum approached Jane McVellion.

"There very much *is* such a thing as excessive force," he said shyly. Jane gave him a vicious glare.

"Not when I'm around. Now get ready." Dinlum hesitated, but timidly went to his locker to get suited up. Rick Farkass then walked up to Jane, himself already arranged. He smiled cockily at her.

"Don't get too used to being called chief, 'cause *I'm* gonna be the one who ends up as the permanent chief!"

Jane gave him a blank, impatient stare. Then she punched him straight in the nose. He stumbled back, covering his face and whining. "Quit making that sound. It's pathetic, even for you." Rick glared at her as he slowly turned away and hunched back over to his locker. Cat Vilner tapped Jane's shoulder. Jane spun to face her.

"What do you want?" Jane asked, a bit calmer but still irritable. Cat shrunk a little, but maintained some confidence.

"Well, we took some applicants for the force, but since we didn't have a chief at the time, we just held onto them," Cat explained.

"I don't care," Jane said, turning away from Cat.

"Well, since you're the interim chief now, we figured you could review the applications," Cat continued. Jane groaned unhappily.

"Fine. Give me the damn applications," Jane said, turning back around and holding her hand out. Cat placed the two applications in her hands. She briefly looked one over. Then she swapped the papers around in her hand and looked over the second application. Finally, she sighed and ripped both up. Cat gave her a look of surprise. "What?" Cat stayed silent, returning to her locker. As soon as Jane heard Alan's voice outside the station, she ordered everyone to move out.

*　　*　　*

Lunch would begin shortly, and DT Sacks, John Dash, Marta Girasol, Toby Smalls, and Jaime Slewdjack sat together. They waited, but nothing was coming out of the dispensers. People started getting antsy. Some just left, while others started banging angrily on the dispensers. Rose Anderson and Casey Goodwill just sat and watched the security station.

The crowd grew louder and more restless. Five minutes after lunch was supposed to be served, the loudspeaker system that had remained largely unused suddenly blared to life, catching many residents off guard. High pitched feedback silenced the crowd as they all ducked down and covered their ears. The feedback faded out after only a few seconds.

"Attention, atten- This thing is working, right? Yeah, it looks like it. Attention, citizens," a voice boomed across the entire bunker. While everyone chatted with confusion, the security force slowly surrounded the crowd, almost completely unnoticed.

"Well, if it isn't the honorable Lord Berkoff!" someone shouted sarcastically. This was followed by a few nervous chuckles. The security force quickly moved in, pinpointing the source of the comment. Within seconds, a baton was raised above the crowd. It came down swiftly and was immediately followed by a loud smack and a cry of pain. The entire crowd shifted anxiously as nervous murmurs sprung up here and there, but everyone went silent as Alan began speaking again.

"As you may or may not be aware, our chief of security, a Mr. James House, died tragically a few days ago due to natural causes. Given that his role was vital to our community, we have been working tirelessly to find a replacement. Unfortunately, since we have been unable to agree on one, there will be an interim chief of security, Officer Jane McVellion. Obey her rules, treat her as you would any permanent chief of security, and everything will be as it was." Alan paused for a minute.

"Despite her title of Interim Chief, she still has the full power and authority that a, for lack of a better word, 'full' chief has. She may enforce any law she sees fit, and she can also deliver any punishment she deems is appropriate. That is all for now." Alan paused once more. "As a side note, lunch is cancelled for today." A cacophony of groans raised from the crowd, and many people started yelling up at the High Rise, which prompted more baton swinging. After only a few seconds of baton swinging, the crowd quickly, but uneasily, settled down.

"Why are they attacking people? They can't do that! Can they do that?" Toby asked, keeping his voice low and horrified at what was happening around him.

"I get the feeling that this is only the beginning," Dash said. Everyone nodded silently in agreement as screams of pain and surprise rang out around them. Except for Toby, who was looking around with an expression of abject horror on his face.

As the security force backed out of the crowd, those who had been hit were given a hand up. Marta spotted one man sitting on the ground with a large bruise and some blood on his head. She quickly stood up and trotted over to him. He looked up as she extended her hand. He gratefully took it and she pulled him up to his feet.

"Thank you," the man said.

"*De nada*. You should probably go see the doctor," Marta suggested. The man nodded and smiled, and walked off, still holding his head. The rest of her friends slowly gathered with her.

"Who was he?" Jaime asked.

"No idea," Marta replied. The others nodded.

"It was very nice of you to help him," Toby said, the sadness from the scene moments ago mixing with signs of hope.

"It's just the right thing to do." Without much else to say, the group slowly went off their own ways.

*   *   *

"Thanks for agreeing to help me out," Dr. Marie said as she finished patching up the last person who had come in with baton injuries. Zachary Zyz was standing guard in her office, his gun drawn as he watched as Dr. Marie sent the last patient out the door.

"I'm only doing this to help fulfill Chief House's last request," Zyz stated. "And also because I swore to protect this country and its citizens. And I get the feeling McVellion and President Berkoff are both threats to the American citizens living here. The interim chief has already made an announcement to the security force that they can use as much force as they want.

She even added that excessive force doesn't exist down here. Not as long as she's in charge."

"We can't let her stay in that position," Dr. Marie said. "And the same goes for Berkoff."

"Agreed. But which one should we prioritize? Because we can't effectively fight both of them at once," Zyz responded.

"Well, if we remove McVellion first, then Berkoff will probably just get another replacement in a matter of days. Maybe a few weeks at max. But she's been in charge for less than an hour and already *her* security force sent half a dozen people in with head wounds."

"They're not all like that. There are some good people on the force," Zyz said.

Dr. Marie thought for a moment. "You could run for the position of security chief! You already have my vote, and I'm certain the vice president will support you. Berkoff might be a bigger threat, at least in the long run, but right now McVellion could do way more damage. And it'll be much easier to at least get her out of her current position. And we have to do is find a permanent security chief. Hopefully before McVellion does even more damage."

"Toaden specifically selected me to watch the chief of security, not *become* the chief of security. Who would make sure the chief stayed in line if I became the chief?" Dr. Marie simply crossed her arms and gave him a disappointed look. "I see your point," Zyz said, mildly embarrassed. "But even with your and the vice president's support, I still need one more vote."

"We know Berkoff would vote no. Dr. Harrack would probably just follow him, and I don't know about Winkle," Dr. Marie said, thinking. "I would've assumed him being friends with Berkoff, he'd be like Harrack and just support him regardless. But he surprised me the last time. Though, given his line of questioning of McVellion, I would think he'd also vote for you." She paused. "Assuming the vice president's trust in you was not misguided."

Zyz gave her an unhappy stare, but did not reply to her comment. "I'll do it. Even if I don't get voted in, at least we can show Berkoff and McVellion that we won't just let them take over without a fight," Zyz said finally. Dr. Marie let out a small sigh of relief.

"Good. If you want, I can tell you what Winkle asked last time. That way you can prepare," Dr. Marie said.

"No. I'd rather get the job on my own merit," Zyz stated.

"This isn't the time to be playing the boy scout," Dr. Marie sighed. "But fine. We'll do it your way. I have to finish filling out all these medical reports, anyways." With that, Dr. Marie sat down at the terminal in her office and began typing. Zyz then made his exit.

*   *   *

After most of the people had shuffled home, a select few stayed behind, mostly just to discuss things, and even one or two still banging on the food dispensers. The security force had mostly cleared out, but a few still remained to make sure the citizens followed what they were told. John Dash, DT Sacks, Toby Smalls, and Jaime Slewdjack had all left, but Marta Girasol was among those that stayed behind. As she sat at a table in deep thought, a figure snapped her out of her thoughts by sitting across from her. She looked up and recognized the man she had helped up shortly after the announcement. The blood was gone and the bruise had been covered by bandages.

"Oh. Hi," Marta said blankly.

"Thanks for helping me out, earlier," the man said.

"Don't mention it. Glad to help."

"I wish everyone thought that way," he man said with a downbeat sigh. They were silent for a moment.

"Were you the one who shouted the Lord Berkoff thing?" Marta asked. The man laughed.

"No... no, that wasn't me. Though I wish it was," he said, his smile still slightly present. Another silence fell upon them.

"Got a name?" Marta asked.

"Daniel," the man said. Marta waited a second.

"Got a *last* name?" Marta asked.

"Butler," Daniel said simply. "You?"

"Marta Girasol." she said. Daniel stretched his hand towards her, and the two shook hands. "So I take it you weren't a fan of the president's latest decision?"

"No. I'd really rather not have this turn into some sort of dictatorship or military state. I know the president isn't the *only* one in charge, but he seems to be getting away with a lot. I don't like it." Daniel paused, then opened his mouth to continue, but another man quickly interjected himself into their conversation.

"You might want to be a little quieter. I heard your conversation from over there." As he said that, a couple of security officers walked right by the table. One glared at the three of the sitting at the table. Then they were gone. The other man then turned back to Daniel and Marta. "It's probably not the best idea to shittalk the fuhrer in front of the gestapo."

"*Gracias*," Marta said, lowering her voice.

"We have to do *something*. We can't let them keep doing stuff like this. And this is only the beginning. Things *will* get much, much worse if we don't take care of this problem as soon as we can," Daniel said.

"Yes, but we're gonna need more people if we actually plan on doing anything effective," the man said. "There might be only twenty soldiers, but they're all fully armed. Even with forty people, we still couldn't win in a fight."

"Then we shouldn't fight," Marta said.

"Well, what you you suggest then?" the man asked skeptically.

"I actually have an idea," Daniel said, thinking.

"Well, I don't know what you're planning, but it better be good," the man paused. "My name's Rex, by the way."

"You gonna share your last name, too?" Marta asked.

"That is my last name," Rex stated plainly.

"Oh," Marta said. She paused awkwardly. "Marta Girasol."

"Daniel Butler," Daniel said. He held his hand out to Rex, but Rex ignored it.

"Now tell us what your plan is," he said.

"We should go somewhere more private," Daniel said. The other two agreed, and the small group soon departed the dining area.

*　　*　　*

Rose Anderson and Casey Goodwill had also decided to stay in the dining area, despite what they had witnessed. They were in deep discussion about the event that had just happened and how injustice was all around.

"I just can't believe this sort of thing would be allowed. Somebody needs to be held accountable," Rose said with frustration.

"Oh, this sorta thing happens all the time, without anyone ever being punished," Casey said in an agitated tone.

"I know this happens in all those third world countries, but this is still supposed to be America!" Rose said exasperated.

"When was the last time you watched the news?" The two were so involved in the conversation, neither of them noticed the two male security officers approach them.

"Well, hello there, ladies," one said smirking, but in a friendly tone. Rose and Casey turned to the men, both with displeased and distrustful expressions.

"May we help you?" Rose asked curtly.

"What do you want?" Casey snapped. The security officers exchanged a glance.

"Well, we couldn't help but notice you were talking about how we were... how did you put it? Something about injustice?"

the same security officer said, the faux friendly tone now gone. "Whatever it was, you better get used to it, because that's the way things are gonna be from now on. We're in charge now, and if you don't like it, too bad!" He chuckled nastily. "Now beat it before I decide to stop being so nice!"

"This is our table. We've sat here everyday since we got here. There's nowhere else we can go," Rose said.

"Not that we would go anywhere if we could," Casey added. The officer sneered.

"Not our problem. Right, Roy?" the first man said.

"Please just listen to him so he'll shut up," the other security office, Roy Bant, said.

"We aren't going *anywhere*," Casey said. She crossed her arms, and stared at Roy, while Rose had an apprehensive look on her face. Roy sighed. The first officer frowned.

"Right. Well, I tried being nice. You're on your own now. Rick, do whatever you will," Roy said, turning away. As he slowly walked away, Rick Farkass grabbed each of them by the arm. Yanked both of them onto their feet, he quickly pulled them away from the dining area, jerking their arms roughly as he went.

"Can you not be so rough?" Rose pleaded in a scared voice. Rick remained silent as he dragged them behind the first row of houses after the dining area. Rick glanced around and confirmed that they were alone. Once he was confident they were, he shoved both woman against the back of a house. Both let out surprised and pained gasps and collapsed to the ground with a thud. They looked up at Rick, who was looking down at them. Casey was extremely infuriated and Rose was quite afraid.

"Consider this a warning. Next time, do what I tell you too, and I *might* not be so rough," Rick said, thrusting his finger in their direction. Neither moved nor responded. Happy with himself, Rick turned and began walking away, happily whistling to himself.

"Disgusting. The world would be better off without people like him," Casey snarled. Rose gently nodded in agreement, rubbing her arm where Rick had grabbed it. Her entire body was shaking slightly.

*   *   *

By the time Zachary Zyz returned to the dining area, almost everyone else had gone away. Only two or three other security officers were still around. A few people had returned and were once again sitting back down. Among them were Casey Goodwill and Rose Anderson, who had reclaimed their table. Although Rose still appeared quite frightened. Roy Bant and Rick Farkass were nowhere to be seen. However, before Zyz had the chance to observe the scene, he was approached by Lucy Desin. As she greeted him with a small smile, Zyz noticed a small bruise on her forehead.

"Are you okay?" Zyz asked with significant concern.

"Huh? Oh." Lucy reached up and lightly touched the spot on her forehead, then lowered her hand back down to her side. "Yeah, I'm fine. When the other officers were hitting the people in the crowd, I stepped in between one of the officers and the person he was about to hit. He didn't notice me in time," Lucy answered.

"Have you seen Dr. Marie yet," Zyz asked. Lucy shook her head.

"Not yet. I've just been sitting in the security station, waiting for the headache to go away," Lucy said. She noticed the concern on his face, and widened her smile slightly. "Don't worry, it wasn't a bad one."

"I know. I was with the doctor when she was patching people up. Some of them were pretty bad."

"Yeah, I should probably go see her soon. But we need to talk about how we can keep something like this from happening again. This can't stand," Lucy said, her smile disappearing. "This is not what I was expecting when I was assigned to the force. It's a disgusting abuse of power."

97

"I think most of us can agree on that," Zyz said.

"I guess I should go see the doctor now, huh?" Lucy said with a sad laugh. Zyz nodded. Before she had the chance to head out, three figures nearby started walking towards the pair.

*   *   *

DT Sacks, John Dash, Jaime Slewdjack, and Toby Smalls hadn't felt like staying in the meal area after the event at lunch. They had decided to go check up on Howard Skittering, since it had been a while since any of them had seen him, and Marta Girasol had said she'd catch up with them later. The majority of people had gone back to their houses, and, as such, the "streets" in between the houses were mostly empty. A few other people also wandered around alone or in pairs, but most of them were ignoring the other groups of people around them.

"You can almost feel it," DT said, breaking a pervasive silence.

"It?" Toby asked, turning and tilting his head to the side to look at DT.

"The helplessness. The feeling that everything is drifting out of reach. That you have no control over your own life. That there's nothing that can be done about any of it," Dash explained, staring straight ahead.

"I don't think it's *that* bad," Jaime replied.

"It will be soon. Once things like this start, they snowball faster and faster," Dash said.

"How do you know that's gonna happen?" Jaime asked.

"Because that's what usually happens. Look at World War I. It started with the assassination of a small European nation that most people probably couldn't point to on a map, and quickly spiralled into the biggest, or 'greatest,' war. I can assure you that almost every major conflict started out with something that seemed small and insignificant at the time," Dash explained.

"But this is a smaller scale than most issues. I don't even think there are enough people here for this to qualify as a country," Jaime said.

"Remind me to tell you about the Knights of Malta, sometimes," Dash coolly responded. "But I digress. Let's just hope it doesn't get that far."

"Yeah, hopefully it doesn't," Jaime agreed.

"Can we talk about something else, now?" Toby asked.

"Y'know, I actually applied to join the security force the other day," Jaime said.

"Really?" DT asked.

"Yeah. But after today, I'm glad I'm not a part of it," he said. Within a few seconds of finishing that sentence, he suddenly sniffled. Another few seconds later, he began crying, stopping to slump against a house. The others looked at him with concern.

"Are you okay?!" Toby asked, crouching down next to him.

"No. I didn't even want to come here in the first place! But my parents... when we got the letter saying I had been selected in the lottery to come live in a bunker to preserve American ideals, they told me I *had* to go. I didn't want to leave them, but they wanted me to be safe. And they figured it would be safer here than out there. If only they saw this place now." Jaime was soon overtaken by tears as he sobbed loudly. Concerned looks passed between the others.

"I'm sorry to hear that. Your parents sound like good people. I'm sure they just want what's best for you. They couldn't have guessed what would happen down here. No one could," Toby said.

"Yeah, they were," Jaime said, smiling a little as he sniffled and wiped away a tear. "They always put me first, even before themselves. They were always so worried about me. That's why my father taught me how to shoot. In case I ever needed to defend myself. Until he admitted he just didn't want me blowing my head off if I ever got my hands on a gun." Jaime laughed a little more. "It's funny. Normally, you'd think parents would try to keep dangerous things away from their kids. But my parents thought differently." He stopped for a moment to let a few more tears roll down his cheeks. "Anyways, like I was saying, my father took me out to shoot everyday until I could shoot flawlessly." He paused for a beat. "I was only ten at the time. Anyways, that's why I applied to the security force."

The group waited patiently and silently as Jaime cried himself out. After about five minutes, he made one last sniffle and stood up.

"Ready to go?" Toby asked softly. Jaime nodded gently, smiling and wiping his cheek again. Toby smiled back, and the small group resumed their journey.

*   *   *

"Dr. Marie, what are we doing here?" Percy Winkle asked. The Council had gathered, at the behest of Dr. Marie. Zachary Zyz stood in front of the large conference table. "I know you lot have nothing better to do than have petty political squabbles, but unlike you, I actually have plenty to do."

"Like what?" Dr. William Harrack asked. His hair was messy and unkempt.

"Do you remember about thirteen years back when the US government sent the seal team into North Korea to take out, oh what was his name... ah! Kim Jong something or other, and dismantled their entire government?" Percy asked.

"Yes?" Harrack asked cautiously.

"Well, a few years back, I managed to... *acquire* his entire DVD collection," Percy said, with more than a little pride. "Plus the Playstation 5 *and* 6, just to name a few. I could go on, but I'd much rather finish this up and get back to it than just tell you about it."

"Didn't he have a ton of porn in that collection?" Harrack asked with tangent interest. Percy's face quickly turned bright red.

"Well, maybe I don't have his *entire* collection," Percy stammered out. Then he quickly added, "I also have to make sure the garden's automatic sprinklers, harvesters, etcetera are functioning properly."

Alan looked at Harrack. "Dr. Harrack, how is that nutrition experiment coming along, by the way?" he asked. Harrack returned his look with a tired expression.

"It's taking a lot longer than I thought it would. It should be *easy*. But I just can't seem to get the formula down. I can't figure out what keeps going wrong with it," Harrack responded, the exhaustion clear in his voice.

Toaden glared at him. "You promised the government you were the one scientist who could make a concentrated nutrition block. Something, as you said yourself, could 'contain a person's entire daily nutritional intake in one bite,'" Toaden said.

Harrack stared at him for a solid twenty seconds before responding with, "You're a politician. Don't lecture me about promises." Toaden's glare intensified, and Alan cracked up into laughter.

"Good one," Alan said as his laughter quickly died down.

Dr. Marie cleared her throat. "Well, if you're all finished, I'd like to get started," she said.

"Yes. Can we *please* get this over with?" Percy seconded, his face still quite a bit red.

Dr. Marie took a deep breath. "I have gathered the Council together because I believe I have found a suitable replacement for the chief of security," Dr. Marie said in as formal a way as she could. Zyz remained motionless, as he had this entire time. Percy sighed impatiently.

"Just introduce your candidate?" Percy said, dismissively waving his hand. Before Dr. Marie could introduce Zyz, he introduced himself.

"Officer Zachary Zyz. Former United States military. I have been on multiple missions to the Middle East, and I was also present in the undeployed reinforcements for the Korea mission you yourself talked about earlier. I have experience with leading small platoons. I'm certain my file can fill you in more fully about my service history."

"I can vouch for Officer Zyz. I personally selected him to make sure the chief of security stays in line," Toaden added. Percy nodded with a mildly impressed expression on his face.

"As interesting as that is, let's just start with a preliminary vote to see where everyone stands," Percy said.

"You already know my vote," Dr. Marie said.

"I also vote yes," Toaden said.

"I vote no," Alan said simply.

"No surprise there," Dr. Marie scoffed. Everyone looked at Harrack. He glanced around the room. Both Alan and Dr. Marie were shooting him intense glares. His eyes shifted between the two of them repeatedly. Finally, he sighed and looked down at the table.

"I vote against this decision," he said. Alan smiled and Dr. Marie rolled her eyes.

"So that's two for, and two against, correct?" Alan chimed.

"Correct," Percy confirmed.

"I guess that just leaves you, Mr. Winkle," Dr. Marie said formally. All eyes turned to Percy. Percy sat up straight and puffed out his chest.

"I'm afraid I can't vote 'yes' on this matter," Percy said.

"What?!" Dr. Marie yelled, losing her composure and jumping up from her seat.

"Dr. Marie, calm down. Right now," Percy ordered sharply. Dr. Marie slowly sank back into her seat, her expression still furious. Percy sighed sympathetically and continued more gently. "I know you want Interim Chief McVellion out of this position as soon as possible, but it has only been a few hours since President Berkoff appointed the position to her. And despite my own expectations, Alan told me she's already managed to whip the security force back into shape. And while I'm sure your officer here can do the same, Chief McVellion has already proven herself to be reliable and effective. Even if your officer here is a better fit, let's at least give McVellion a few weeks as interim chief. If she doesn't work out, then we will revisit this issue. But let's not constantly change the chief of security hourly. So, as owner of this bunker, I am officially declaring that meetings of this kind will not be held again until McVellion has been given sufficient time for us to see whether she continues to be an effective leader." Dr. Marie stuttered for a response, but her mind came up blank. "Well, I think that concludes this meeting. And hopefully any meetings of this kind for a while." Percy stood up, and the others in the room uneasily followed suit, except Dr. Marie, who remained seated. She stared dumbfoundedly at Percy as he walked towards the elevator.

"What has he been telling you about McVellion?" Dr. Marie asked in a low, guttural growl, mimicking Interim Chief McVellion's own natural speaking voice. Percy turned to face her as he reached the elevator. He then turned his head to Alan.

"You didn't lie to me, did you Alan?" Percy said in a low tone. Alan quickly mustered up the most convincing smile he could manage and looked back at Percy, who was now scowling distrustfully.

"Of course I didn't! You know me, Percy. I don't lie to my friends," he said, his awkward smile wavering.

"The officers attacked a crowd of civilians under her orders," Dr. Marie continued. Percy continued to glare distrustfully at Alan, then slowly turned and pressed the button on the elevator.

"Well, sometimes the population needs to be reminded of their place. But I'm sure that the president will tell the interim chief not to do it again. And if it does happen again, then we'll meet again to discuss a new chief of security. And a new president," Percy said. The doors dinged open and he stepped inside. Alan bared his teeth and let his smile disappear. He turned to Dr. Marie.

"I'm sorry your little plan failed," Alan said with mocking snarl. She didn't acknowledge him, and instead stood and walked to the elevator. Zyz lightly put his hand on her shoulder, and she suddenly snapped around, grabbing his hand. Once she realized it was him, she loosened up a bit and released his hand. He motioned towards the elevator, and the pair stepped in. Toaden and Harrack started walking towards the elevator, but Alan grabbed their shoulders and pulled them back.

"Are you okay?" Zyz asked, after the doors had closed. She nodded.

"Yeah. I could just... use a nap right about now," Dr. Marie replied weakly.

"I hope you know it was nothing personal," Percy said.

"Shut it," Dr. Marie said.

Alan immediately turned to Toaden as the elevator doors closed. "I thought we were friends. Why do you keep voting against me?" Alan asked. Toaden simply looked at him. There was a hint of indignation in his expression.

"We're not friends. I don't even know where you'd get that idea from. Even if we *were* closer than just colleagues, my responsibility is to the citizens first, not to you," Toaden responded harshly.

"Fine. But don't forget who the president is, and who the *vice* president is," Alan snarked.

"I already told you that you have less power than you think," Toaden said, then pulled away from Alan to walk to the elevator. "And thanks for making me wait for the elevator to come back up."

"I think Percy made it clear that what you told me wasn't the truth," Alan accused. Toaden kept his back to Alan as he waited for the doors to open.

"Maybe it was a lie. But I'm only trying to do what's best for the citizens of this bunker. And I can say with certainty that you being president is *not* what's best for this bunker," Toaden said.

Frowning viciously, Alan walked over to the small, red couch that was set up next to the glass table. he reached behind one of the cushions and pulled out a small calibre pistol. Harrack immediately jumped forward, catching Alan off guard, and easily snatching the weapon from Alan's hand, just as the elevator doors opened. Toaden stepped inside the elevator and turned around just as Harrack thrust the gun under the nearest cushion, falling onto the chair it was stationed on. All Toaden saw was Harrack gently slide off the chair, silently landing on the carpeted floor. Harrack hopped back to his feet just in time to see Toaden's judgemental expression as the elevator doors closed. Alan turned to Harrack.

"I wasn't *actually* going to shoot him! And when did you suddenly care about human life?" Alan asked.

"I'm trying to help you!" Harrack almost shouted.

"Yeah, I'm sure you are," Alan snapped sarcastically.

"I'm trying to stop you from fucking yourself over! How do you think the vice president would react if he saw you pointing a gun at him? It doesn't matter if you were actually going to shoot him. It doesn't even matter if the fucking thing was unloaded! All he would've seen was the gun. You're smarter than this," Harrack said, exhausting himself.

"You may have a few good points. But *don't* do that again. You're lucky I still consider you a friend, and that you make a convincing argument, otherwise I might take offense at your actions," Alan said.

"*Offence*?! I just stopped you from *getting caught pointing a gun at the fucking vice president!*" Harrack yelled. The room became silent, save for Harrack's heavy panting. Harrack slowly calmed himself down over the next few minutes. Finally, he exhaled deeply. "Fine. If you don't want my help, then

I won't stop you next time. Have fun getting caught. I hope this is all worth it," Harrack said calmly. He slowly turned and walked over to the elevator, stepping lightly across the floor.

"It *will* be worth it. You'll see. Now get out of my sight," Alan growled as Harrack pressed the button. He just sighed in exasperation. The doors opened and he stepped in. He faced the back of the elevator without turning around until the doors closed.

Now alone, Alan clenched his fists, his arms beginning to shake. Angel slowly opened up her hiding space and peered out. Seeing the room was clear, she stepped out and stretched. Alan's arms continued shaking harder and harder until he finally screamed in anguish. He brought both of fists down upon the glass table. It shattered, sending papers and glass shards spilling all over the floor, as well as causing Angel to jump in surprise. Alan's hands turned into bloody messes, glass embedded into them. He stared at his hands, shaking harder than ever, as the blood flowed down his arms freely. His screams intensified greatly.

*   *   *

DT Sacks and John Dash stood in the middle of Howard Skittering's house as the others waited outside. They surveyed the house. It had an almost abandoned appearance. Broken things laid strewn across the floor. The bedside lamp had been tossed on the ground, the bulb shattered. The sheets were torn off the bed, and it appeared everything on the shelf had been tossed off in all different directions. Nothing looked like it had been moved in some time, and a very thin layer of rock dust covered everything.

"What happened in here?" DT asked, picking a book up off the floor.

"I'm not sure. Someone could've broken in for whatever reason. Maybe they even fought with Howard. But I get the feeling that's not what happened," Dash replied. DT looked at him, then turned back to the house.

"So what *do* you think happened?" DT asked, continuing his inspection.

"He may have snapped. 'Gone off the deep end,' as I've heard a few people say. But I think he did this, himself," Dash answered, slowly examining the room.

"Well, whatever happened, Howard probably needs help. We just have to find him, first. Where do you think he went?"

"Why do you keep asking me like I know everything?" Dash asked back.

"Well, you always *seem* like you know more than everyone else. So if there's anyone to ask, it's you," DT replied, carefully stepping around the broken glass.

"That's a fair assessment. I can't really argue against it. Let's see... we haven't seen him at any meals since Tony Weitson died, and it doesn't appear he's been in here in awhile. Look at the dust," Dash answered. "Unfortunately, that doesn't tell us where he is now. Just that it's been awhile since he's seen his house."

"My question is, why would he just leave his door unlocked? Anybody could just walk right in and do anything. Like us," DT asked.

"Let's meet up with the others before asking any more questions. If they think the same as you, then I'd rather not have to repeat myself," Dash said. DT nodded in agreement.

"Yeah, okay," DT replied. The two turned and exited the house.

Outside, the other two were waiting. Toby Smalls had been pacing back and forth in front of the house. Jaime Slewdjack had just been standing with his arms crossed.

"What happened? Is your friend okay?" Jaime asked.

"The house has been empty for a while," Dash said. Toby stopped pacing and looked at them. "Toby, you knew Howard longer than the rest of us. Do you know where Howard could've gone?"

"I only knew him for a few minutes before I met the rest of you. Maybe a day, max," Toby replied. "I know as much as you do."

"Understandable. Recent events have made it hard to keep up with everything," Dash said.

"It has been busy lately," DT concurred.

"We haven't seen him since Tony's death, so maybe that has something to do with what happened to him," Dash continued thoughtfully. "But it still doesn't tell us where he *is*."

"Well, we should find him sooner rather than later. Let's just hope nothing too bad has happened to him already. From the look of his house, I'm not really expecting this to end well," DT said.

"How bad is it in there that you're talking like he's already dead?" Jaime asked.

"Go take a look for yourself, if you want," DT said. Dash and DT stepped aside as Jaime and Toby both entered the house. Less than a minute later, they both exited.

"Yeah, we should get moving," Jaime said. Toby closed the door as he stepped out. Without another word, the small group headed away from Howard's house.

*　　*　　*

"Ah! Could you use something that stings a little less?" President Alan Berkoff said as Dr. Linda Marie dabbed his hands with hydrogen peroxide-soaked cotton balls.

"No. Now hold still," she said with a professional tone. The surgical mask muffled her voice ever so slightly. Using a high definition camera attached to the backside of a large screen that blew up the image the camera was transmitting live, she could see nearly every detail of Alan's torn open hands. She turned to Dr. Phillip Genson, who was standing behind her. "That's the cleanest I can get it." Dr. Marie stood up and let Dr. Genson sit down in front of the camera. Dr. Marie sat down next to Dr. Genson, holding more hydrogen peroxide and cotton balls.

"You really should be under anesthetic for this," Dr. Genson stated as he grabbed a pair of tweezers. With perfectly steady hands, he removed one of the larger shards that had barely broken through the skin.

"Not with *her* around," Alan said nastily, glaring up at Dr. Marie. Dr. Genson removed another shallow shard.

"Despite our political differences, I am a doctor first. I swore an oath, and I do *not* plan on breaking it," Dr. Marie stated, still in the same professional tone. "*Especially* for you." Alan's nasty look didn't abate. Dr. Genson continued removing the shards that hadn't gone deep.

"You still haven't said how you managed to do this in the first place. There isn't much glass down here for you to break. At least outside of the housing area," Dr. Marie said quietly after a moment of silence.

"And I'm not going to say," Alan said stubbornly.

"I need that info for the official report," she said flatly. Alan groaned, then yipped and turned to Dr. Genson. Dr. Genson looked up at him.

"My bad. That one was deeper than I thought it was," he said, then returned to his work. "That's all the easy ones. If you want anesthesia, speak now or forever hold your peace."

"I appreciate the thought, but I'll still pass," Alan said. Dr. Genson shrugged.

"Alright. I warned you." Alan continued to let out yelps and whines of pain. "Try to keep still. It'll hurt a lot more if you don't."

"Anyways. You were saying how you got these injuries," Dr. Marie said.

"No I wasn-*OW!*"

"Hold still." Dr. Genson moved the hand he was working on over to the side and began working on the other hand.

"You were saying?" Dr. Marie asked. Alan let out a frustrated huff.

"Fine. After the rest of you left, I tripped and fell onto the glass table in the High Rise. I reached out to break my fall, and... this happened," Alan explained.

"There. Was that so hard?" Dr. Marie asked. Alan turned to glare at her, but yelped again before he had the chance to change his expression. Dr. Marie managed not to snicker. "Too bad, though. I really liked that table. Who's gonna clean up that mess, though?"

"Not my problem," Alan said.

"Almost done," Dr. Genson said. "After I stitch you up, it may be awhile before you regain full control of your hands. Try not to do anything requiring your fine motor skills. And don't do anything that would put too much strain on your hands. Everything else you should be fine." Dr. Genson carefully removed a very fine piece of glass lodged deep into Alan's hand. Alan bit his lip, letting out a low but steady whine, and used all of his self control not to move his hand. However, his will was slipping and he beginning to twitch very slightly. But Dr. Genson managed to get the last piece out before Alan lost his will, and Alan breathed a sigh of relief. "Dr. Marie, disinfect him again while I grab the sewing kit."

Dr. Genson stood up and Dr. Marie sat down, grabbing Alan's wrists and placing them in front of her. He glared at her as she held the cotton ball against the top of the hydrogen peroxide and quickly flipped it upside down and back again.

"That's too much!" Alan protested. Dr. Marie didn't look at him as she moved the cotton ball closer to his hand. However, he pulled it away before she could. She then looked up at him impatiently.

"No, too much would be dumping this entire bottle on your hands. Would you rather get an infection and have us chop off your hands in a month, or would you rather feel a little stinging now?" Alan grumbled and begrudgingly reached his hands out towards her again. "That's what I figured." Alan continued yelping as she dabbed the cotton ball all over his cuts. After less than a minute, she and Dr. Genson switched places again.

"Now, let's try to do this quick so Dr. Marie doesn't have to do that again," Dr. Genson said. "You know the drill, don't move, and it'll hurt a lot less." Dr. Genson then began stitching Alan's wounds closed, which he naturally continued to whine and yelp about throughout.

*　　*　　*

Dash and the others waited at the dining area until dinner started, at which point they began asking if anyone had seen Howard recently. While they were unsuccessfully trying to locate their friend, Interim Chief Jane McVellion had told Zachary Zyz to take the night off. While he naturally found her offer extremely suspicious, he decided he needed a night away from the force to hopefully be ready to continue the fight against the president and the interim chief. Skipping dinner, he headed straight to his house.

Despite the fact that they had a small surplus of homes, quite a few people didn't use theirs. Percy Winkle had his mansion, Alan Berkoff usually slept in the High Rise, Dr. Marie and Dr. Harrack both tended to fall asleep in their respective offices, and a few security officers slept in the security station. Unless they were on night duty. Zyz decided he didn't want to sleep in the security station that night.

Dinner was just starting, so most of the residential area was lifeless. As he walked through the W section, he squinted to see in the auxiliary's low light. As he squinted, he suddenly realized the main lights in the section of the bunker he was in had been shut off. He looked up to confirm his observation was correct. Once he confirmed that lights were off only in the section of the bunker immediately surrounding him, he began scanning the area for any signs of trouble. His eyes quickly adjusted the low light. He didn't see anything. He slowly returned to his walk, keeping an eye and an ear open, and sticking close to a row of houses.

After a few light, quiet steps, he suddenly stopped again, hearing just the slightest sound coming from the alley right next to him. After squinting at it for a few seconds he didn't see anything. As he was about to turn away, he heard another slight sound come from the same direct, but slightly above him. He looked up in time to see a dark figure in the air. Before he had time to react, the figure landed a kick on his face, knocking him off balance. As he struggled to keep his footing, the figure sprung towards him. Before he could even regain his balance, he felt a needle prick in his arm. However, the assailant didn't manage to inject the needle's contents into him before his reflexes took over. In less than a second, he had launched his body straight at the attacker. He felt the needle come out of his skin as the assassin was caught off guard.

The two slammed into the ground, Zyz feeling the force of the impact travel through his assailant's body. Taking quick advantage of the opportunity, Zyz got back onto his feet. He drew his pistol - the only weapon security officers were allowed to take with them when they weren't on active duty - and turned around but the attacker was already on their own feet. Before he had time to react, the assassin kicked the gun out of his hands. Another sweeping kick knocked his feet out from under him, and Zyz fell onto his side. He saw the assailant thrust their arm downwards, holding an object like a knife. But Zyz was already rolling away, and whatever object it was smashing into the ground. As Zyz rolled onto his knees, he saw the object was a syringe.

Getting to his feet he quickly went to knee his assassin in their face, however the attacker reflexively jumped back, avoiding the attack. Zyz quickly stomped on the syringe, smashing the small glass object. Zyz and his assailant were now a good few feet apart. Zyz finally got a good look at the assassin, who was dressed in all black, including a black mask that covered their entire head. That was all Zyz could observe, as his attacker didn't waste a single second, the assailant suddenly pulled something off of their waist, rapidly wrapping both hands around it and pointing it at Zyz. Zyz dodged to the side, practically diving in between two houses. As he was moving, he heard three distinctive gunshots, and felt one just graze his back, right above his waist.

He landed in the alley with a thud. His mind was going too fast for even him to keep track of. The main thing he thought about was how the assailant had to be using a silencer, noting the gunshot's high pitch, low volume, and low echo. He silently but quickly crept through the alley to the other side of the house. Turning the corner he pressed his body against the house and panted as quietly as he could. He silently moved along the wall, constantly checking either side of the house for the attacker. As he remembered his assassin's first attack, he looked up towards the roof. Nothing was there. As he continued along the side of the building, looking in all three directions, he finally reached the edge of the house. As he checked around the corner, seeing it was clear, he turned back and saw the assailant standing on the roof of the house, looking over the edge at the other side corner, gun in hand. As his attacker looked across the area beneath them, inevitably seeing him. Zyz sprinted around the corner as the assailant fired off two more shots, one of them just grazing his arm.

The assassin glided over to the edge of the house that Zyz had just run around, however as they reached the edge, they looked down with only enough time to see him jumping up towards them and grab their leg. He yanked his attacker off the one story structure, however the assailant still managed to squeeze off a single shot, which carved out a small crevice in the top of Zyz's shoulder. Feeling the blood begin to run down his arm, Zyz slammed the assassin into the ground. Despite this, his attacker managed to keep their grip on their gun. Jumping to their feet, Zyz grabbed their arm and smashed his knee right in their stomach. Somehow still unfazed, the assailant swiftly kicked him in his ribs twice, then yanked their arm out of his grip.

Zyz grasped for the gun, grabbing the end of the silencer. He hoped his grip was good enough and pulled on it. Even though his assailant was caught off guard, they managed to keep their grip on it, sliding towards him. Zyz punched them in the face, finally managing to catch a break as the attacker lost their grip on the gun and stumbled back. However, it was short lived as his assassin quickly regained their composure and launched themselves at him. Zyz was caught off guard once more, and received a kick to the stomach. The silenced pistol flew out of his hand and went skidding into the darkness.

Zyz tried to ignore the pain in his stomach as the attacker came at him with their fist heading straight for his face. Zyz managed to catch the punch, but at the same second he wrapped his hand around his assassin's, his knee was kicked in and the assailant forced him against the house. Stepping back, his attacker threw their foot above their head, slamming it into his face, also smashing the back of his head against the house. Zyz slowly sunk back against the house, gripping the sides of his head. The assassin did a spinning kick again hitting his head, sending Zyz sprawling through the alley on his stomach, towards the "street" they had started their fight. His head was pounding, his vision was blurry and he couldn't see anything, and he couldn't hear anything besides the ringing in his ears.

Despite being virtually incapacitated, Zyz attempted to feebly crawl forwards, away from his assassin and out of the alley. As he crawled blindly, he suddenly felt a foot stomp down on the center of his back. However, the assailant didn't have much weight behind their stomp, and Zyz, mustering up the strength through nothing but pure adrenaline, placed his hands firmly on the ground and forced himself up. He felt his attacker's foot follow his back upwards, before flying off somewhere behind him. He stumbled forward, attempting to run but not being able to do more than shamble forward. As Zyz struggled to move, he felt his foot bump into something, sending it skittering just in front of him. Before he hand time to wonder what it was, he felt something slam into his back at full force. He tumbled forward once more. As he landed on the ground, he felt the object he had kicked digging into his stomach. He reached under his body and blindly grabbed for it. He managed to wrap his fingers around it and discovered it was the gun the assailant had knocked out of his hand only minutes earlier.

Getting his fingers into a proper grip around the trigger, he threw all of his body weight to one side, quickly rolling over onto his back. He already had the gun pointed up. Still mostly blind, he didn't waste a second firing in the direction his assailant had to be to have knocked him down. As the shots echoed out loudly across the bunker, Zyz didn't stop until he had unloaded the entire clip. Once the gun stopped firing, he just laid back and accepted that whatever would happen next was out of his control and passed out.

*   *   *

Very few people noticed the dark section of the bunker. Those who did, thought little of it. Dinner was winding to a close. The crowd had been unusually chatty, though they had good reason to be. DT Sacks, John Dash, Toby Smalls, and Jaime Slewdjack all convened at an empty table. None had been successful in narrowing down the location of Howard Skittering.

"It's starting to get late. We should pause for the night," DT said, tired.

"He's already been on his own for a few days. One more night shouldn't make a difference. Honestly, right now I'm a little more worried about Marta. I have seen her here at dinner, and I'm a little worried," Dash replied.

"I think I'll stick around for a little while longer," Toby started. "I'm-" Before Toby could finish his sentence, a long series of gunshots rang out across the bunker. Despite echoing, it was very clear where the shots had come from. The entire crowd immediately stopped what they were doing and began moving towards the sound. Some ran ahead of all the others, while the majority moved at a slower pace. A decent fraction of the crowd moved at a fairly quick speed, falling in between the runners and the shamblers. Nobody knew what to expect.

The security force quickly mobilized and was dispatched, still ending up behind most of the crowd. Pushing their way through the shamblers, they eventually caught up with the ones going at a medium pace, but the runners ended up at the scene before the security force. Once the security officers reached the scene, they had to force the runners away.

October 4, 2031

Most people hadn't slept too well after the previous night's event. Many still made it to breakfast the following morning. While they nervously ate what little food they could keep down, President Alan Berkoff was breathing down Dr. William Harrack's neck as he worked. This was because Harrack was working on something quite different to his normal experiments.

"Can you *please* take a few steps back?" Harrack asked impatiently. Alan grumbled, but obliged. Alan's hands were wrapped up in a thick layer of cloth bandages. "Thank you." Harrack continued his examination on the woman sitting on the table in the back of his office. She was sitting with her back to him, and he was looking at her left side, just above the waist. He was sitting on a chair significantly lower than the table, wiping at the burnt flesh. The table's occupant stayed remarkably quiet. "What is this, a gunshot wound?" Harrack asked as he worked.

"What's it matter to you?" Alan snapped.

"It doesn't. Just wondering." He continued to work for another couple of minutes in silence. "Well, if it *is* a gunshot wound, you're incredibly lucky it didn't go deeper. At least this didn't break the skin." Harrack continued for another few moments in silence. "How did you even *get* a bullet wound? The only guns that were shot off were-"

"Just stop asking, okay?!" Alan said angrily, crossing his arms and tapping his foot impatiently.

"This is why you brought her to me instead of Dr. Marie." The woman sitting on the table shifted her head slightly, causing the long, blonde hair she had draped around her neck to fall over Harrack's hands. She quickly combed it back up with her fingers. "She's the agent you were talking about. And she's the one who tried to kill that officer last night, isn't she?"

"Stop asking questions," Alan said.

"I saw him this morning. He looked bad," Harrack paused to look at the five foot six inch, one hundred ten pound female sitting in front of him. "Well, I have no idea how you managed to do what you did. But I will say I'm genuinely impressed."

"Would you stop talking?" Alan said.

"You realize I didn't have to help you, right? And you're starting to make me regret agreeing to this," Harrack said. He looked up at the back of Angel Puer's head. "You don't talk much, do you?"

"Jeez, how'd you figure *that* one out, Sherlock," Alan snarked. Harrack returned to tending her wound.

"If I weren't almost finished, I'd kick you out of my office right now," Harrack said. "So what happened to your hands?"

"That's it. Kill him," Alan said to the woman sitting on Harrack's table. Harrack tensed up as he expected the worst, but all the woman did was turn to look at Alan disapprovingly. When Harrack was still alive a few seconds later, he placed the wet gauze he had been using to clean her skin down on the table next to her and sat back. "Finished." He turned around in his chair to face Alan. "Now will you leave me alone?"

"Gladly," Alan said. Angel gracefully slid off the table onto her feet. Alan turned around and walked out the door with a huff. He tried to open the door, but with his hands bandaged up, he was unable to grip the handle. After a minute, he gave up, grumbling to himself. Angel silently nodded at Harrack, then opened the door, allowing Alan out, before proceeding out the door herself. Harrack sighed.

*   *   *

DT Sacks met up with Toby Smalls, John Dash, and Jaime Slewdjack at breakfast.

"Should we keep trying to look for Howard today?" Toby asked. DT looked at Dash.

"Didn't you mention something about wanting to find Marta?" he asked.

"I mentioned I was worried about her. If we haven't found Howard by now, he's either fine, or we're too late to help him," Dash said.

"We can't just give up on him!" Toby said.

"I didn't say we should," Dash replied. "I'm just saying, don't get your hopes up too high *if* we find him." Toby frowned unhappily.

"We haven't tried checking the bar," Jaime suggested. Toby's frown changed into a thoughtful expression.

"I didn't think he was the drinking type, but..." Toby said, his voice faded away as he retreated deeper into thought.

"It's worth a shot," Dash added.

"Yeah. I think we're out of other places to check, anyways," Jaime said.

"Let's go," Toby said, jumping up.

"Can we at least finish eating, first?" Jaime asked. Toby looked down at his food and didn't answer.

"The bar isn't going anywhere," Dash added, taking a bite of an apple.

"I guess not," Toby said, slowly sitting back down. They finished their meal in silence. Once they were finished, the group stood up and departed the table.

*   *   *

The elevator the in High Rise opened, and Interim Chief Jane McVellion, Officer Cat Vilner, Officer Rick Farkass, and Officer Roy Bant all stepped out. Cat was holding an empty cardboard box, and Rick was holding a broom and dust pan. Jane pointed at the shattered table, the glass and files still all over the floor.

"Bant," she said. "Pick up that table and get it out of here. I don't care what you do with it."

"If you can't fit it into any of the thrash shoots, then just put it in the back of storage," President Alan Berkoff said absently from his seat. He was sitting at the far side of the large conference table, staring out over the bunker almost indifferently.

"Yeah, what he said," Jane added.

"Alright," Roy, the largest and most muscular of the three officers, said. He walked over to the table and heaved up the metal frame of the table. With a huff, he carried it back to the elevator. Stepping inside, the doors closed and he disappeared. Jane turned to the other two officers.

"Vilner, pick up all of the files and place them in that box. Farkass, sweep up all the glass," she ordered. Cat walked over to the mess, carefully kneeling down on a section of the carpet that didn't have any apparent glass in it. She began to pick up the files, shaking any glass shards off of them. Rick just turned to Jane.

"I hope you enjoy this while it lasts, because one day, *I'll* be the one ordering *you* around!" Rick boasted. Jane gave him a mildly irritated stare.

"If you miss a single piece, I will shove the glass down your throat," Jane said flatly. Rick gulped nervously and looked at the mess. He turned back to Jane.

"But most of it is on the carpet," he said weakly.

"Then use your hands," Jane said. Rick sighed, then walked over to the glass. He started by sweeping up what had fallen next to the rug. Jane walked over to the conference table and sat down across from Alan, who was still facing away from the rest of the room and staring out the window.

"You're gonna regret this when *I'm* chief," Rick said with a vaguely threatening tone.

"Oh, be quiet," Alan said, tired and annoyed. Rick sighed again and continued working silently. After a few minutes of silence, Jane turned back around to the officers.

"Vilner. Since I'm not your partner now, and Officer Zim died last night, I'm making you partners with Officer Desin," she said. Cat looked up from the floor.

"But Officer Zyz survived," she said.

"What?!" Jane said with clear anger, shooting forward.

"Yeah. I mean, he doesn't look *good*, but he's alive," Cat continued. Jane slowly leaned back in her chair.

"Then Desin is your partner until Zippy is better," Jane said dismissively. Cat picked up a light file.

"I think some stuff is missing from this file," Cat said Alan spun around slowly in his chair.

"What's the name on it?" he asked.

"'John Dash,'" Cat read. A slight chill went down Alan's spine, but he retained his composure.

"No, nothing's missing. It's just a light file," he said. Cat nodded and placed the file in the box. At this point, Rick was picking very small shards out of the rug with his fingers. A minute later, Cat put the last file in the box. She stood up, picking up the box.

"I think that's the last file," Cat said.

"Good. You may leave," Alan said, dismissing the officer. "Just drop the box in the storage room downstairs, first." Cat nodded and headed for the elevator. Jane looked down at Rick.

"Are you done yet?" she said impatiently. He looked up at her indignantly.

"I'm picking glass out of a carpet with my fingers. *Of course I'm not done yet!*" he yelled. Jane growled.

"Fine. Then take the carpet with you and finish it somewhere else. I don't want to have to see your face anymore," she said, turning away. Rick frowned angrily, but obliged. He folded the side of the rug filled with glass over the other side, then folded it again. He picked it up and stashed it under his shoulder. Carrying the rug, broom, and dustpan, he headed for the elevator. In a few seconds, he was gone. Alan smiled.

"Is there any particular reason you like pushing him around?" Alan asked, standing up and walking around the table.

"Yeah. I don't like him," Jane replied. Alan laughed.

"There's another reason you sent him out, isn't there?" Alan asked.

"Yeah. That officer is still alive?!" Jane snapped at Alan.

"Yes. But don't fret. We may not need to kill him," Alan responded, confidently smiling.

"Why not?! What if he gets *my* job in a few weeks? Do you know what would happen!?" Jane said, fuming.

"I'm sure we scared him off. Even if we didn't, Dr. Marie would probably try to keep him from running again, just to save his precious little life. She cares about people too much," Alan explained.

"I still don't want him alive. And isn't he a soldier? Don't they have some stupid code of honor, or something? We should kill him while he's weak," Jane said.

"Well, you do have a point. Do what you will, I won't stop you. However, I have more important things to worry about, so this one is all you. Just keep in mind that the doctor is probably watching him twenty-four seven. And if he's actually made any friends on the force, they'd probably be there, as well," Alan said.

"Why don't we just kill the doctor and their friends?" Jane asked.

"As much as i dislike her, she is still the only doctor we have down here, besides the surgeon." Alan held up his hands, still bandaged. "And if we get hurt again, we may need her." Jane grumbled unhappily, but didn't argue further. Alan continued smiling.

*　　*　　*

Zachary Zyz was lying motionless on a cold steel table. His eyes were closed. The sound of typing on a nearby computer could be heard. A light was suddenly turned on over his body, shining directly on him and covering him in light. Groaning, he sluggishly moved his arm up to his face, shielding his eyes from the light.

"I'm sorry," a female voice said, and the light turned off. Zyz let his arm fall back by his side. He smacked his lips together and coughed. His mouth felt like it was stuffed with cotton.

"W-water," he gasped out. Someone obliged, helping him sit up then holding the cup of water to his lips, tilting it gently. He drank the entire cup. "Th-thanks."

"Don't mention it," the voice said. As Zyz's senses adjusted, he was able to identify the voice as belonging to Dr. Linda Marie.

"W-wha-what happened," Zyz asked hoarsely, trying to sit up further. Dr. Marie gently guided him back down, and he obliged.

"You took one hell of a beating. Severe concussion, several bullet wounds, three missing teeth and a few smaller things. I don't know how you managed to survive. But you're gonna be out of commission for a while. Though now is a worse time than ever to be associated with the security force. Still, this is one hell of a way to hang up your kevlar vest," Dr. Marie explained. "I don't suppose you saw who did this?"

"No," Zyz coughed out. "Had a mask. Couldn't see anything." He tried sitting up again. "More water, please."

"Here you go," Dr. Marie said as she handed it to him.

"Thank you," he said, and slowly drank it all. He let out a satisfied sigh. "I'm not quitting the force."

"What?" Dr. Marie said.

"I can't quit. There's nothing I can do from the outside," Zyz said.

"Well... I can't really argue. But at least wait until your injuries are healed and I can make sure you don't have permanent brain damage. You took some really bad hits. I'm surprised you're awake as soon as you are. But please lay back down. You really shouldn't be up." Zyz listened to the doctor's orders and laid back down.

*   *   *

Toby Smalls, Jaime Slewdjack, John Dash, and DT Sacks reached the bar just as Mickey November was unlocking the doors. He turned to them as he inserted the key into the lock.

"Ain't it a bit early for drinking?" Mickey asked.

"You're the one who's opening the bar at this hour," Dash snapped back.

"Hey, got me there," Mickey said, then let out a gruff laugh.

"We're just looking for our friend. We haven't seen him for a few days, and this is the only place we haven't checked yet," Toby explained.

"Your friend? That's *real* specific. Sorry, can't help you out with just that," Mickey said. He turned away from them and finished opening the doors. Stepping inside, he flicked on the lights. The small group followed him in.

"Well, has anyone been coming often for the past few days?" Jaime asked. Mickey thought for a moment as he began setting up the bar for the day.

"Can't say I recall. Unless you count all of them that got here after the lunch incident," Mickey said. Toby sighed sadly.

"Well, thanks anyway," Toby said, and began trudging towards the door. Jaime looked sympathetically at Toby, then turned back to Mickey.

"Have you had to remove anyone for being rude or disruptive? From what I heard, this guy wasn't always the nicest person around," Jaime asked. Mickey just looked at him.

"Can't say my customers are the most polite crowd, but I ain't had to throw someone out," Mickey said, then looked away. The door opened behind them, and Tia Valentine stepped in. Jaime sighed in defeat and turned to DT and Dash.

"Either or you got anything to add?" he asked. Neither said anything. Jaime sighed again, and the three of them headed for the door, which Toby was slouched against.

"Actually, there is that one weird guy..."

Jaime spun around to face Mickey again. "What weird guy?"

"He showed up a few days ago. Walked around the bar randomly, muttering to himself. Never ordered a drink, though. When he started bothering the other customers, I hadda kick him out. He's been hanging around outside ever since. Doesn't come inside anymore, though. No matter how many times I try to get rid of him, he always comes back. No idea if he's your friend, but I'd really appreciate it if you can get him outta here," Mickey elaborated.

"We'll check it out," Jaime said. The group then headed out the door. They walked around the building. Not seeing anything on the side, they rounded another corner to the back of the bar, where they spotted a curled up figure lying motionless on the ground. The figure could be smelt from a few feet away. Jaime and DT both cringed, and Dash took a few steps backwards. Toby managed to fight the smell and walked forward, putting his hand over his mouth and nose. The others hesitated, but eventually followed. Jaime lifted his shirt's neck up and covered the bottom half of his face with it.

"I didn't think it was possible for someone to smell this bad this soon," DT commented, breathing through his hands.

"You'd be surprised," Dash responded. He wasn't covering his face, but was instead just holding his breath.

Toby leaned down and lightly shook the figure. The figure stirred and groaned, confirming the figure was a male. The man looked up. His face was covered in the same rock dust that had coated Howard's house, as well as everything else that wasn't cleaned regularly.

"Howard? Is that you?" Toby asked, unable to recognize the grimy face. The man seemed to slowly register his surroundings. After a few seconds of looking around, he focused on Toby's, his expression in a blank stupor.

"T-Tony?" he asked weakly, his voice hoarse and gruff.

"No, it's Toby. Not Tony," Toby said in a gentle, comforting voice. Jaime and DT both caught the hints of anxiety in it.

"Tony? But... you're dead..." Howard Skittering slowly sat up. As he looked at Toby, his eyes suddenly grew wide in fear. Jaime felt a chill go down his spine.

"Howard, it's Toby. With a b," Toby said, the anxiety quickly growing.

"Have I died? Are you here to take me away?" Howard asked frightfully. "I don't want to go..."

Dash stepped forward. Howard's head snapped around to look at him. "Freddy? I... I *told* you not to drive! You had too much to drink, and... and..." Dash opened his mouth to say something, but before he had the chance, Howard suddenly jumped up, causing Toby to jump back in surprise, narrowly avoiding being hit my Howard's flailing arm. As he jumped back, Toby lost his footing, tripping and falling onto his butt.

"I'm not letting you take me! I'm not dying today!" Howard yelled. Before anyone could stop him, Howard shot forward and ran around the corner, out of sight. His screaming could still be clearly heard. "The dead are here! The dead are here to take us! We're all gonna die! We're all gonna die here! No one will survive!"

The group quickly rounded the corner, each with a different expression upon their face. They watched in shock and horror as Howard ran around in circles, emitting a high-pitched scream. A crowd quickly drew around him. As Howard continued ranting madly, quiet murmurs sprang up in the crowd. The murmurs quickly grew louder. Finally someone yelled at him, "Shut up, asshole!" Others in the crowd began doing the same, and soon most of the crowd was vehemently shouting, hurling insults of all kinds at Howard. Some voices were angry, others sounded rather scared. Howard seemed to remain unfazed, continually shouting back about how they were all doomed. Toby started walking forward, but something grabbed his arm and pulled him back. He looked up at Dash.

"I know it's tough, but stay out of this one. I don't think you can help him right now. Let him tire himself out, and once the crowd disperses, then help," Dash said calmly. Toby took another step forward, anyways, but stopped and held his position. Toby looked back at Dash.

"We have to do something, though!" he pleaded.

"I know. And we will. But trust me, you don't want to go up against a mob mentality," Dash replied.

As they watched helplessly, Howard ran right at one woman, grabbing onto her arm. She screamed and shoved him away. He stumbled back, but didn't fall. Still unfazed, he immediately ran straight back into the crowd. The crowd split, allowing Howard plenty of room to slow to a stop. As he did, he turned to his left and again ran right for the crowd. The crowd was caught off guard and didn't split in time, causing Howard to run right into it. Then, seemingly acting in unison, the crowd repelled Howard out, tossing him onto the ground. He was up on his feet again within a minute.

"I can't just watch this!" Toby exclaimed. He only made it two steps before a gunshot rang out. Toby froze, and the crowd ducked down, covering their heads. Howard stood standing above all the others. He also froze, standing like a deer caught in headlights. He blankly stared straight ahead, before swiftly twisting his body around to face the source of the shot. Rick Farkass and Roy Bant were standing outside of the crowd. Rick was holding his gun above his head, light steam gently rising out of the barrel. Roy stood next to him, his weapon undrawn.

"Calm down and stop disturbing the peace, or I'll shoot!" Rick yelled loudly.

"Cool it," Roy said impatient, yet collected.

"Why should I? The interim chief said we can do whatever we want, basically. Besides, if this guy is really crazy, then being calm won't do shit. Ya gotta be-" Before Rick could finish the thought, Howard suddenly rushed at him. Rick was caught off guard and froze out of panic, and Roy was struggling to get his gun out of its holster.

"Don't you see?! We're all dead already!" Howard yelled as he grabbed Rick's shirt collar, yanking Rick's face close to his own. The two spun around as Howard grabbed onto Rick.

"Please don't hurt me," Rick squeaked out. Howard opened his mouth to say something else, but before he could, another shot rang throughout the bunker. Howard stared into Rick's eyes as he slowly sank to his knees, still gripping Rick's shirt. A second shot was fired. Howard's grip finally loosened, and he released Rick's shirt as he collapsed to the ground. Roy was motionless, his gun only halfway out of the holster. Rick hyperventilated as Jane McVellion walked up to Howard's body. She looked at Rick first, who was still panting heavily. Dismissing him, she looked down at Howard. Without hesitating, Jane pointed her gun at Howard's head, and pulled the trigger.

Toby fell to his knees. Jaime crouched down next to him, and wrapped his arm around Toby's shoulder. DT stood motionless, his mouth hanging wide open. Even Dash's eyes were wide with shock.

"I could've saved him," Toby said, his pained voice barely audible.

"No," Jaime said softly. "I don't think we could've. There was something wrong with him that we couldn't have helped with." Tears began flowing silently down Toby's cheeks. Another second later, he held his face in his hands, and began sobbing. Jaime continued to try and comfort Toby as he cried. Dash and DT remained silent.

"For once, I'm glad you're such an idiot," Jane said, turning to Rick. "If you weren't, I couldn't have killed him, myself." She let out a short, deep laugh. Rick still had the expression of horror plastered firmly on his face as he rapidly looked in between Jane and Howard's boy. Roy was stoically quiet.

*　　*　　*

As Howard Skittering's body was moved to Harrack's lab, DT Sacks, John Dash, Toby Smalls, and Jaime Slewdjack returned to the dining area. All were completely silent. Only a few people still remained in the dining area. They sat down, and didn't move, only somberly looked down at the table. Toby's eyes were red and puffy, and he had an apathetic look on his face. The others all had very serious expressions.

"We need to do something. We can't just sit by next time," Dash said. Toby looked up at him, and Dash returned the look. "I was wrong. I didn't think *that* would happen. But that doesn't excuse my inaction. Next time, we'll step up." Toby's expression didn't change, and he looked back down at the table.

"How? We're just a few people. What can we even do? Especially against the entire government?" DT asked, exasperated.

"We find more people. Make a bigger group. Strength in numbers," Jaime suggested, emotionless.

"We could also try finding someone with enough power to actually remove the temporary chief from office," Dash said.

"What if the people are too afraid to go up against the security force? I'm sure most of them would be too scared for their lives. Besides, after the way they treated Howard, I'm not sure I want to work with those people. As for someone who can actually do something, who? Who would actually be willing to fight for us," DT replied hopelessly.

"We could ask Dr. Marie," Toby added.

"I guess it's worth a shot. But what if she doesn't want to help? Then what?" Jaime asked.

"We could try talking to the vice president. I always see him around doing surveys, or something like that. We could even try asking that scientist," Toby said. His apathetic look was dissipating as he became more invested in the conversation.

"I'm not sure I trust any of them, but I guess we don't really have a choice. What else can we do?" DT said. "I mean, aside from nothing."

"We can't just do nothing! Not again," Toby said.

"So should we try to talk to one of the doctors or the VP? Or try to gather up more people to join us?" Jaime asked.

"Well, anything we do carries a risk. Anyone could just tell the security force about us. I'm sure they wouldn't be happy to hear us talking about this sort of thing," Dash said. He leaned on his arm thoughtfully. "I say we talk to Dr. Marie first. If her reaction to Tony's passing was any indication, she cares a lot about people. She can't be happy about what the security force did at lunch yesterday."

"Makes sense to me," DT said.

"Yeah, let's do it!" Toby said. "Hopefully we can get justice for Howard. And all those people from yesterday."

"Well, let's not just sit here and talk about it. Let's go," Jaime said, standing up. The others also stood up, and the group was soon moving towards Dr. Marie's office.

*   *   *

Zachary Zyz had moved from the metal operating table in Dr. Marie's office onto the significantly more comfortable bed in her office. He was sitting up, drinking another cup of water as the door to the office gently opened. Dr. Marie turned away from the terminal she had been typing at to see who had entered.

"Zach!" Lucy Desin exclaimed with worry as she rushed over to him. He didn't even get the chance to put his cup down before Lucy had wrapped her arms around him, pulling him into a hug. "Are you okay?!"

"Yeah, I'm fine," Zyz said with a laugh. She hugged him tighter. He let out a small whine of pain.

"S-sorry," Lucy said, releasing him and backing away. The door opened again, and three more people entered. Two male, one female. Dr. Marie turned to them.

"Can I help you?" she asked. She looked at the female. "Wait... weren't you a friend of Tony Weitson?" Marta Girasol nodded her head.

"Yes," she said.

"Well, how can I help you?" Dr. Marie asked again, this time with more curiosity. One of the men stepped forward.

"My name is Daniel Butler. My associates and I are planning a protest against the oppressive actions of the security force. Between the lunch incident, and the shooting that occurred earlier today, we cannot stand idly by as we are treated as disposable," the man said.

"I see. And how exactly do you plan on 'protesting?'" Dr. Marie asked.

"Nonviolently, of course. Gather up as many citizens as we can. Lead a peaceful protest to the security station. Demand that they recognize our rights as American citizens. Then hopefully garnering more support so we can keep doing it until the security force treats us with the rights we were born with," Daniel said.

"And while he's keeping the officers distracted, Officer Desin will help some of us sneak into the security station and steal their weapons," the other man said. Dr. Marie turned to him with a serious look on her face.

"That would get you arrested. Or worse," she said.

"Which is why we're not doing it," Daniel said sternly, turning to the other man. He frowned.

"I'm not saying we actually use them. I'm just saying we stock up if the peaceful solution fails," the man replied.

"I'm with Rex," Marta said. "I think we need those weapons. Without them, the security force could just execute us all without a second thought." Dr. Marie turned to around and reached up to a shelf full of folders.

"Hold on, not *every* officer is like that! Zach and I aren't like that, and I know a few other officers who aren't, either!" Lucy said defensively. "And I never agreed to let you into the station."

"Well, I'm sure that Officer Zyz, here, would be more than happy to help us out," Rex said, looking at Zyz with an expectant smile. Zyz gave him a stern stare.

"I'm not letting civilians into the security station," he stated plainly. Rex's smile disappeared. Dr. Marie pulled a folder of the shelf. She opened up the file.

"Captain Rex, is it?" she said, reading the file.

"Yes," Rex responded. Marta looked at him.

"Your first name is Captain?" she asked in disbelief.

"It's... a long story," Rex replied. He turned to Dr. Marie. "Why are you reading my file?" Dr. Marie closed the file and put it on her desk.

"I'm just trying to figure out if you're being honest about what you want the weapons for," Dr. Marie replied.

"I'm not the one who has been beating and executing people," he responded sharply.

Before anyone could say another word, the door opened once again, and everyone turned to see who was entering. Daniel, Marta, and Rex moved away from the door to make room for DT Sacks, John Dash, Jaime Slewdjack, and Toby Smalls. The room was quickly reaching maximum capacity. Rex stared suspiciously at the group. Marta and the group were both surprised as they recognized each other.

"Marta? What are you doing here?" DT asked.

"Are you hurt?" Dash asked with mild worry. She smiled.

"I'm fine, don't worry," Marta said. "I'm sorry I kinda disappeared after yesterday." Dash looked at the other occupants of the room.

"You still haven't told us what's going on here," DT said. Daniel and Rex exchanged a nervous look. Marta noticed and turned to them.

"It's okay. I trust them," Marta said comfortingly. Daniel smiled, while Rex remained suspicious.

"If you say they are trustworthy, then I shall trust them," Daniel said.

"No offense, but I'd rather judge for myself if we can trust them," Rex said.

"No offense taken," Marta said, then turned back to the group.

"So what are you guys doing here?" she asked.

"Well… we were thinking of ways to fight against the security force, and we decided to come ask Dr. Marie if she'd help," Jaime explained.

"What is it about me that makes everyone think I'd join a conspiracy?" Dr. Marie asked, giving a confused half-smile.

"Because you seem like you care about people," Toby said. Dr. Marie couldn't think of a response.

"Well, we welcome all people willing to put up resistance!" Daniel said with a wide smile.

"Yeah..." Rex said, suspiciously eying each member of the group.

"We'll be glad to do what we can," Jaime said. DT looked at Zyz.

"What happened to you?" he asked.

"Someone tried to kill me last night. I'm sure you all heard the gunshots," Zyz answered.

"So that's what that was. The security force wasn't saying anything," DT said.

"Who did it?" Dash asked.

"I don't know. They were disguised. They're a skilled fighter, though. I barely got any hits in. And I had combat training," Zyz answered. "I did manage to get a few shots off on them, though. Not sure if any of them connected."

"And no one else came in with any sort of injuries," Dr. Marie said. "If he did manage to hit them, then I'm sure he would go to Dr. Harrack, instead. The two are working together, after all." There was a large amount of resentment in her voice.

"We still need to get the word out. How are we gonna gather support for it?" Marta asked. Jaime stepped forward.

"I'd be glad to help spread the word," he said.

"Me, too," Toby said.

"Well, I already said I wouldn't just stand by and do nothing again," Dash said. DT just shrugged.

"Sure," he said.

"Excellent!" Daniel said, smiling widely.

"I can try my best to keep the security force away. At least the bad officers," Lucy said. DT and Dash exchanged a glance.

"Well, it looks like we have a plan," Daniel said.

"Wait, wait, wait. We still need to organize this. You can't just tell people there's going to a protest and expect them to automatically know when or where it's going to go down," Rex said. The others all seemed to pause to think. Daniel's smile disappeared.

"We could do it in the back of the housing area. There's never anyone back there," Lucy suggested. Rex and Daniel both nodded.

"Yeah, that should work," Rex said approvingly. Daniel smiled again.

"Well, *now* it looks like we have a plan!"

"When should we tell the people to meet us back there?" Toby asked. Daniel's smile disappeared again.

"Dinner. Tonight," Rex said.

"Bit short notice, but I'm better sooner than later," Dash said. Daniel smiled again.

"*Now-*"

"Let's stop wasting time and start getting the word out," Rex said, opening up the door and walking out. The others also slowly shuffled out the door, leaving only Dr. Marie, Zyz, and Daniel. Daniel looked at the other two. Dr. Marie gave him a sympathetic shrug. Daniel sighed and also left the office. Dr. Marie and Zyz exchanged a skeptical look.

*　　　*　　　*

Alan Berkoff's hands were no longer covered in bandages. However, the stitches remained in and scars ran all over his hands, disfiguring them. Alan stared at his hands, as though memorizing every detail of them. They had a slight tremble, and he carefully tried to bend each one of his fingers, slowly flexing it. Occasionally, he would let out a wince of pain, or would be unable to flex a finger completely. The elevator dinged, and he looked up. Standing up, he gently walked over the elevator, and waited for it to open. As it did, he smiled warmly.

"Ah, welcome! Please, come in. Take a seat," Alan said as he welcomed Percy Winkle into the High Rise. The two were alone, at least as far as Percy knew. Alan patted the back of a large red chair that had once been situated around the glass table.

Percy walked past the chair Alan was indicating without acknowledgement, and sat down at one of the swivel chairs on the far end of the conference table. Alan, keeping his slightly faded smile, straightened his back and cleared his throat. He then also walked over the conference table, taking a seat opposite Percy. "Let's skip the pleasantries and get straight to business," Percy said. Alan's smiled waned slightly. Percy cleared his throat. "What the *hell* are you trying to do?!" Alan seemed completely off guard.

"Wh-what are you talking about?" Alan stammered.

"I'm talking about everything you've been doing since that vault door opened. You have no idea how many strings I had to pull to get you in the position of president. I ignored your fuckup that spiraled the world into chaos. I had hoped that it was a fluke, and that you make sure never to do anything like it again. When you came crawling on your hands and knees, begging me to let you in on this project, I had thought you wanted a second chance, an opportunity to prove you can do better. Had I known this is what you would do, this is how you would act, I would've cut my losses and left you in your self-dug grave. You've shown you don't give a single damn about this bunker or the time and money I invested into it! It's clear you only care about furthering whatever demented agenda you may have. I don't really care *why* you're doing all of this, but when you put my entire project in jeopardy, I have to put my foot down." Percy had furiously yelled the entire monologue.

Alan sat motionless, at a complete loss of words. Percy waited with an agitated expression as Alan slowly regained his composure. After almost two minutes, Alan's face finally reconfigured itself, and he sat up, puffing his chest out. "You think it's so easy to lead this place?"

"I know *you're* not running this place. I've talked to Toaden. While he spends all of his days inspecting the bunker and making sure all the systems running smoothly, you just spend all your time goofing off up here. When was the last time you even did something productive?!" Percy replied. "I mean, aside from using your power to appoint a, abusive interim chief."

"At least I'm actually *here*, doing something, while you're off prancing around your fancy mansion, playing with all your expensive little toys. Besides, what am I even *supposed* to do?! Nothing ever really seems to happen around here, and Toaden checks the bunker and systems all on his own. I didn't tell him to do it, and if he hadn't just assumed the responsibility, I might *even* do it! I mean, it's boring as hell, but at least it's *something*."

"If you're looking for *excitement*, then politics was probably the wrong job for you." Alan's anger was briefly replaced with a laugh. Percy waited for him to finish. "I don't know what you were expecting from this position, but I'm sorry you didn't get it. Now start acting like an *adult*, and do your fucking *job*."

"I already told you, *there's nothing to do!* What do you expect from me?!" Alan yelled.

"I *expect* you not to continually be incompetent! Don't hire people who will only abuse their power." Percy stopped as the irony settled on him.

"I'm sure *you* could do *much* better," Alan said sarcastically.

"Currently, I am the fourth richest person alive. I own the single largest munitions manufacturing, research, and development company on the planet. Which I built from scratch, by the way. So, yes. I'm *sure* I could do much better."

"Yes, everybody knows how basically every military on the planet buys their weapons from you. Remind me again how that whole middle eastern controversy went?" Alan snickered.

"Once the product transfers ownership, the responsibility is off of the seller," Percy responded mechanically.

"We both know that's bullshit," Alan replied.

"You'd be wise to shut up, now," Percy snarled.

"Fine. Let's just wrap this up," Alan said impatiently. Percy took a deep breath.

"Against my better judgement, and all common sense, I am giving you *one* final chance to prove yourself." Percy leaned forward in his chair, pointing right at Alan. "I appointed you to president. Which means all of your actions reflect off me. If it weren't for that, I would've fired McVellion the moment I found out you lied to me about what she did to the citizens. But I have my *dignity* to protect, something you don't even seem to understand. Fire McVellion, and *maybe* I'll *consider* letting you stay president. But, after this, the first mistake you make will also be your last," Percy said. The two stared at each other for a long time. Eventually Percy stood up, leaving the High Rise without another word.

*   *   *

Despite still having a large crowd, the dining area was significantly more empty than usual. However, at the very end of the residential area, against the back wall of the bunker, a large crowd of almost forty was gathered. Most were nervously chatting amongst themselves, the entire seemed wary. A smaller group was gathered at the front of the crowd, consisting of Daniel Butler, Captain Rex, Lucy Desin, Marta Girasol, John Dash, Jaime Slewdjack, DT Sacks, and Toby Smalls. As Daniel was preparing himself, Rex turned to the others.

"I gotta say, I'm pretty impressed with the crowd you've managed to draw," he said genuinely.

"You'd be surprised," Dash said, looking at the condensed crowd. Daniel stepped forward and called for the crowd to quiet down. They stopped talking to give him mild attention.

"First of all, thank you all for coming," Daniel started. He paused for a moment and smiled to himself as the crowd focused on him. "Second, I am sure all of you are here because you are tired of the oppressive nature the security force has adopted.

Between the lunch beatings and the execution earlier today, it is clear that things will only continue to escalate. Which is why we have to stop this before it goes too far!" Daniel paused as the crowd let out a small and rather quiet cheer.

"We have to show the security force we won't simply sit by and do nothing as they continue to terrorize us. Which is why tomorrow morning, at breakfast, we will be marching on the security station!" Daniel paused again to allow a slightly louder cheer.

"However, we should prepare ourselves for the worst. This enemy is not one to be taken lightly. They may try to strike us down. They may strike hard. Some of us may be injured during the protest. Maybe most of us. But we must be prepared to take a few blows. We all know what they have already done, and what they are likely willing to do. But we must be willing to take these hits! For if we don't take them now, we shall only take them later. And if we take them later, it may already be too late." Daniel paused, however there was no cheer this time. "I understand if there are any of you that don't want to take this risk. I know I am asking a lot of you. Now is the time to back out, if you so desire. Though I implore you to stay, as we are not only fighting for ourselves, but for everybody. For all who will live down here. We cannot allow the future generations to grow up in a totalitarian regime!" Daniel stopped. Three individuals peeled away from the crowd and slowly headed away from the rest of the crowd.

"What were they expecting," Rex muttered under his breath.

"Well, I'm surprised we didn't lose more," Marta also said under her breath. John Dash nodded in silent agreement.

Daniel then cleared his throat. "I know that you may be scared. I don't blame you. Honestly, I'm a little scared myself. This is a scary scenario. And I'd like to comfort you by saying that everything is going to be okay. That the security force will back down. That they will treat us with the rights we were born with!

But I can't say that. I can't say that this will spontaneously fix everything. This will be an uphill fight. We are at a disadvantage in everything but numbers. The security force may attack us on sight. We will not fight back, however, as that will only give them more of an excuse to beat us and tighten their grip on our lives. We must be willing to take these blows without seeking retribution." Daniel stopped to breath. "What I can say is that this situation will not improve on its own. Inaction will cause things to become worse for all of us. We cannot stand idly by as the security force continues to abuse us!"

"Why shouldn't we defend ourselves? Someone hits me, I'm gonna hit them back!" someone from the crowd shouted. The crowd murmured loudly as a southern accented man with a stetson pushed his way to the front of the crowd. He looked unhappily at Daniel. Daniel coolly responded with almost no delay.

"As I already said, it will give them even more of a reason to continue to oppress us. We cannot solve violence with more violence." Daniel paused and noticed the answer didn't quite please the southerner. The crowd continued to murmur. "We are fighting for justice and our rights. But we must not also forget that the officers of the security force are also people, with the same rights as us. To hit back as they hit us would make us no better than them. We may be on opposite sides, but we are all people. We must show them the same humanity that they do not show us."

"Be better than them? This is a *war*! We don't have room for mercy. We have to take them down, once and for all," the southerner shouted. Lucy stepped up next to Daniel.

"Not every security officer is like that!" she shouted. "Some of them *are* good people! They're just scared of Chief McVellion. I've talked with them, I've worked with them. They're not all bad people! I mean, yeah, not every one of them are good, either. But to say all the officers are the same person is wrong!" The crowd settled down a little. However, the southerner began booing. A few other people joined in, but the majority of the crowd stayed silent.

"You're all the same! I'm sure you're just leading us into a trap. We should tie you up and lock you in one of these houses! Then we need to strike when they least expect it!" the southerner yelled. Some people in the crowd shouted in agreement. Lucy shrunk back with a fearful expression.

Dash leaned close to Marta. "Remind me to tell them about the Milgram experiment sometime," he whispered.

"Everyone, calm down!" Daniel yelled as he stretched out his arms. "I know they've violated our rights, but we can't turn on one of our own just because she happens to have the same uniform as our oppressors. If we're going to fight for justice, then shouldn't we grant the officers the same justice? Once we reinstall a democracy into this bunker, then we shall judge each officer individually, based on their individual actions. This bunker was created to uphold American values. Shouldn't we try to do the same?"

"American values? Our American *rights* are being stepped on! You've even said so, yourself! And I'm willing to do anything necessary to get them back," the southerner said.

"He's right!" someone in the crowd shouted, which was followed by a small cheer. More people seemed to be backing up the southerner. As Daniel's mind rushed to think of a response, Rex stepped up next to him, and loudly cleared his throat. The crowd didn't respond.

"Everyone, *quiet!*" Rex shouted at the top of his lungs. The sound reverberated off of the stone walls, and the crowd was shocked into silence. Even the southerner appeared surprised. The crowd slowly returned their attention to the front. Some had guilty or scared expressions, while others, like the southerner, seemed more irritated. Rex quickly spotted the unmistakable stetson and scowled. "Alright. Since you're so outspoken against this plan, maybe you'd like to tell us your name?"

"Jeremiah Shoostand," the southerner said irately.

"Okay, Jeremiah," Rex said in a calm tone. "I can tell that you want to end the security force's abuse as soon as possible. I can't blame you. I think we all agree that things are pretty bad. That we are being denied basic freedoms and rights. But what you're suggesting is too risky. Not to mention, this group is kinda small, especially for something like this. We could grow this revolution much larger, but if we just attack the security force, it may scare others into supporting them. We have to show that we aren't savages." Rex paused for a breath. Jeremiah silently, but intently, listened, his arms crossed.

"Alright, fine. You make a good argument, I'll admit that. But if your plan fails, *I'm* trying *mine*," Jeremiah said. Rex sighed in defeat and slowly nodded.

"I think that's all. You should all go home now. Rest up, sleep well. You're gonna need it. We'll meet here tomorrow, before breakfast," Rex said. The crowd lingered a moment longer, once again murmuring. Then it slowly dispersed, the crowd's members returning to their homes. Jeremiah was one of the last to leave. Soon enough, only the original eight planners of the protest remained. Rex turned to the others.

"That goes for all of you, too," he said. Daniel looked at Rex.

"That was a well put together speech. Consider me impressed," Daniel said.

"Well, it's easier to talk someone like that down when you agree with them," Rex said. "I still don't think your peaceful protest is going to get us anywhere."

"Well, I suppose we shall see tomorrow morning," Daniel said with a smile. He then departed, whistling an old time show tune to himself. Rex turned back to the other six.

"I guess Marta wasn't wrong about you four. You pulled through better than I expected," he said.

"Thanks," DT said. Rex turned to Lucy.

"Are you *sure* you don't want to help us into the security station to stock up on weapons?" he asked.

"Wait, *what?!*" Jaime asked, surprised.

"Right, that was before you entered the doctor's office," Rex said thoughtfully.

"The answer is still no. I'm not helping you sneak into the station," Lucy answered.

"Under what circumstances would you agree to do it?" Rex asked. Lucy crossed her arms impatiently and didn't answer. Rex sighed. "Fine. I won't press any further. But if you change your mind - and I hope you do - then let me know." He turned to the others. "Would you guys help sneak in?"

"No. I'm not touching a weapon," Toby replied firmly. DT and Dash exchanged an unsure glance. Jaime stepped forward.

"Yeah, I'll help. But I agree that this is a bad idea," he said.

"Don't worry. We'd only use them as a last resort. It's meant more to just keep them from hunting us down," Rex explained. They stood in silence for a few moments longer.

"So I guess that's it," DT said.

"Well, we should all go get some sleep, too. See you guys here tomorrow morning?" Marta asked. They all nodded at varying paces. The small group stood in place for another moment, as if they were stuck. After only a couple minutes that seemed to stretch on forever, the group finally moved away, heading back for their beds.

October 5, 2031

The next morning, Alan Berkoff was relaxing on a lavish sofa in the High Rise. He was once again flexing each of his fingers. He was able to flex his fingers further, and made less pained winces. Angel Puer sat on a nearby chair. As he tested his fingers, Alan looked up at Angel.

"Why didn't you kill Will when I asked you to?" he asked. She looked up at him. After a moment of silence, she pointed at the empty area in the room where the glass table had once been.

Alan followed her finger. After looking at the spot for a moment, he let out a short laugh. "Fair point," he said. He then looked back at Angel, who made a circle above her head with her index fingers. Alan took a minute to interpret the motion. Then he let out another short laugh. "Yeah, I probably could've come up with something a bit more inconspicuous."

Alan went back to examining his hands, and Angel looked around the room. Something caught her attention, and she focused on the window. Standing up, she walked over to the window, and looked down. Alan noticed her and stood up himself. As he walked up next to her, he looked out and saw a large group of over thirty people marching through the residential area. As they moved closer to the dining area, in became increasingly clear that they were moving as a singular unit.

"What the hell are they doing?" Alan asked. Angel didn't respond. As the crowd entered the dining area, they stopped moving. However, they did not disperse, instead continuing to stand together. "I don't like this. Keep an eye on them." Angel gave a single nod of acknowledgement. As they watched the security force exit the security station to face the crowd, Angel swiftly turned around, walking over to the elevator. Alan heard the elevator doors open, then close another second later.

With the security station empty, Angel was able to sneak through without being seen. Walking into one of the large storage rooms in the back, which was clearly labeled "Authorized Personnel Only," she looked around at the multiple military-grade boxes. Most of them proudly displayed "Winkle Enterprises," followed by a short description of what was in the box. Angel looked at the box labeled "Winkle Enterprises Projectile Explosives" as she passed it. She stopped at a box in the back of the room, labeled "Winkle Enterprises Long Range and Sharpshooters." She removed the lid from the box. Inside of it, were numerous shiny, unused, and dismantled sniper rifles, careful packed into identical styrofoam holders. On top of the stacks of rifles, was a small case, seemingly out of place. Angel removed the small case from the box and replaced the lid. She then turned and walked out of the store room.

She also reached behind the box and grabbed a dark grey outfit. She quickly pulled the pants and shirt over her own, pulled the gloves on, and changed her shoes. She then quickly tied her long hair into a large bun, and stuffed the mask into her pocket. Outside, the security force blocked the view of the station, and they were all facing away, allowing Angel to sneak out of the station, and around the crowd without detection. Giving the crowd a large girth - not that anyone would notice her with the crowds gathered - she walked around the side the residential area, still carrying the small case. Once she was a few houses in, she stopped and looked around. The area was empty, and the rows of houses cut off the view of the dining area.

Confirming she was alone, she tossed the case onto the roof of one of the houses. She quickly sprinted at an alley in between that house and the one just behind it. When she was close to the building, she sprung herself upwards. As she was about to hit the building, she planted her legs firmly on the side pushed. She turned her body around in midair, landing on the house she had tossed the case onto. She pulled the mask out of her pocket and put it on. She didn't have a clear view of the dining area. Grabbing the case, she crouched down and cautiously moved along the rooftops. Hopping onto the next house in the row, she now had a much clearer view of the dining area.

She opened up her case, revealing another dismantled sniper rifle. This one, however, was a different model than the stacks of one in the Winkle Enterprises box. Angel's rifle was also much less shiny, with scuffs and scratches indicating multiple uses. She took the parts out and began screwing them together, including a large silencer on the end. Once the rifle was assembled, she laid down flat on the roof of the building, and loaded a bullet into the chamber. Peering through the scope, she adjusted it as necessary.

*   *   *

The security force was lined up, in between the protesters and the security station. The crowd was chanting "Give us justice! Give us our rights!" over and over. Jane McVellion stepped in front of the other officers. Someone at the front of the crowd raised their hand, and the crowd slowly chanted quieter and quieter. The same person then stepped forward. Daniel Butler and Jane McVellion stood face to face, both intensely staring at each other. She glared at him, then glanced at the crowd behind him briefly, before returning her glare to him. Her face was impatient, and slightly confused. However, she did not appear angry.

"What the hell are you doing here?" Jane asked.

"We are protesting the security force's abusive practices, under *your* leadership," Daniel stated. Her expression became even more confused.

"It's only been two days," Jane said.

"It's been more than enough time for your officers to beat us, and to execute a man," Daniel said, raising his chin up but maintaining eye contact with Jane. Jane's confusion was replaced with anger.

"Just get out of here. This is the only chance I'm giving you," Jane ordered.

"We are not leaving until the atrocities you've been committing come to an end," Daniel said. Jane bared her teeth and removed her baton from her belt.

"Leave now," Jane demanded forcefully.

"We are *not* leaving," Daniel said, equally forceful. The entire dining area was motionless as the two stared at each other. Then Jane raised her baton, and brought it down upon Daniel's head. Daniel stumbled back, but regained his defiant posture, seemingly ignorant of the drops of blood rolling down the side of his face. He stepped back up to Jane. The protest behind Daniel also took a collective step forward. Jane looked in between them and Daniel, and snarled. Jane raised the baton again and struck him again, much harder. Daniel stumbled back again and lost his balance. The crowd seemed to hold its breath and Jane gave a satisfied half smile. But pushed himself up again, his head bleeding much harder, once again taking up the same spot in front of Jane. Jane's smile disappeared.

Jane growled which soon turned into a full-blown animalistic yell. She hit Daniel again. He fell down again, this time laying motionless on the ground. The protesters shifted nervously, and quiet murmurs sprung up amongst them. Jane stared down at him, bloody baton in hands, breathing heavily through her mouth. When he didn't move for another few seconds, Jane calmed down, placing her baton back on her belt. She looked up at the rest of the crowd.

"Get out of here!" she shouted, her deep voice carrying through the bunker. The crowd, more nervous than before, took a few steps back and began to break up slightly. A few people from the protest stepped forward. Jane didn't notice and turned back to the rest of the officers. "Throw this piece of shit in the back." As she started to walk back to the security station, cheers suddenly emerged from the crowd behind her. Jane stopped in surprise, and slowly looked over her shoulder. Daniel was once more standing. Despite being covered in blood and swaying gently on his feet, he held the same position, not back down.

He continued to stare defiantly at her. Jane fully turned around and marched back to her same spot. She stared at him silently for a moment. He continued to stare back. Jane drew her pistol and pressed the barrel in between Daniel's eyes. Without hesitation, she pulling the trigger. His body immediately fell backwards, sprawling out on the ground as he fell. Both the protesters and the security force went completely silent, remaining completely motionless. Jane smiled as she stared down at Daniel's body, the gun still in her hand. She turned to the crowd, her fury unabated. The crowd turned their attention to her, many still stunned.

"If you're still here in the next two minutes, I'll have you all *shot*!" She yelled, waving her gun around carelessly as she spoke. She stared at them for another few seconds, then holstered her gun. She turned around to face the row security officers, still lined up and unmoving. She started approaching them. "Go back into the station and grab your rifles!" she ordered.

Before she could reach the other officers, though, someone with a southern accent suddenly yelled "Attack!" Jane stopped, but before she could turn around, the crowd was charging forward, leaving only a few protesters standing back. Marta Girasol had tried to rush forward, but Captain Rex had grabbed her from behind and held her back. Marta looked at Rex angrily. It was just them, John Dash, DT Sacks, Jaime Slewdjack, Toby Smalls, and Lucy Desin, who was wearing her casual clothes, remaining.

Jane had just enough time to look over her shoulder before someone ran into her. She stumbled, but didn't have any time to react before the rest of the crowd slammed into her, knocking her to the ground. She covered her head as the mob trampled over her. The security officers, most of which were still stunned, didn't know what to do as the mob rapidly closed the distance.

A few had regained enough sense to draw their batons before the mob reached them. The mob smashed into the line of security officers, the two groups melding together to create a gigantic brawl. The mob managed to knock down a few officers who were still trying to process the situation. However, there were still a few officers who weren't caught off guard. Those who had managed to get their batons out quickly swung them, hitting as many of the rioters as they could. A few of the rioters went down, but they still managed to push the officers back, trying to knock them off of their feet.

"What gives?" Marta asked angrily. Rex just looked at Lucy. Lucy looked back, a horrified expression on her face.

"Alright, fine," she said simply. Rex, Marta, and Jaime followed Lucy around the scuffle. Dash, DT, and Toby stayed behind and just watched with shock.

The security officers had much heavier protection, and once the shock wore off they began to push back against the mob. The officers pushed back harder against the mob, forcing the mob to back away, and allowing some officers who had been knocked over to get back to their feet. They quickly joined back in, forcing the mob back even further.

"We should go," Rose Anderson anxiously suggested to Casey Goodwill as the two watched a table on the edge of the dining area.

"Go where? Besides, I'm curious to see how this ends," Casey responded. "It's not like we're in danger over here."

Some intuitive rioters had managed to snag some batons off of the fallen officers. As they started to use the batons against the officers, the remaining security officers tried to coordinate strikes on the highest threats. Even with the batons, the security officers' kevlar vests and body padding allowed them to keep the upper hand, and the rioters only managed to slow down the officers as the officers continued to push back the mob.

As one man raised a stolen baton, he has suddenly hit in the face with another baton before he could swing his. The man's stetson flew off as he fell to the ground. He lifted his face up from the ground long enough to see it get trampled and destroyed. Jeremiah Shoostand gritted his teeth and pushed himself back up, narrowly avoiding a baton swing. As he jumped away, he quickly looked around and spotted a younger security officer standing on the edge of the crowd.

The young man looked scared. He was staying out of the main brawl, unlike a lot of the other officers. Jeremiah eyed the holster on the officer's belt. He smiled nastily. Johnny Dinlum watched in horror as more and more people on both sides were injured and injuring each other. The young officer glanced to his left for just a second, just in time to see a baton inches from his face. As the baton connected with Dinlum's face, he staggered back. Jeremiah grabbed the handle sticking out of the holster and jerked it out, then kicked the young officer squarely in the chest. Dinlum collapsed onto the ground, and didn't get back up.

At the same time, Roy Bant was busy with another citizen who was trying to wrestle the baton out of his hands. Roy spotted Jeremiah running straight at Dinlum. Roy managed to shove the woman back and managed to smash her head with the baton before she could regain her balance. She went sprawling into another protester who had just successfully gained a baton from another officer. As the woman protester fell onto him, he caught her, looking up to see Roy just as he turned away. The protester lowered the woman onto the ground and went after the officer.

All of this was happening as Jeremiah attacked Dinlum. Before Jeremiah could properly hold the gun, Roy had already dashed over and grabbed at it. Jeremiah was caught off guard and almost lost his grip, but he managed to hold and, and the two tried to wrestle it away from the other. The two tried to push the barrel of the gun towards the other, both fighting to get their finger on the pistol's trigger. Roy suddenly jerked the gun barrel towards him, and Jeremiah's hand slipped. Grasping desperately to keep the gun in his grip, he accidentally hit the trigger, sending a stray bullet flying away from the brawl and into the dining area.

The gunshot caused much of the brawl, on both sides, to retreat back to their respective sides. The two sides, both with many disoriented, bleeding, or still laying on the ground, took advantage of the ceasefire to try to get their bearings and judge the damage. There were naturally some who had ignored the gunshot and continued to fight. But most were just trying to catch a breath.

Jeremiah and Roy were among those still actively fighting. The two continued to struggle over the gun. One security officer noticed the gun they were fighting over and stepped towards them. Both of the men were too focused on the gun to notice her. The protester who Roy had pushed the woman into suddenly tackled Roy, causing him to lose his grip on the gun. The two then grappled with each other, both grabbing the other's shirt collar and trying to punch the other.

Jeremiah knelt down onto one knee and began breathing heavily as Roy and the other protester continued to fight right next to him. Angel waited for them to move out of the way so she had a clear shot on Jeremiah. The security officer who had stepped towards them drew her own gun. Jeremiah saw her approach and pointed the gun up at her.

"Stop!" she yelled. She raised her gun. Jeremiah stared down the sight on Dinlum's gun. Jeremiah didn't hesitate to fire. Before she knew what was happening, the bullet entered Cat Vilner's left eye. Nobody noticed that the gunshot seemed to echo only once. The bullet flew through Cat's head, exiting out the back of her skull and taking most of her brain with it. As her brain flew out of her body, it spread outwards, splattering all over the ground and people standing near her. Her body stood straight up for a moment longer, her fingers still tightly clutching her gun. Her bloody and matted hair came loose, some of it fell over the front of her face and covered her now-empty left eye socket. She remained upright for another second. Then her body collapsed to the ground.

No one moved. Not even Roy, who was standing over the over protester he had just been fighting with. Jeremiah realized that all was quiet. He smiled, and stood up straight. He cleared his throat to gain everyone's attention. He opened his mouth to say something, but before he had the chance to say anything, he suddenly launched forward onto the ground. Jane McVellion stood behind him, baton in hand. She stood over him as he tried to push himself up. Bending down, she hit him repeatedly until he stopped moving. While most of the crowd remained shocked and motionless, a few wiser members of the mob made the decision to run. No one stopped them.

As Jane finished beating Jeremiah, and ordered the security force to arrest all of the protesters they could, Casey Goodwill cried for help as she knelt over Rose Anderson. A red spot was slowly growing on Rose's shirt, right where the stray bullet that was launched when Roy and Jeremiah fought over the gun had struck her.

*   *   *

Dr. Linda Marie was sitting in her office, alone except for Zachary Zyz, who was still recovering. She was typing away at her monitor.

"You should take a break," Zyz commented. Dr. Marie sighed and spun around in her chair to face him.

"And do what?" Dr. Marie asked.

"Didn't you bring a book, or some other form of entertainment with you?" Zyz responded. Dr. Marie turned back to the shelf above her monitor and stood up. She pulled a large book of sudoku puzzles down. Sitting back down, she grabbed a pencil with her left hand and opened up the book to about halfway through. She set the book down on the table and began looking at the page she had opened to.

That was when the shot rang out. Dr. Marie and Zyz both snapped to attention. They were motionless for a minute, then both stood up and cautiously walked to the door. Opening it up, they walked outside. They caught the tail end of the brawl, with many bloody and beaten, and lying on the ground. As the two watched helplessly, an officer yelled, and the second shot promptly ended the brawl, and the security officer's life. Some of the people in the crowd suddenly sprinted away. "I'm going to need some supplies from my office." She returned to her office, leaving Zyz standing there. Zyz took another step towards the battlezone, but then suddenly grabbed his head and winced in pain. He walked to the nearest table, and sat down, waiting for his headache to subside.

Only a few minutes later, Jane McVellion stood at the entrance to the security station as the able security officers were bringing all of the protesters they could catch into the station. Only a handful of people, both protesters and officers, were still on the ground. Most of the protesters who were still standing had made a run for it, and were given chase by only a couple security officers. The officers were unable to catch many of them, and a decent amount of protesters managed to escape. Many had still been arrested, however. They managed to catch Jeremiah Shoostand, who defiantly spat blood at Jane as he was taken into the station. She responded by taking her baton and giving him a hard blow to the stomach. He doubled over, and was dragged inside.

Dr. Marie looked across the aftermath, holding the mobile medical kit she had gone back to her office for. She didn't linger long, quickly going to work. Dr. Marie walked to one of the few people still lying on the ground. The man was sitting up, covered in cuts and bruises, and breathing deeply. Dr. Marie set down the kit and crouched down next to the man. Before she could even speak to the man, two security officers walked over and yanked the man to his feet. He yelled out in pain. They ignored his pained yelps and began dragging him to the station. Dr. Marie stood up.

"Excuse me," she said firmly. The security officers didn't acknowledge her. Frustrated, she marched up to them, cutting them off and stopping in front of them. The officers stopped with angry expression.

"What do you want?" Rick Farkass snapped.

"This man is officially my patient, and I am not finished examining him," Dr. Marie stated, still firm. Rick, who had no visible injuries, scoffed.

"You got a problem, take it up with Chief McVellion. She told us to round all these people up. I'm sure you can give them a checkup after we get them nice and comfy in their cells," Rick said. Without waiting for a response, he pushed Dr. Marie out of the way and the two officers continued to lead the man away. Dr. Marie continued to march after them with determination.

"I won't let you move these injured citizens without proper medical attention," Dr. Marie informed Rick. Rick looked around. Almost all the protesters, both conscious and unconscious had been rounded up and taken into the security station. Most of the security officers recovered enough and had picked themselves up. There were only a few scattered bodies still on the ground.

"Well, I think you're a little late for that. But I'm sure all those corpses would love your attention," Rick replied. The two officers dragged the man inside the station, leaving Dr. Marie helpless to stop them. She sighed and walked to the nearest body on the ground. Cat Vilner laid with her brain spread out behind her. Dr. Marie didn't stay with her for long. The next body she came across was a man in his late thirties, laying in a pool of blood. Again, she didn't stay with Daniel Butler for long.

As she looked around, trying to see if there was anyone the security officers hadn't dragged into the station, she noticed a couple sitting at a table. Neither appeared to be moving. Dr. Marie briskly trotted over to them. As she got closer, she realized they were both women. One was covered in blood, her eyes wide open. The other woman was holding her hand, silently staring at her. Dr. Marie sighed and took the first woman's pulse. Casey Goodwill looked up at Dr. Marie. Dr. Marie wordlessly shook her head. Casey went back to staring at her friend's body. Dr. Marie gently closed Rose Anderson's eyes. Standing up, she began walking to the security station.

Jane McVellion watched as the last protester was brought inside the security station. As she turned to enter the station herself, she noticed something in the corner of her eye. She turned back around to see Dr. Marie approaching the security station. Jane groaned as Dr. Marie walked up to her.

"I demand to see every person in that building, your officers included," Dr. Marie said professionally. Jane, who had cuts and bruises herself, snarled at Dr. Marie.

"Fuck off," Jane replied nastily. Before Dr. Marie could say another word, a voice from inside the station called for Jane. Annoyed, Jane entered the station. Dr. Marie tried to enter the security station, but was promptly pushed back out. Two officers then came out and stood guard, preventing Dr. Marie from entering.

As Dr. Marie attempted to talk her way past them, Jane reappeared from the station. Seeing Dr. Marie was still there, she audibly growled, then removed her baton from her belt and threateningly approached Dr. Marie. Dr. Marie held her ground until the moment Jane smacked her across the face with her baton. Dr. Marie let out a loud yelp of pain and crumpled to the ground. Zyz immediately rushed over, completely forgetting about his headache. As she picked herself off the ground, he helped her up. Dr. Marie ignored the gash on her cheek and picked up her medical kit. After one more depressed glance at the security station, the two turned to leave. After a few steps, they heard commotion behind them.

They turned around in time to see the body of the protester who had fought with Roy over the gun being thrown onto the ground in front of the station. The officers went back inside, and the entrance was empty except for the man's body. Dr. Marie and Zyz exchanged a glance. Zyz tried to get Dr. Marie to keep walking away, but she pulled away from him and marched back to the security station's entrance.

Dr. Marie bent down and began to examine the man, placing her medical kit next to him and opening it up. She quickly took his pulse, then sighed in defeat. Before she could commence her examination, two security officers appeared from the station, and grabbed the man's body. Dr. Marie stood up as they began dragging him away.

As Dr. Marie was about to object, Jane reappeared in the doorway, brandishing her bloody baton. Dr. Marie took a few instinctive steps back as Jane held a menacing gaze on her. Dr. Marie stood there for another second, and Jane took one large step forward. Dr. Marie quickly bent down and packed up her kit, making a quick exit from the security station. She joined Zyz, and the two returned to her office.

More officers then came out and began dragging Cat and Daniel's bodies away. A couple of them approached Casey and Rose. After scanning the couple, they grabbed Rose's arms and pulled her off the seat. As they dragged her across the ground Casey jumped forward, screaming loudly and grabbing onto Rose's hand, not letting go.

"Please. Oh, God, no. Why... Don't let it be this way. This isn't happening. This can't be happening," she continued to cry as she followed her friends body. The officers threw Rose on top of the small pile of four bodies they had stacked up outside of Dr. William Harrack's office. The officers walked away, but Casey continued to hold her friend's hand and cry.

*   *   *

Marta Girasol, Captain Rex, John Dash, DT Sacks, Jaime Slewdjack, Toby Smalls, and Lucy Desin had all returned back to their original meeting spot in the back of the residential area. Rex was doing inventory on the guns they had managed to collect. They were all completely silent.

After a few minutes, Rex looked up at the others. "I could use some help with these," he said. The others just stared at him.

"Can we do it later?" Marta asked. Rex sighed and continued on his own.

"That..." Toby choked up before he could get more than a word out.

"That was fucked up," DT finished for him.

"That doesn't even begin to describe it," Marta replied. They continued to stand around in silence, the only sound being Rex counting the weapons.

"What do we do next?" Dash asked, breaking the silence. Rex stopped counting and looked up at him.

"We... we, uh..." he paused to think.

"Well, whatever we do, we can't give up," Jaime said, determined.

"Agreed," Rex said.

"But that still doesn't give us a plan. Daniel's peaceful protest didn't work, and that Texan's violent protest didn't work, either," DT said.

"We could take the security force out, one by one. While they're on patrol!" Jaime suggested.

"We're *not* killing them!" Lucy almost yelled. "Besides, hasn't there been enough death? Isn't one dead security officer enough for you?"

"She isn't the only one who died," Rex said.

"And I'm not saying we *kill* them. I meant take out as in disarm," Jaime replied.

"Though we could kill them if we wanted," Rex said.

"No," Toby stated firmly. Everyone looked at him. "We shouldn't fight anymore. We-"

"You saw how well nonviolence went for Daniel," Marta said gently. "I'm afraid we're past that point."

Toby opened his mouth to say something, but the only sound that escaped was a small squeak. Then he suddenly collapsed onto the ground, crying hysterically. Everyone just looked at him sadly, unsure what to do. In another minute, Rex finished counting the weapons and zipped them up in two large duffle bags. He tossed one bag to Marta. It landed at her feet. She glanced at it, then returned her attention to Toby. Rex sighed. Another few minutes later, Toby had cried himself out, and was sitting quietly on the floor. Rex stood up, tossing a duffle bag over his shoulder.

"As much as I think we should make our next move as quick as we can, I... understand now isn't a good time. Go home, get some sleep. We'll meet up again soon," Rex said. He then took his leave, walking away with the duffle bag. Shortly after, Toby stood up and began walking away. Marta grabbed her duffle bag, and they all walked away.

*　　*　　*

Alan decided to cancel breakfast that day. The dining area remained devoid of citizens for hours, regardless. Angel had wanted to spend some time in her house outside of the hidden compartment she was often crammed into. Percy Winkle stood in the High Rise with him as he watched a few security officers mop up the blood that covered the ground down below. Alan could clearly see it, despite the dark color of the rock and he height of the High Rise. He slowly turned to face his fellow Council member. Alan seemed to be in a dazed state. Percy was infuriated.

"This is a complete fucking mess! You *do* realize that, right?" Percy shouted angrily at Alan. Alan almost didn't seem to register what Percy had said.

"I..." Alan stammered, almost at a loss of words.

"How could you let this happen?!" Percy yelled, even louder. Alan flinched, and instinctively ducked down. Percy stared at him in frustration. After cowering for a moment, Alan seemed to regain his senses. He cleared his throat and stood up straight.

"How is this my fault?! I'm not the one who started the revolt!" Alan said defensively.

"Maybe not, but your temporary chief of security was responsible. Her actions directly caused the deaths of three civilians and one security officer! The worst part is, I *told* you to remove her! Why didn't you just listen to me?! This is a complete disaster! And it all could've been prevented, if you had just *listened* to me, and fired that woman. She may be responsible, but this is all on you," Percy yelled.

Percy stared at him and sighed disappointedly, his anger dissipating. As disappointment and regret replaced his anger, he turned away from Alan. "But what was I expecting from a political reject? Clearly I was wrong to give you my sympathy. But it's time to correct my mistake," Percy said with a somber tone. As Percy looked away from Alan, Alan walked over to one of the couches, reaching behind a pillow.

"You're just lucky I don't like leaving leadership positions open," Percy stopped to look back at Alan, who was standing patiently with his hands behind his back. "You stay stay in charge until the rest of the Council can settle on a replacement. We'll probably have to vote in that soldier as chief of security, first. I've changed my mind on that matter, so it won't be difficult. I'll gather the Council together later today. After that, we'll begin the search for the new president."

"But I can stay in charge until then?" Alan asked. Percy sighed.

"Yes. You can stay in charge until then," Percy said. Then he narrowed his eyes and stared directly in Alan's eyes. "But *don't* do anything you'll regret."

"Percy, you are a true friend."

"Cut the crap. I'll see you at the Council meeting later today."

Before Alan could respond, Percy walked over to the elevator and pressed the button. Alan let his hands fall to his sides. They were both empty. As Percy had his back turned to him, Alan started looking under different pillows. The elevator opened, and Percy stepped on. Another second passed, and the elevator was moving downwards.

"Where the hell did Will put that gun?" Alan asked angrily to himself. Finally he sighed in defeat. "I guess I'll just have to have McVellion handle this."

*   *   *

Dr. William Harrack stared at the pile of bodies outside of his office. A fifth body was laying next to the other four, still gripping the hand of the one on top of the pile. As harrack watched, the fifth body adjusted her arm, mumbling lightly in her sleep. He sighed and walked towards the security station. Unlocking the chain link fence, he stepped inside. He pressed the numbers into the keypad to the security station, but as he opened the door, he was suddenly pushed backwards. He stumbled, and then looked up angrily.

"Oh, sorry. We thought you were the other doctor," the security officer said apologetically.

"I don't care what you're doing in there, but I need at least one officer to help move the bodies outside of my lab. You idiots just piled them up, and I can't move them myself," Harrack snapped.

"Uh, I'll go talk to Chief McVellion," the officer said, then stepped back inside and closed the door. Harrack grunted impatiently. Less than a minute later, the door opened again and Rick Farkass was shoved outside.

"Hey! You didn't need to push me!" he yelled at the other officer. The other officer just shrugged and closed the door. Rick spit at the door and turned to face Harrack. "They told me I'm on body duty."

"It's not my fault you had to go and kill people," Harrack retorted as he turned and began walking back to his office. Rick followed him.

"Don't blame us! The chief killed the first dude, and the rest of the deaths had nothing to do with us!" Rick said defensively as he struggled to keep Harrack's pace.

Harrack sighed. "It doesn't matter whose fault it is. I still have to take care of the dead, regardless." The two didn't exchange any words the rest of the short walk to Harrack's office. As they stood in front of the door, they looked down at Casey Goodwill, still sleeping and holding Rose Anderson's hand. Rick sighed sadly.

"I threw these two against a building once. Just for talking badly about the force," he let out a sad laugh. "I thought... I thought if I defended the force's honor, I... I don't know. It all seems so insignificant now."

"It's a bit late for a change of heart," Harrack stated factually. Rick choked back a tear.

"I know," he said with heavy sorrow. Putting a straight face back on, he and Harrack leaned down and picked up Rose's body. As her body was lifted away, Casey slumped over to the side, Rose's hand sliding out of her own. She slowly stirred awake. She lifted her head up just as the door to Harrack's office closed. She stood up, tired and sleepy, and walked over to the door. She tried to open it, but was met with an unwelcome and familiar face.

"Please stay out here. Dr. Harrack is busy at the moment," Rick said. Casey looked behind Rick, but couldn't see into the back room.

"Where's Rose?" Casey asked sleepily.

"She's..." Rick sighed. "Just go away. Take a shower. You've been sleeping on a pile of corpses," Rick said gently.

"I wanna see Rose," Casey said stubbornly.

"I'm sorry, I can't let you do that. Go home," Rick said, a little harsher.

"Let me see her," Casey demanded, now more awake.

"I can't let you do that," Rick said forcefully. "Now please leave."

"No!" Casey yelled, and tried to force her way into the office. Rick was stronger, however, and managed to shove her out of the office, quickly slamming and locking the door. Casey immediately started banging on it, demanding to see her friend.

"What the hell is all that racket?" Harrack asked irritatedly as Rick entered the back room. Harrack was just sitting down at his monitor. He placed a small device down on his desk.

"Her friend," Rick said, pointing to Rose, who was laying in the crematory. Harrack sighed.

"Determining cause of death would be a lot easier with an official report of what happened." Harrack swiveled in his chair to look at Rick. "You were there. How could this woman have gotten shot?"

"The only shots that were fired were by Chief McVellion before all hell broke loose, and when that one citizen shot Officer Vilner." Rick paused to think for a moment. "There was another shot fired at some point, but I didn't think it hit anyone."

"Well, apparently it did," Harrack said. "As far as I can tell, she was shot right in the dining area. I'd ask her friend what happened, but she doesn't seem to be in the mood for thoughtful discussion right now." He waited another moment. "Either way, she was killed by a standard security force sidearm. And since the entire security force was in that brawl, it had to have come from that stray bullet."

"There were two officers who were off at that time. Officer Zyz and Officer Desin. But both of them had their weapons, including their sidearms, checked in at the time," Rick said. "I noticed them earlier."

"Stray bullet it is," Harrack said, finishing the report on his monitor. After saving and closing the document, he stood up and walked over to the crematory. He turned it on, and Rose Anderson's body was engulfed in flames. Harrack let it run for another minute, then switched the device off. Nothing was left but ash. In the moments of silence, both men noticed the banging on the door had stopped. "Let's get the next one."

The two stood up and walked to the door. Rick took the lead, unfastening his baton from his belt and cautiously unlocking the door. He peered outside slowly. Casey Goodwill was nowhere to be found. Rick breathed a sigh of relief and gently swung the door open. He replaced his baton on his belt and stepped outside, with Harrack in tow. They stepped over to the pile of bodies and picked up Cat Vilner's body. As they lifted her up, some congealed blood fell out the back of her head and splattered onto Rick's shoes. He groaned in displeasure.

They brought her body inside, and fastened it into the cremator. Harrack took one look at her face. "She was shot by the civilian?"

"Everyone saw it. Happened right in the middle of everything," Rick responded. Harrack picked the small device up from his desk, placed it against Cat's arm and pressed a button. A few seconds later, he nodded and sat down at his monitor. He placed the device next to him again. The death report only took him a few minutes, and then he turned on the cremator once more.

"Halfway done," Harrack said humorlessly. They carried in Daniel Butler's body. They placed him in the crematory. Harrack once again placed the small device against Daniel's arm. "Daniel Butler," he said after a moment. "They said he was going to run for president one day. Of the country, not the bunker, I mean. Everyone talked about how he was going to be the next black president." Harrack looked at Rick.

"He's the one Chief McVellion shot in front of everyone," Rick confirmed. Harrack finished up his report within a few minutes. The crematory was used for the third time in a row.

The pair walked outside once more, and picked up the final body. Bringing him inside, they set him up in the cremator. Harrack once more used the device. "Gary Tills, eh? What killed him?" Harrack looked up at Rick. Rick shook his head. Harrack sighed and returned to the body. He looked over Gary for a minute. "No visible injuries." Harrack took a small pair of surgical scissors and snipped off Gary's shirt.

"Is there anything else you need me for?" Rick asked.

"I don't think so. I'll come to the station if I need anything else," Harrack said, not looking up as he began to inspect Gary's bloody chest. Rick nodded and excused himself. "That's weird. This bullet hole is... I need to talk to Berkoff." Harrack stood up, and quickly exited his office, heading straight for the security station.

*   *   *

"I need you to do something for me," Alan Berkoff said to Jane McVellion. Jane snarled.

"I'll do it later. There's a bastard who killed an officer locked up downstairs. And he pissed me off," Jane replied angrily.

"You don't have to do it yourself. Just send some officers to Percy Winkle's mansion," Alan said.

"You want me to order them to kill him?" Jane asked impatiently.

"No, I don't think anyone would be willing to kill him. Besides, they can't get into his mansion without his permission, and I'm sure once he sees them outside, he won't want to come out. Not that I'd mind if he was killed," Alan answered.

"Alright," Jane agreed. She turned away and headed for the elevator. Before she reached it, it dinged and opened. Harrack stepped inside. He glanced annoyedly at Jane for a second, then walked past her. Jane boarded the elevator and went back down. Harrack marched up to Alan.

"I have a body in my lab with a bullet hole that's too big for any of the guns that the security officers carry. *Especially* the sidearms," he stated, wasting no time. Alan sighed.

"My agent attempted to... *neutralize* the gunman who took the life of that unfortunately officer. Unfortunately, she didn't have a clear shot. Other people were in the way. When he fired, she also fired, but hit one of the other people. I'm guessing that's who you have in your lab," Alan explained. Harrack thought for a moment.

"Well, I can't just put that in the report, can I?" he asked.

"No. Just say he died from injuries he sustained during the revolt," Alan answered. Harrack sighed.

"Alright," he agreed somberly. Without another word, he exited the High Rise.

*   *   *

Lunch passed without incident. But by the time lunch was over, Jeremiah Shoostand was barely more than a bloody pulp handcuffed to a metal chair. They were alone in the interrogation room in the back of the security station. As blood poured from countless wounds all over his body, Jane McVellion punched him across his face. She looked at her fists, which were covered in blood and bruises, and flexed them, wincing slightly. Jeremiah let out a small, gurgled laugh, which caused him to cough up blood. Jane turned around and snarled, equipping her baton. She proceeded to smash him in his stomach. This caused him to double over and cough up even more blood. But when he finished coating the floor in blood and spit, he looked up at her and smiled. He even tried laughing again, but it came out a gurgled horror of a sound, and just caused him to spew out more blood.

Jane gave a good whack straight to the chest, knocking the wind, and more blood, out of him. Jeremiah just smiled again. Furious, Jane stomped out of the room. Jeremiah let his head flop forward. She was back again in a few seconds. Immediately, she marched straight to Jeremiah, who tried to give a defiant smile, but couldn't get his head back up in time. Jane marched behind him and grabbed his hair, pulling his head back. Jeremiah yelled out. Jane held a small pocket knife against his forehead, right at his hairline. With his head pulled back and Jane leaning over him, Jeremiah was able to make eye contact with her. He stared into her eyes defiantly and she stared back. Jane growled at him, then took the knife away from his forehead. He continued to stare into her eyes.

Jane thrust the knife into his left eye. Jeremiah screamed, and struggled to get out of Jane's grip. However, she just pulled his hair back even harder. As he squirmed with excruciating pain, she began to wiggle the knife around in his eye socket. Jeremiah's screams of pain were unrestricted, and they filled the room. Jane's smile only grew. Jane used the knife to scoop some of his liquified eye out of the socket, then calmly walked around Jeremiah. Jeremiah continued screaming for another moment before his screams started to fade. Panting heavily, he looked up at Jane. She smiled at him and approached him once more. She wiped the knife, still covered in his eye fluid, across his cheek, creating a slick cut. A wide but vicious smile was across her face. As the two looked at each other, Jeremiah slowly formed a weak, wavering smile. Jane's own smile immediately disappeared. Yelling in frustration, she departed the room once more. Jeremiah's weak smile dropped off his face.

Jane didn't return to the interrogation room for a few minutes. When she finally returned, she promptly unlocked Jeremiah's cuffs and pulled him his his feet. He tried to keep up with her as she dragged him out of the room, but wasn't able to and ended up being dragged across the floor by his shirt collar. She dragged him out of the station, where nine of the captured protesters had been lined up in a row. They were each blindfolded, and on their knees. Security officers stood behind them, wielding assault rifles and full riot gear. A small crowd of onlookers was already gathering. Jane forced Jeremiah to his knees in front of the row of protesters. She forced his head to look at the other protesters. Jane stepped away from Jeremiah as another officer grabbed his head.

"Make sure he doesn't look away," Jane ordered. She walked over to the first man in the line. "What's your name?" Jane asked.

"Ted. My name is Ted. Weston. Ted Weston," the man nervously stammered. Without hesitating for a second, she took out her gun and shot him in the head. Everybody, even the security officers, jumped at the sudden gunshot. She walked back to Jeremiah and pressed the gun against his head.

"Beg me to stop and kill you, instead," she said calmly.

"Fuck you," he gurgled out, spitting more blood at her. She turned away from him and walked back to the row of protesters. Before she could reach them, Johnny Dinlum intercepted her.

"Stop. This isn't right," he said soft, but firm. Jane snarled, and shoved her gun in his face, pressing it against his nose.

"Don't you *dare* tell me what to do," she snarled. She held the gun against his face a moment longer, then shoved him to the side. He stumbled and Jane continued to the line of hostages.

"What's your name?" Jane asked the woman who was now at the end of the line.

"My name is Janet Smith. Please, if we can just..." Jane didn't let her finish her sentence before executing her. Jane returned to Jeremiah again. With the gun once more pressed against his head, she stared into his face.

"Beg me to kill you, and spare them, and I'll let them go," Jane said quietly. Jeremiah looked like he was about to spit at her again, but glanced at the terrified faces of the seven remaining hostages.

"Fine. Stop. Kill me, not them," Jeremiah forced out through gritted teeth. Jane smiled.

"Not good enough," Jane said. She turned back to the row of captured protesters. Before she had time to walk back over to them, one of them stood up on his own, then sprinted away from the security station, despite being blindfolded and handcuffed.

Jane quickly shot at him, but missed. The crowd that had gathered screamed and scattered. Rick Farkass also fired, but his bullet flew over the runner's head, missing completely. Then Roy Bant aimed and fired. The man fell.

"Bring him back here," Jane ordered. Roy and another officer immediately dragged him back over, still alive and conscious. "What's your name?" Jane asked.

"Screw you!" the man shouted. Jane shot his right shoulder. The man screamed in pain. "Ernest Handler, alright!" he shouted. Jane executed him without a second thought.

"Kill me!" Jeremiah shouted before Jane could even turn around. "Just stop and kill me already! That's what you want, right? Don't kill them! Kill me! Kill me..." Jeremiah roared furiously at first, before breaking down into bloody tears. "Are you happy now?" She laughed and slowly turned away from the remaining hostages. She looked at the other officers.

"Let the rest of them go. I'm sure they've learned their lesson. And, if not, we have their IDs," she said. The other officers quickly took off the hostages' blindfolds and uncuffed them, releasing them. Jane was staring into Jeremiah's eye. She marched back over to Jeremiah and dismissed the officer holding him. She aimed her gun and shot him point-blank in his neck, severing his carotid artery.

Jane watched with a nasty smile on her face as Jeremiah floundered onto the ground and began jerking around. He tried gasping for his neck, but the handcuffs prevented him from doing so. Then, with one final kick of a boot, he was still.

October 5, 2031
General Report Log-12
Doctor Linda Marie
Subject: Fatalities

"The number of fatalities from the disastrous event this morning have just doubled from four to eight. The only positive to all this is that McVellion released all of the prisoners she had arrested after the riot. A few of them came straight here. I did my best to fix them up, but they won't be fine. Physically, they'll heal. But I can't even imagine what being in that situation would be like. They should've had a therapist down here. Even if all of this wasn't going on, this whole situation is highly stressful. I can't help but feel partially responsible. I should've tried to convince them not to go through with their protest. Even though I didn't think things would go the way they did, eight people died today. And I could've tried to prevent it. But I didn't. I hoped that maybe they would actually make a difference. Clearly, I was wrong. There doesn't seem to be any move we can make against McVellion that wouldn't end horribly. We can't just sit back and give up, but what can we do?"

End of log.

President Alan Berkoff

Vice President Eustace Toaden

Chief Researcher Dr. William Harrack

Chief Physician Dr. Linda Marie

Head of Security ~~James House~~ [DECEASED]

Security Force (20):

Roy Bant - Joshua Black - Robert Cansky - Winston Castor - Peter Corrad - Lucille Desin - Jonathan Dinlum - Richard Farkass - Jacob Faunt - Aranai Fielding - Kate Finn - John House - Barney Keeling - Roberta Kisk - Jane McVellion - Joseph Nine - Scott Samona - ~~Catherine Vilner~~ [DECEASED] - Gordon Yackit - Zachary Zyz

Citizens (90):

Bing Abbot - Ann Akai - ~~Rose Anderson~~ [DECEASED] - Jacob Ardune - Robert Beaner - Sarah Barnes - Cherry Beau - ~~Dylan Beecut~~ [DECEASED] - Margaret Belcher - Andrew Bigelow - Alfonzo Bogardanzi - ~~Daniel Butler~~ [DECEASED] - Marino Cantopus - Booker Cooper - John Dash - Jet Dashel - Mark DeFrana - Samuel Dunkard - Barry Eldren - Jeremy Finickle - ~~Candice Finnell~~ [DECEASED] - Haiten Fish - Henry Flagelmeier - Maxwell Geck - Dr. Phillip Genson - Marta Girasol - Casey Goodwill - Chandler Haal - ~~Ernest Handler~~ [DECEASED] - Garrison Hartford - Alfred Hatton - John Heegan - Mario Henderson - Nancy House - William House - Conrad Jackman - Vincent Jax - ~~Harry Jenkins~~ [DECEASED] - Leyna Kase - Martin Kievan - Wanda Lamon - King Liardi - William Lovell - Mary Lovell - Geoffrey Lowell - River Maple - Oliver Markus - Delegan McHarvan - Diana Mint - Gilbert Nose - Mickey November - Conor O'Reilly - Patrick Peaskill - ~~Jim Penn~~ [DECEASED] - Jonathan Peterson - Angel Puer - Richard Reel - Captain Rex - Doug Roberts - Hank Rockell - Dishtowel Sacks - Jillian Sampson - Nadia Schwartz - Argus Scott - ~~Jeremiah Shoostand~~ [DECEASED] - Robert Simpson - ~~Howard Skittering~~

[DECEASED] - Jaime Slewdjack - Toby Smalls - Harold Smidt - ~~Janet Smith~~ [DECEASED] - Nicolas Smithson - Meegan Spoon - Sean Tilling - ~~Gary Tills~~ [DECEASED] - Barnaby Tob - Colin Vacett - Tia Valentine - Amelia Vanisha - ~~Anthony Weitson~~ [DECEASED] - Hannah Welt - Dean Wentell - ~~Theodore Weston~~ [DECEASED] - Andrew Wicker - Peach Williamson - Dell Willis - Percy Winkle - Denger Woof - Laney Youth - Johnson Zip

Alan Berkoff paced nervously around the High Rise. As he nervously chewed on his nails, he suddenly heard a ringing. Freezing, he turned to the source of the ring. He looked at the wood-paneling in the wall just in time to see a landline slide out of another secret compartment wall on a drawer. He cautiously walked over to the device. Any and all communications to the outside were impossible. The steel reinforcement on the bunker blocked all telephone and internet signals, not unlike a faraday cage.

"H-hello?" Alan asked slowly as he answered the phone.

"Why the hell are there armed officers outside my house?!" Percy Winkle snapped nastily from the other end. Alan let out a slight sigh of relief.

"I regret to inform you, Mr. Winkle, that you are under house arrest due to treason," Alan answered.

"Treason? I should have *you* arrested for treason! It's not even like I was gonna have you arrested! You'd be free to do whatever you wanted, as a *citizen*. Believe me when I say that I will *not* let this pass. As soon as I get the Council together-"

"Sorry, to cut you off, but I have some very important duties to do on that cushion right over there. I'm sure you understand," Alan interrupted.

"Ber..." was all Percy said before Alan hung up on him. Alan began shaking slightly and went back to nervously pacing back and forth.

*   *   *

"I think the rebellion is dead," Captain Rex said to Marta Girasol. The two were sitting alone in the back of the residential area, less than a full day after Daniel had made his rallying speech. DT Sacks, John Dash, Toby Smalls, and Jaime Slewdjack were all in their houses, and Lucy Desin was with Zachary Zyz.

"*Tiene que haber algo que podamos hacer*," Marta muttered.

"Daniel is dead. One of us died in the battle. Another five people were executed. I'd be willing to fight back against the security force, but I can't do it alone. Even if all of your friends agree to help, which we both know they don't all agree, we still can't take them on," Rex said.

"Well, maybe others will think like you and come back?" Marta suggested.

"Are you kidding? Between the beatings and executions, I don't think anyone is still willing to fight. They're probably all scared into submission," Rex replied hopelessly.

"Not all of us." Rex and Marta looked up in surprise as they were approached by a young woman. Her short brown hair was up in a bun. Rex jumped to his feet defensively.

"Who are you?" he demanded.

"Nadia Schwartz," she said. "And I'm still willing to fight the security force."

"I don't suppose you can fire ten guns at once," Rex said.

"I can't be the only other one still willing to fight," Nadia said confidently.

"No, you aren't." All three of them turned as a short man slowly approached them.

"And who are you?" Rex asked.

171

"Garrison Hartford. I'm willing to fight, and I have experience with firearms," the man replied.

"See? And I'm sure even more will join," Nadia said to Rex. The smile on her face almost spread to Rex.

"Especially once they realize that the security force is going to abuse them whether or not they fight back," Garrison said. Marta stood up.

"Don't forget about Lucy, and that other guard. Zach, I think she called him? I'm sure he would help," Marta said.

"Yeah, and at least one of your friends was willing to help. The young redhead," Rex said.

"I don't really know him too well," Marta responded with a hint of skepticism.

"He tried to sign up for the security force when they had that application period," Garrison said.

"How do you know that?" Marta asked.

"Because I also applied at the time," Garrison responded. A flash of suspicion crossed Rex's face, but it quickly disappeared.

"Well, it's a start," Rex said with a sigh.

"Now all we need is a plan," Nadia said.

*   *   *

"You're going to do *what*?" Lucy Desin asked, shocked, as she and Zachary Zyz walked along back edge of the bunker.

"I'm going to officially withdraw from the security force. Tomorrow," Zyz repeated. He stared straight ahead and refused to look at Lucy.

"Why? The security force needs someone like you, now more than ever!" Lucy said.

"It's gone beyond being able to fix the force from within. I'm certain Interim Chief McVellion will shoot the next officer who questions her. I refuse to take part in any further actions of the force," Zyz responded.

"So what am I supposed to do?" Lucy asked.

"Find John House. The last thing James House said to me was to protect his brother in the event of his death," Zyz said. "I've been so distracted by everything that's been happening, I've barely done anything to fulfill James' last wish. But it's time I rectify that."

"Does John even know you spoke to James before his death?" Lucy asked. Curiosity had replaced her angry worry.

"No. Only Dr. Marie knows. And she probably hasn't told anyone else," Zyz stopped. When Lucy said nothing after a few moments, Zyz continued. "I need to speak to James' other two siblings. Nancy and Bill, I believe."

"What should I do about John?" Lucy asked.

"Tomorrow morning, meet up with him in the station and bring him... where did you say the resistance group meets?" Zyz asked.

"All the way in the back of the residential area," Lucy replied. Zyz nodded.

"I'll try to get James' siblings, and we'll join up with them," Zyz said. Lucy nodded.

"Understood. This shouldn't be too difficult, right?" Lucy said, smiling. Zyz sighed.

"Just be careful around McVellion. You know the plan. I'm going to find Nancy and Bill. I'll see you tomorrow," Zyz said softly. Lucy nodded.

"Okay. See you tomorrow." With that, the two split up, heading in their own separate directions.

*　　*　　*

Zyz immediately went to the security station to retrieve James' letter, which was still in his vest. However, it wasn't until dinner that Zachary Zyz managed to find Nancy House. He had gone to both her and Bill House's homes, however neither had appeared to be home. While Bill was still nowhere to be seen,

Nancy sat alone with a food tray in front of her. Zyz recognized her from a family photo James had taped to the front of his locker. Ignoring her food, she was instead staring at the security station. She didn't notice Zyz until he sat down at her table.

"Who are you and what do you want?" Nancy instantly asked.

"My name is Zachary Zyz. I'm on the security force, and I-"

"I don't want any trouble," Nancy said, suddenly fearful. She stood up to leave.

"Wait!" Nancy paused, frozen. "I'm resigning from the force tomorrow. I'm here because I talked with your brother shortly before his death." Nancy immediately sat back down, suddenly invested in Zyz's words.

"Really? What did he say? Did he tell you anything? Did he even say anything? Was he hurt? Was he in pain? Please don't say he was suffering too badly," Nancy asked rapidly. Smalls streams of tears ran down her face.

"He was completely healthy the last time I saw him. But he was worried for his life. He asked me to give this to you in the event of his death," Zyz said. Zyz pulled James's hand-written note, now slightly crumpled, from his pants pocket and handed it to Nancy. She immediately snatched the note and began furiously reading it.

"It's his handwriting," she said distantly. "It's messy and scribbled, but it's his..."

"I'm sorry I didn't get it to you sooner. I've been preoccupied," Zyz said apologetically. Nancy didn't seem to register his words. She finished reading the note, and slowly looked up at Zyz.

"I know I probably shouldn't trust you, but I... this is the first thing to bring any sort of closure since James's death. I can't just... walk away from it," Nancy said.

"Should we show this to your other brother?" Zyz asked.

"John or Bill? Wait... what about John?!" Nancy exclaimed.

"Don't worry about him. I'm currently working on getting him away from the force," Zyz reassured.

"He's not like the other officers. He wouldn't help beat those people," Nancy said, more tears streaming down her face. "He's a good person."

"I'm sure he is," Zyz said gently, offering a smile. Nancy stared blankly into face as the tears slowly stopped rolling down her cheeks. Zyz waited in silence for her to speak.

"We should show this to Bill," she said. Zyz nodded and stood up. "Wait a second." Zyz looked down at Nancy, who was still sitting. She looked back at him. "Why was he scared for his life? Who made him scared?"

"President Berkoff," Zyz answered simply. Looking down at the table, more tears streamed down Nancy's face as her expression twisted into one of rage. She clenched his fists, the letter getting crushed. However, she quickly began using breathing techniques and soon calmed herself down.

"We need to get justice," she stated. Zyz nodded.

"I know some people who are already working on that," Zyz said. Nancy's head snapped up.

"They know about James?"

"Not exactly. They're more focused on the security force, but I'm sure they'd be willing to help get justice for your brother," Zyz explained. Nancy seemed conflicted for a moment.

"My older brother ran the security force once. My younger brother is in it. I don't want them to be demonized," Nancy stated.

"And they won't. James had nothing to do with this, and we're getting John out of it," Zyz replied.

"I guess. But what's going to happen to the security force, them?" Nancy asked.

"I'm sure we'll try to reform it. With less... *sadistic* officers," Zyz answered.

"Well, let's go get Bill. Then I'd love to help and make sure our family name doesn't go down in infamy," Nancy said with a sad smile. She then stood up, and the two headed for the residential area.

"He wasn't at his house when I checked," Zyz said as they walked.

"He doesn't like to answer the door. But he'll do it if he knows it's me," Nancy responded.

*   *   *

"Bill, it's me!" Nancy yelled as she banged on his door. Zyz stood off to the side with his arms crossed. "Come on, baby brother! Open up!" She continued banging on his door for almost a minute.

"I don't think he's here," Zyz said.

"He is," Nancy said calmly. She kept banging on the door. She paused for a minute, and then tried turning the handle. The door opened. She glanced briefly at Zyz, then stepped inside. Zyz followed. It was dark inside the house, and Nancy tripped over something on the way to the desk lamp next to the bed. She flicked it on, filling the messy, disorganized room with light. Bill House, who was laying on his bed and holding a mostly empty bottle of whiskey by the neck, groaned and rolled over on his side, away from the light. "Bill!" Nancy yelled, putting her hands on her hips. Bill jumped up, losing his grip on the bottle, which slid to the floor.

"What the hell?" Bill asked, dazed and clearly hungover. Nancy bent down and picked up the bottle.

"I could ask you the same thing," she said, shoving the bottle in his face. He squinted and pushed her arm away.

"It's not like there's anything better to do down here," he grumbled. Nancy sighed.

"I just want you to be safe and happy," she said.

"Yeah, whatever." He stood up and walked into the bathroom. "So what do you want?" he asked as he washed his face. Nancy pulled out the wrinkled letter.

"I have a letter from James. Before he died," Nancy said. Bill turned off the water.

"I don't care," he said, staring into the mirror. Nancy took a step back.

"How could you just... *not care* about this?!" she asked, aghast.

"Is that all you wanted?" Bill continued. Nancy waited a minute before answering.

"Well... no. There's a group that wants to reform the security force, and-"

"Not interested," Bill said, then closed the bathroom door.

"What," Nancy said flatly.

"I fully support the force the way it is," Bill said. Nancy and Zyz could hear him urinating.

"How can you support anything they've done?!" Nancy yelled through the door. The toilet flushed and Bill emerged a moment later.

"Because it doesn't affect me. I'm just keeping my head down. I'll be fine. I'm not like those idiots who tried to attack them," Bill said. He looked around his room. "Shit. I'm gonna have to steal more whisky from the bar, aren't I?"

"Forget about that!" Nancy yelled. "How can you just sit by while other people are murdered in public?!"

"Because they got themselves into that mess. And it's not my problem, even if they hadn't," Bill said as he sat down on his bed. He looked up at Nancy. "Do what you will, but don't try to drag me into it. You're lucky I don't tell the force about what you said." Nancy didn't say another word. She just silently put the letter back in her pocket and walked out of the house. Zyz gave one final glance at Bill and followed Nancy out. "And never call me your baby brother again!" Bill yelled out the open door.

October 6, 2031

In the morning, Lucy Desin looked at the patrol schedule that had been posted in the security station. She quickly scanned the paper, looking for John House's name. As she turned to leave a deep voice suddenly called her name. Lucy froze and slowly turned around. Jane McVellion towered over her.

"What are you doing here, Officer Desin?" Jane asked. Lucy steadied her nerves.

"I was just checking my patrol schedule," she said. Jane grunted.

"You have the day off," Jane simply replied.

"O-oh?" Lucy said.

"Yeah. Officer Zyz isn't back, and Officer Vilner is dead," Jane explained.

"I see," Lucy said, masking her confusion. The two stood there for another moment.

"Now get out of here," Jane said annoyedly, before turning and walking away. Lucy breathed a sigh of relief and quickly exited the security station. She jogged into the residential area. She looked around for a moment, but didn't see anyone. She ran down an alley and checked the next "street." She spotted a couple of security officers slowly patrolling a little farther down, walking away from her. Lucy quickly jogged after them. It took her a moment to catch up to them.

"Officer House!" she yelled as she got near. The two officers stopped and turned around.

"Officer Desin?" John House asked with confusion as she slowed to a stop in front of them. "What's wrong?"

"Oh, uh, nothing," she said, slightly out of breath. "Can we talk? In private?" The two turned to look at John House's partner. He shrugged.

"Hey, just so long as we get our story straight, I don't care what you do." His partner then walked away. "I'm gonna go home and take a nap. Wake me up when you're done." John House turned back to Lucy and the two began walking together.

"So what's so important you need to talk to me alone?" he asked with a slight laugh.

"It's about the security force," she said. John House let out a sad sigh.

"Isn't everything these days?" he asked rhetorically. "I wish there was some way to change things."

"Well, there might be," Lucy replied. John House looked at her with curiosity.

"What do you mean?" he asked.

"I don't really know how to explain it, but come with me. I know some people who do!" Lucy said, then began jogging to the back of the residential area. John House followed, struggling slightly to keep up.

*　　　*　　　*

Before breakfast, the resistance was slowly gathering together at the back of the residential area. Captain Rex, Garrison Hartford, and Nadia Schwartz were already waiting. Marta Girasol approached with Jaime Slewdjack, Toby Smalls, John Dash, and DT Sacks in tow. Toby and DT both yawned and sat against the bunker wall, leaning back and closing their eyes. The others stood together.

"How are we doing on numbers?" Dash asked.

"Not sure yet. Lucy went to get her old partner to join back up. We haven't seen her since," Marta said.

"Let's try to get everyone together before we start planning," Rex said.

"Agreed," Dash said. They stood around for another moment without saying anything.

"So what's up?" Nadia asked.

179

"Not much," Garrison shrugged. "Just planning on overthrowing a police state." The others laughed, except Dash and Rex, who both just smiled.

"Feels good to laugh," Jaime said with a smile still on his face. They were quiet for a moment before Jaime spoke up again. "Who's that?" he asked, peering into the residential area. The others turned to where he was looking. A small group of four people was approaching them. At least one of them was wearing a security uniform. The small group spread out wider, and Rex stepped over to a duffle bag that had been placed against the backside of the last house in that row. The group, now spread out, tensed up nervously and stared at the small group approaching. Once they were closer, Marta breathed out a sigh of relief.

"It's Lucy!" she said loudly. The others relaxed and Rex walked away from the duffle bag. The ground, consisting of Lucy Desin, Zachary Zyz, Nancy House, and John House made their way over. Lucy quickly introduced Nancy and John House to the others.

"So are these the guys who are finally going to explain what's going on?" John House asked.

"Aren't you going to try and reform the security force?" Nancy asked.

"Well, that's one way of putting it," Garrison muttered.

"First, we need to dismantle the current security force," Rex said.

"Dismantle?" John House asked.

"Don't worry, we're going to try not to kill anybody," Lucy said.

"I don't think they're going to go down that easily, though," John House said.

"Agreed. Which is why we're stocking up and preparing for a fight," Rex said.

"But we're going to try and avoid actually killing any of them, right?" Lucy asked, concerned.

"I don't know if we'll be able to handle this situation without a few deaths," John House replied. Lucy turned to him.

"But they're not all bad people! You know them, some of them are just scared to defy Chief McVellion!" Lucy said.

"And some of them are more than happy to go along with her trigger happy ways," John House replied.

"We can't just destroy the force!" Nancy said. "Think of James."

"What about James?" John House asked.

"This security force is the legacy of the House family, now. We can't just let it be remembered as the group of nasty people which had to be destroyed!" Nancy said. The others gave her a blank stare.

"Legacy? What the hell are you talking about?" Rex asked.

"Yeah. This has nothing to do with James. Or our family," John House said.

"Regardless, we shouldn't get rid of the force. What's gonna keep anarchy away?" Nancy said, crossing her arms.

"We'll build a new force. Start from the ground up. Get the support of some of the higher ups, and get all new officers," Jaime said.

"What about the current officers?" Lucy asked.

"Arrest any of them that were directly involved in any of the oppressive actions that have been taking place over the past few days," Rex said, then stopped to think. "All the others, I don't know. I don't think it would be wise to put them back on the force."

"Fine by me," John House said.

"But why not?" Lucy asked. Marta sighed and walked over to the wall where Toby and DT were still sitting against, although more awake. Dash followed her over. The four sat against the wall, away from the arguing group. After sitting in silence for a moment, Marta let out a sad laugh.

"Never imagined this is what I'd be doing when I walked through that vault," she said.

"I'm glad I met you guys, but sometimes I wish I wasn't here," Toby said.

"I don't think any of us wishes we were here," DT replied.

"This was all a mistake," Toby said, then sniffled.

"I'm sure they're going to open that door any day now," Dash said. The others looked at him.

"You still think they can make peace outside?" DT asked. Dash looked at the others.

"It's what I'm hoping for," he said.

"Well, I'm sure they will," Toby said with a sad smile.

"*Más vale que abran esa puerta y nos saquen de aquí,*" Marta said. She sighed. "I am still glad I met you guys, though. You're the closest friends I've had since I left Puerto Rico."

"I think you guys are my first real friends," DT said. "I didn't really have any in the outside world."

"I was never really one for friends," Dash said solemnly. Toby smiled.

"You guys are awesome," he said. DT laughed and the other two smiled.

"Thanks," DT replied, still smiling.

"I wonder what life would've been like if the security force didn't try to kill us all," Marta said.

"Well, for starters, it would probably be a lot more boring," DT said. The others looked at him. He looked back. "I didn't say boring was bad. I wouldn't mind boring right now."

"I think I'd prefer less excitement, too," Dash concurred. Marta sighed and rested her head on Dash's shoulder. He looked down at her.

"Hope you don't mind," she said, noticing his glance.

"It's fine," he said, and looked back at the other group, who was still arguing.

"Can we stop fighting, already?! We're in a war!" Rex shouted. The four sitting against the wall stood up and walked over to the larger group.

"This isn't war," Zyz said. "And let's try to keep it that way."

"Either way, we need a plan. We can't just take them head on," Rex said.

"So let's think strategy," Nadia said.

"I can spy on the force and let you know what they're up to," John House said.

"Alright, that sounds like a start," Rex said. "Though I'd prefer Desin to do it. No offense, I trust her more."

"It's fine. I understand," John House said.

"McVellion already told me to take the day off. Probably will until Zach returns," Lucy said.

"Which I won't. Thanks for reminding me, I need to hand in my resignation," Zyz said.

"Don't do that quite yet. The more spies the better," Rex replied. Zyz took a moment to reply.

"I'll consider it," he said.

"Well, I better get back before they notice I've been gone for too long. Hopefully Pete hasn't been waiting for me," John House said. He looked at Lucy. "Do you have a radio on you?"

"No, I left mine in the station with my other stuff," she said. John House took his radio off his belt and handed it to her.

"I'll grab yours when I get back to the station. At some point we'll swap them." With that, he departed.

"I should get going, too. I don't think I'd be much help with planning," Nancy said, also departing.

"Anyone else want to head out?" Rex asked. Nobody moved. "Alright, then."

"So what's the plan?" Garrison asked.

"Well... for now, there's not much we can do. Let's hope House gets some good info we can use. But we can't just rush into something. We need to be smart, not quick," Rex replied.

"The longer we wait, the more time the security force has to make things worse," Nadia said.

"Rex is right," Zyz said.

"Your name is Rex?" Nadia asked, suppressing a giggle.

"It's my last name," Rex replied.

"What's your first?" Garrison asked. Rex sighed.

"Captain." Nadia laughed.

"Your name is *Captain Rex*?!" Garrison burst out.

"Yeah, well, both of my parents were obsessed with boats. Especially the navy." Rex paused. "I'm here trying to escape *them* more than anything else."

"But does, like, your birth certificate say 'Captain Rex' on it?" Nadia asked. Rex sighed and nodded. Nadia laughed harder.

"I think that's enough for now. We'll meet up again soon to discuss further plans," Rex said. No one objected, and the group broke up.

*   *   *

John House heard Jane McVellion screaming from outside the security station. He sighed as him and his partner braced themselves, pushing through the doors and walking inside. They were instantly enveloped by the booming voice of Jane McVellion.

"Find them!" was all John House heard. Two very nervous officers immediately ran into the back room. Jane looked up at John House and his partner. "House! Corrad! Where have you been?!"

"We thought we saw some suspicious activity, but it turned out to be nothing," Peter Corrad said. John House quickly seconded the statement. Jane grunted and turned away from them, walking into one of the storerooms. As Peter walked to his locker and took off the heavier parts of his uniform, John House quickly walked over to the rack of radios in the back of the station locker room, and plucked the one above the Desin name tag. He attached it to his belt as Jane walked out of the storeroom right next to him. He nervously glanced at her. She ignored him.

The two officers quickly reappeared. "They aren't back there," one reported. Jane yelled again.

"They have to be *somewhere!* Weapons don't just disappear," she yelled. Roy Bant approached her calmly, holding a clipboard with a few sheets of paper.

"According to inventory, they were all here before the riot. It wasn't until after that anyone notice they were missing," he reported. She snatched the clipboard out of his hands and stared at it. After a second she threw it at him. The clipboard bounced off his kevlar vest and clattered onto the floor. Roy had no visible reaction. Jane was quiet for a moment. Then she turned to Roy.

"Anything else?" she asked.

"The only officers who weren't on duty during the riot were Officer Desin and Officer Zyz," Roy reported. Jane snarled.

"Take that useless partner of yours, and *find them!*" Jane shouted at Roy. Roy nodded an acknowledgement, then quickly trotted away. Jane turned to John House, who had gone to his locker and was now removing his vest. "House! Corrad!" The two officers snapped to attention. "Pick up that clipboard and do complete inventory. *Now!*" The two immediately sprung to work. The two walked into the first storeroom.

"This is gonna suck," Peter said as he stared at the full room. "Why do you think she's making us do this? From the sound of it, she just had Bant do inventory."

"Maybe she just wants us to double check. Let's just get this over with," John House said with a sigh. Peter looked down at John House's belt.

"Hey, your, uh, radio is on," Peter said.

"Huh? Oh, thanks," John House said, taking the radio off his belt and switching it off.

*   *   *

By the time John House had turned his radio off, Lucy Desin was in full sprint down the residential area. She had almost reached her own home as the lunch crowd was dispersing, slowly returning to their own houses. As she weaved in and out of the moseying crowd, she quickly burst out ahead of them all. She continued running at full speed for another minute, panting heavily, until she reached Zachary Zyz's house. She immediately banged on the door. Zyz slowly opened the door and stared at her. Her clear panic and exhaustion immediately caused him to straighten his back.

"What's wrong?" he asked with urgency.

"I heard on the radio, they discovered the guns were missing. They know we're the only two officers who weren't in the brawl," she explained quickly. Zyz nodded. "She sent Officer Bant and Officer Farkass to pick us both up."

"Bant and Farkass? Well, in that case, I don't think I can get away by telling them I was in Dr. Marie's office the entire time," Zyz said thoughtfully. "Not that I would. I don't want to leave you as the only suspect." She smiled at him.

"It's fine. I'm guilty. You're not. I agreed to this plan, now I have to deal with the consequences. Go to the doctor and get your alibi," she said.

"And what about you?" Zyz asked.

"Don't worry about me. I can handle myself. Oh, one last thing." She took the radio off her belt and gave it to Zyz. He took the radio and looked at her with a concerned expression. She smiled wider at him. "I'll be fine. Trust me. I'm sure I'll see Rick and Roy before you do, so I'll try to buy you enough time to clear your name."

"You still don't have an alibi, yourself," Zyz said.

"Well, that's my problem. Not yours." She wrapped her arms around him and gave him a hug. He winced slightly, but hugged back.

"I don't like this," Zyz said.

"I know. But it's gonna be fine, okay?" She released him and lingered for another moment. "You're an awesome partner." Zyz smiled sadly. She cheerfully smiled again. "I'll see you at the next rebel meeting." And with that, she was off again, sprinting back up the residential area. As she re-entered the crowd of citizens returning from lunch, she slowed to a light jog. The crowd wasn't particularly thick, and she could see pretty far down the "street." As she looked ahead, she saw two figures wearing security uniforms in the distance. Without thinking, she dodged into an alley and popped out into the next street over. She looked ahead. The crowd was much thinner and she didn't see any uniforms. She continued jogging up the street and weaving through alleys, until she slowed to a stop in front of Captain Rex's house. She banged on his door.

"Who are you?" he yelled through the closed door.

"Lucy!" she shouted back. Rex cautiously opened the door and peered out. Once seeing she was alone, he opened the door wider.

"What is it?" he asked curtly.

"They discovered the missing weapons. They know it was either me or Zach," Lucy explained.

"Oh," Rex said. "I can't hide you in here."

"I don't want you to. Just give me one assault rifle," Lucy said.

"Finally changed your mind about killing officers?" Rex asked as he disappeared into the house. Lucy stepped forward and stood in the doorway. Rex crouched down next to his bed.

"I didn't. I just want them to think it was me," Lucy said.

"And what are you gonna tell them when they only find one gun?" Rex asked as he pulled the duffle bag out from under his bed.

"Don't worry about that. I won't be saying a word to them," Lucy replied. Rex looked up at her as he unzipped the bag. He looked at her for a moment before nodding in understanding. He looked back down at the open duffle bag, and pulled out a large assault rifle.

"Good luck," he said, handing it to her. She grabbed it and smiled. Rex handed her a couple magazines, which she placed in her pants pockets.

"Thank you."

"And... I'm sorry," Rex said.

"I agreed to the plan. You have nothing to be sorry for," Lucy said, still smiling. She once again lingered for a moment as her smile slowly faded off of her face. Rex zipped the duffle bag back up and slid it under his bed. He stood up and looked at her. The two stood in awkward silence as neither moved. Finally, Lucy smiled again and let out a nervous laugh. "Seeya at the next rebel meeting," she said sadly. Rex gave her a sad smile.

"Yeah. Seeya there," he replied. And just like that, she was gone. Once again she was jogging down the street, weaving in through alleys. However, holding a large assault rifle garnered unwanted attention. She wasn't far from her house.

"Officer Desin!" a voice behind her shouted out. Lucy slowed to a stop, nervously sweating. She didn't turn around.

"What is it?" she yelled back, still facing away from the voice.

"Chief McVellion wants to see you," Rick Farkass again shouted. "Wants to talk to you about missing weapons." Lucy stood perfectly still. "You wouldn't happen to know anything about that, would you?" The voice was getting closer. "After all, multiple concerned citizens just saw you-" Rick didn't even finish the sentence before Lucy suddenly darted into an alley. "Hey!" Rick and Roy Bant began running faster down the street, but before they got far, Lucy popped out from behind the corner and fired off a few rounds at the ground in front of their feet. Rick screamed. Both officer jumped back and dashed into an alley, themselves. All the citizens that had been in the area screamed and ran. Lucy jumped back out, occasionally spraying cover fire every time they moved out of cover. Roy popped out and fired back. A shot hit Lucy's hip, and she began limping as fast as she could as she returned fire. Roy dodged back behind the house. Lucy then disappeared into an alley.

"Call backup," Roy said as he ran out and began pursuing her. Rick got out his radio and quickly flicked it on, sweating and clearly panicking. Roy ran across the street, and pressed himself against the house next to the alley Lucy had run into. As he moved closer to the alley, he quickly snapped around the corner, aiming his gun into the alley. It was empty. Keeping his gun drawn, he crouched and began cautiously walking through the alley. As he neared the other side, he once again pressed himself against the far wall. Edging closer to the corner of the house, he took a deep breath as he once again snapped around the corner, gun drawn.

The street was empty. Slowly walking out of the alley, he suddenly heard breaking glass. He had barely enough time to comprehend the sound before a frenzy of bullets forced him to retreat back into the alley. Taking one last cautious look around the corner, he realized that Lucy Desin's house was right across the street. He spotted shattered glass in front of the window to it, before more bullets forced him to retreat out of view. He sat and waited for backup.

Roy kept an eye on the house until more security officers arrived. Any time one of them tried to get close to the house, a bullet storm erupted and smashed into the ground near them. Jane McVellion and Roy Bant stood face to face behind the house directly across from Lucy's.

"What the hell is going on?" Jane demanded.

"It's Officer Desin. She's barricaded herself inside her house, and fires at anyone who gets close," Roy reported.

"Desin? She always seemed like a little bitch to me. Whatever," Jane said dismissively. "Let's just get in there and kill her."

"Something isn't adding up, though. Why was she just walking down the stree-"

"Shut it, Bant. I don't care. Just kill the bitch," Jane interrupted. Roy opened his mouth, but closed it again without saying anything. Jane stood there for another moment. She turned away from him, facing all the other officers. She grumbled and leisurely strolled to one of the farther alleys, disappearing into it. Roy sighed.

"Alright, everyone!" he shouted. "Be ready to fire together! She can't aim at us all at once!" As he took his position in an alley, he stood with John House and Peter Corrad.

"Finally some action, huh?" Peter said excitedly. "I was beginning to think I was gonna die of boredom."

"Yeah... fun," John House said, offering a nervous and insincere smile. Peter didn't catch on. Roy flicked on his radio.

"Prepare to fire in five. Four. Three. Two." Without having to say the last number, officers in four separate alleys across from Lucy Desin's house open fired, all aiming for her window. Lucy returning fire, most of her bullets slamming into the ground in front of the alleys, far from any of the officers. Many of them still ducked back. John House also fired at the ground in front of Lucy's house. The only other present officer who wasn't firing into Lucy's window was Rick Farkass, who was cowering in the back end of one of the alleys.

Lucy stopped returning fire after only a few seconds, and another few seconds later, Roy ordered all officers to stop firing. They complied, with the exception of a few who fired a couple more rounds after being ordered to stop. The assault lasted less than twenty seconds. All was quiet once more, and the officers patiently waited for some sort of signal from Lucy. No such signal ever came. Roy turned to John House and Peter.

"Advance," he whispered. The two nodded in acknowledgement, and John House peeked around the corner. When no bullets came in his directions, he stepped out from the alley. Still no bullets. Crouching down, he took a few cautious steps forward. All was still. Peter followed John House out of the alley. As they advanced on the house, the tension seemed to grow. John House sighed and suddenly rushed forward. Peter, unprepared, stared after him for a minute, before quickly following. The two rushed up to Lucy's house, and pressed themselves against the front wall. John House took a deep breath, then stepped away from the wall and turned the doorknob. It was locked. John House closed his eyes and kicked the door in.

When he opened his eyes, the first thing he saw was Lucy Desin, laying face down, near the far end of the house. She was laying in a slowly growing pool of her own blood. John House sighed sadly and turned around, facing the alleys full of officers.

"It's clear!" he shouted. The other officers came out of cover, most casually walking with their weapons by their side. As the large crowd of officers gathered around the entrance, Roy Bant and Jane McVellion entered the house. John House and Peter Corrad also entered, leaving little room for any other officer. Roy looked at the garbage chute, which was propped open with the assault rifle jammed into the hinges.

"Why would she try to get rid of the gun? It's not like destroying evidence would make her seem innocent," Peter commented.

"It must've been what she did with the other guns," John House said, his mind rushing. "It's still a good gun, y'know?"

"Must be what happened," Roy said skeptically. Jane walked over to Lucy, stepping through her fresh blood. Jane gave her a swift kick. John House cringed and looked away. There was no response from Lucy. Jane rolled her body over with her foot. As Lucy flopped onto her back, the others could see that her eyes were open, her mouth still open in an expression of terror. Bullet holes riddled her shoulder and upper chest. Jane laughed for a moment, then turned to the chute. She grabbed the gun and yanked it out.

"Wait!" Roy yelled. But Jane was already holding the gun. Jane looked up at him with confusion. "It could've been a trap," Roy said softly. Jane snickered.

"Whatever. She's dead. Let's get out of here," Jane said, then pushed through all the other officers and out the door. All the other officers soon began dispersing, leaving only Roy, John House, and Peter. Peter tilted his head and looked at Lucy's body. Then he turned to John House.

"Didn't you know her?" Peter asked.

"Not any better than you," John House said coldly, then turned and exited the house. Peter shrugged and followed, leaving Roy alone in the house.

"Something still doesn't add up," he said to himself. Then he sighed and exited the building. "Hey!" he shouted. "Someone still needs to take her body to Harrack's office!"

*   *   *

Dr. William Harrack received Lucy Desin's body not long after. He filed the death report, automatically notifying Dr. Linda Marie of Lucy's passing. A few hours later, dinner rolled around, and the rebels met in the dining area. Most of them had barely eaten anything recently. The tables had a maximum occupancy of six, so the large group had to split up. Toby Smalls, Jaime Slewdjack, DT Sacks, and John Dash sat at one table, while Captain Rex, Marta Girasol, Zachary Zyz, Garrison Hartford, Nadia Schwartz, and Nancy House sat at another. All of them had unfinished food in front of them. Both tables were silent for a long time.

"Well, shit," Garrison said, finally breaking the silence.

"I can't believe she's gone," Zyz said, staring at the table. "She deserved better."

"Who's gonna tell us the security force are good people, now?" Nadia asked with a nervous laugh. Zyz glared at her and she quickly went silent.

"I still think it just needs a little restructuring, is all," Nancy said with a weak smile. Zyz let out a sad sigh.

"Dr. Marie asked me to bring her some lunch. She hasn't eaten anything in a few days," Zyz said, picking up his food tray, which was full of mostly uneaten food. "Oh, I almost forgot." Zyz took the radio out of his pocket and put it on the table in front of Rex. He quickly grabbed the radio and hid it in his own pocket.

"Thanks," Rex said. Zyz nodded in appreciation, and departed. Rex sighed. "This was a tremendous loss." Marta bowed her head. Nadia put her hand on Rex's.

"I know," Nadia said.

"But, we can recover. We have to expect casualties in this war," Rex continued. Marta picked her head up.

"Is that all she is to you? A casualty?" she asked impatiently.

"She was a great help to the cause. So she's more than just '*a* casualty,'" Rex replied.

"*En serio?* She was also a person. A good one," Marta said, standing up. A twinge of guilt and sorrow spontaneously manifested on Rex's face. His lips twitched upwards for a second, as if he were about to cry. Then he closed his eyes and took a deep breath, and straightened his face.

"We'll make sure her death isn't in vain," Rex replied with a stone face. Marta sighed and walked to the other table, sitting down next to John Dash.

"I hope that doesn't mean you plan on killing any of the officers," Nancy said.

"Nah. If he said something about avenging her, then yeah. But... yeah," Nadia tried to explain. Rex just glanced at her.

"No. We're not going to kill them," Rex said. "Not unless we have to."

"We should try to at least honor Lucy's memory by not killing the people she swore by," Nancy said resolutely.

"This is a war. If we have to kill, we will," Garrison said, equally firm. The table continued debating the issue quietly.

"What's going on over there?" Toby asked as Marta sat down.

"Don't ask," Marta replied with a frustrated sigh.

"Oh," Toby said.

"So what happens now?" Jaime asked.

"I assume we keep going. If we were going to stop because of a death, then this resistance wouldn't exist right now," Dash said.

"He's right," Marta said, looking at the table. "This was *una pérdida trágica*. But we can't let it stop us." She let out a sad sigh.

"It's okay. We'll have to make sure it's the *last* death that happens around here. For a while, at least," Dash said, and offered a small smile. Marta was still staring down at the table and didn't notice.

"Yeah," she said.

"Well, I like that idea," Toby said. "No more death. Let's hope we can actually do it!"

"I wouldn't get my hopes up," DT said.

"Yeah. Things look like they're only gonna be getting nastier. It's nice to hope for the best, but we should expect the worst," Jaime said, looking at the table the others were sitting at. "But, no matter what, we need to stop the security force." Jaime paused. "Even if we have to do things we don't want to."

*　　　*　　　*

Alan Berkoff was sitting in the High Rise. The phone had been ringing off the hook. Alan continually ignored it. At multiple points, Angel Puer had shoved the phone's drawer back into the wall. However, Angel finally knocked the phone off the receiver, and it dangled below the drawer by the cord. They could still hear Percy Winkle's voice fuming through the phone. After almost a minute of non-stop yelling, Angel placed the phone back on the receiver. It continued to ring.

Angel barely heard the ding of the elevator over the ring of the phone. She rushed back to her hidden compartment and closed the door. The elevator opened a few seconds later, and Alan turned just as Vice President Eustace Toaden walked in.

"Where have you been?" Alan asked loudly over the ringing. Toaden stepped into the High Rise and briskly walked to the phone.

"I've been trying to do damage assessment," Toaden said as he picked up the phone. "Hello?" Toaden asked. Toaden then stood quiet and just listened. After a minute, he turned to Alan. "You put Winkle under house arrest?!" Toaden yelled in disbelief. Alan just stared at him.

"It seemed appropriate at the time," Alan said softly. Toaden sighed.

"You have to realize you can't be doing any of this," Toaden said. He stood up, slowly. He approached Toaden, leaning over him. His shadow covered Toaden's face.

"I'm the president. I have free reign to do as I wish," Alan said. His voice was threatening, but also unsure of itself. Toaden frowned deeply. Alan flashed him a smile and laughed.

"This isn't funny," Toaden said sternly. "This is still America!"

"No, this is the bunker," Alan snapped back. Toaden seemed caught off guard. Alan then snickered as his mind raced. "Can we continue this conversation later?" he asked casually.

"What? No! This is a very pressing matter, and-"

"And we should convene the entire Council to discuss it," Alan interrupted.

Toaden cleared his throat. "I don't know what you're planning, but I can assure you that whatever you're planning will not work," Toaden said firmly.

"So, are we done here for now?" Alan asked boredly, turning his back on Toaden. Toaden gave him a suspicious glare.

"Not even remotely. But I guess we'll discuss this with the Council further."

"Then can you leave me alone, now?" Alan asked as he sauntered away.

"Fine. But this isn't over," Toaden warned. He stood there another moment. After a moment of silence, Toaden left the High Rise.

"Shit," Alan said to himself, now alone.

October 7, 2031

Dr. Marie looked up from her desk as she heard the ding signifying her office door was being opened. Zachary Zyz walked through the door, carrying two trays of breakfast.

"Thanks," Dr. Marie said as he placed both trays on the desk.

"Don't mention it," he said as he pulled a stool up and sat down next to her. Dr. Marie pulled her tray closer and sighed. Zyz picked up a banana and began unpeeling it.

"I'm sorry about your partner," she said, her food still untouched. Zyz looked over at her. "I never said that yesterday."

"You didn't say much at all yesterday," Zyz replied, then bit into the banana.

"Because It's my fault she's dead," Dr. Marie replied. Zyz turned and looked at her. He finished chewing and swallowed.

"It's not your fault," Zyz said. "I don't even know how you think that."

"Because I knew how wrong this all could've gone. That day in my office, when everyone met..." her voice, full of regret, slowly faded. Then she cleared her throat and continued. "I should've said something. Told them how dangerous it would be. I could've prevented eight deaths that day. Officer Desin makes it nine. That's nine deaths I could've prevented."

"People like Butler, the other protesters. They wouldn't have stopped, no matter what you told them. Even if he knew the outcome, do you think Butler would've given up his protest? Sure, he would've done things differently, but it wouldn't have *stopped* him. Nothing would've. As for Lucy... Officer Desin..." Zyz couldn't finish the sentence.

"She should still be alive. She didn't need to die," Dr. Marie responded sadly, staring at her food. She let out a short, sad laugh. "I just wish there was *something* I could do. I just feel so helpless." Zyz sighed.

"You could always join the resistance," he suggested. She looked up at him, offering him a small smile.

"It's still alive?" she asked.

"Captain Rex is still running it. It's not large, but it's definitely alive. And I don't think it's going anywhere soon, especially since Lucy just gave..." Zyz choked up and stopped for a moment. Dr. Marie lightly patted his back.

"It's okay," she said gently.

"She gave her life for the resistance," Zyz forced out. "And I'm sure as hell going to make sure she didn't die for nothing."

"Oh, I am so going to look forward to bringing Berkoff down," Dr. Marie said with conviction. Zyz looked up at her.

"Berkoff? I know he had something to do with Chief House's death, but what does he have to do with the security force?" Zyz asked, Dr. Marie looked at him.

"He's behind *all* of it. He used his veto power to make McVellion interim chief after the Council voted against her becoming the full chief, and I'm certain he was responsible for the death of James House, I just can't prove it. It doesn't help that Harrack is his little lapdog," Dr. Marie said angrily. "Not to mention I heard from the vice president that he put Percy Winkle under house arrest. I don't know why, but if I had to guess, I'd say it was because Winkle was catching on to Berkoff's schemes and tried to get rid of him. Every single tragedy that has happened in the bunker since it closed can all be traced back to *him*. I've been fighting him since he first tried to get McVellion elected as chief of security, but he always has some slimy trick up his sleeve."

"I guess we've been so focused on fighting the symptoms, we forgot to look at the cause," Zyz said, standing up. "We have to get this info to the rest of the resistance."

"When people are being executed in the middle of the street, it's easy to forget things like politics." Dr. Marie paused. "There's a Council meeting later today. At lunch. Toaden thinks Berkoff wants to resign, but I'm sure that Berkoff is planning something." She paused for a minute. "Get the resistance together. Right now." Zyz nodded, and was out the door. Dr. Marie grabbed a bunch of food off of her tray and shoved it into her lab coat pockets, then followed him out.

*　　*　　*

It didn't take long before all eleven surviving members of the resistance were gathered once more in the back of the bunker, now with Dr. Linda Marie.

"What's going on?" Nadia Schwartz asked curiously.

"There are... more people than I was expecting," Dr. Marie said with slightly surprise.

"Hopefully it's enough," John House said.

"Let's skip the pleasantries and get right to business," Captain Rex said. He looked and Dr. Marie and Zachary Zyz. "Zyz, why are we here?"

"Dr. Marie is willing to help us out," he said simply. All eyes turned to her.

"President Berkoff is behind everything that's happened with the security force," she said bluntly.

"What?" DT Sacks asked, shocked.

"I'm not surprised," Garrison Hartford said, crossing his arms.

"I remember the announcement," Rex said. "I figured he was just in charge of delivering it, though."

"No. This entire thing is because of him. I'm pretty sure he murdered Chief House, too. I had evidence, but it disappeared," Dr. Marie continued.

"I watched Chief House write the letter, myself," Zyz said. "Before Dr. Marie lost it."

"I didn't lose it!" she said aggressively. "It must've been stolen, or something."

"How?" Zyz asked skeptically.

"We don't have time for this!" Rex yelled before Dr. Marie could speak.

"Thank you," Dr. Marie said softly. "I'm pretty sure Dr. Harrack has been helping him cover up multiple suspicious deaths. Obviously I can't prove it. But what I do know is that he used his power to make Officer McVellion the interim chief after the Council voted against her becoming the next chief of security."

"He really is responsible for everything that happened," Toby Smalls said.

"That's good to know, but how does it help us stop the security force?" Jaime Slewdjack asked.

"Well, it doesn't help with things right now, but I'm telling you that even if we manage to get rid of McVellion, Berkoff probably isn't going to stop anytime soon," Dr. Marie said.

"Well, we can take care of him once the security force is dealt with," Rex said.

"There's a Council meeting later today. I have a very bad feeling about it, though. Berkoff agreed to it, so I'm sure he's going to try something. Toaden thinks he's going to resign, but I don't think so," Dr. Marie explained.

"Want us to make an extraction plan?" Rex asked.

"I'll be right down below you. If you need to get out, I can get you out," John House said.

"Let's just make a rendezvous point," Zyz said.

"Yeah. We need you on the inside," Rex said.

"I know, I just..." John House paused. "After what happened to Officer Desin, I can't be around those people anymore. I just can't."

"We'll get justice for her, don't worry," Rex said. "We need to know what the security force is up to."

"Yes. We will," Zyz said firmly.

"I'm sure the officers were just doing their jobs, and Officer Desin-"

"We *will* get justice for her," Zyz said uncompromisingly, cutting Nancy House off. She quickly shut her mouth.

"What's a rende-who point?" Marta asked.

"It's basically a place that people agree to meet at during a specified time," John Dash explained.

"Oh, I see," Marta said.

"On a similar note, we should find a more official meeting spot. At least so we aren't out in the open," Rex said.

"What about the houses?" DT asked.

"Maybe, but they're too small to fit all of us," Rex said.

"Then we use more than one house," Dash said.

"That could work," John House said.

"Alright, but whose houses?" Rex asked.

"You can use mine. It's pretty far back, plus we'd see anyone long before they got to us," Zyz said.

"Any more volunteers?" Rex asked.

"There are also plenty of empty houses," Dash said.

"We can't just go into a dead person's house and use it for ourselves?!" Nancy said, upset.

"Well, it's not like we have many options," Nadia said.

"Why don't you volunteer your house, then?" Nancy snapped.

"Why don't you?" Garrison asked. Nancy didn't have a response.

"I'm sure most of those... 'unused' houses are locked. How would we get in?" DT asked.

"The security force has spare keys for each house," John House said.

"And I'm sure Dr. Harrack collected the original off of the deceased before cremating them," Dr. Marie said. "He may be a piece of shit, but he's not an idiot."

"We should spread out our forces, just in case one of us gets found out," Rex said. "But we still don't have a centralized meeting place."

"My office would still be a little too small. And all of you guys coming and going would be pretty suspicious," Dr. Marie said.

"We have two radios, now. We could *try* to fit ourselves into two houses and talk over that," John House suggested.

"What if the security force overhears us?" Nadia asked.

"There's private and public frequencies. We just need to use the private ones. Even if two radios try to message the same private frequency, the second one would basically get a 'call busy' signal until the first disconnected. Sure, they could talk to us, and we could talk to them, but as long as we have our radios set to each other's private frequency, they can't hear a word we're saying," John House explained.

"I'm still not sure it's the best idea, but it's all we have," Rex said.

"What's the next step, then?" Dr. Marie asked.

"Well, you can get us the keys from Harrack," Marta started.

"Then go to the Council meeting," Rex said. "We'll have you covered from the ground. But please be careful. If Berkoff is as big a threat as you think he is, this could be dangerous."

"I didn't think he was anything more than a scheming politician, but... I don't know anymore," Dr. Marie said with worry. "I'll be careful, don't worry."

"Good luck," Marta said. Dr. Marie nodded and smiled.

"I'll try to get the spare copies first. If that doesn't work, we can try Dr. Harrack," John House said.

"It's harder to tell which one is more risky," Dr. Marie said with a slight laugh. "Well, we shouldn't waste any time. It won't be long before the Council meets."

"Let's go, then," John House said. With that, the two departed.

"So what now?" Nadia asked.

"We wait for them to get those keys," Rex said.

*   *   *

John House braced himself and walked into the security station. All the officers who weren't on patrol were idly going about their business. He casually walked through the locker room, glaring at other officers every so often. Whenever anyone would look at him, he quickly turned his head away. No one seemed to notice his glaring.

"Hey, John!" Peter Corrad said excitedly, jumping up from a bench and trotting over. "Where ya been?"

John House forced a smile onto his face. "Just out," he said.

"Cool," Peter said, smiling widely. John House's smile slowly faded off of his face. Peter awkwardly stood there for another minute. "Well, seeya for patrol." Peter trotted back to his locker and sat down. He stretched. John House turned away and continued walking further into the security station. He walked into one of the smaller storerooms off to the side of the building. It had been converted into the security force's armory and supply station. While it had heavy riot gear, it also contained more mundane things that might be needed. Walking past all of the emergency gear, John House stopped at a metal desk. He bent down and opened the top drawer on the right side. He pulled out a medium sized metal box and opened it. Inside were one hundred and twenty separate keys. Each one was imprinted with a number.

"Shit," John House said to himself. He glanced over his shoulder through the door leading to the security station. Nobody with within sight. John House turned back to the box. He stared at it for a moment, thoughtfully. After a few second, he sighed. He began grabbing handfuls of keys and shoving them into his pockets. He could only fit about a quarter of the keys into each pocket before it looked suspicious. With roughly half of the keys now in his possession, he closed the box, put it back in the drawer, and closed the drawer. He then turned and walked out of the storeroom.

As he began walking through the locker room again, he nervously glanced at Peter Corrad, who was happily chatting with another officer. Peter didn't seem to notice John House yet, and John House held his breath as he walked by. Continuing past Peter, he quickly made it to the door. He stopped only to open it up, then stepped outside, closing the door behind him. He let out the breath he had been holding in a sigh of relief, and quickly made his way through the door in the chain link fence, once more returning to the back of the residential area.

*   *   *

Just under an hour later, Dr. Linda Marie walked into the security station, promptly marching past every office. She paid no extra mind to John House, who sat next to Peter Corrad on one of the benches. Dr. William Harrack, Vice President Eustace Toaden, and Percy Winkle were already standing at the elevator. The three turned to look at her as she stood in line with them. Toaden pressed the elevator button. They waited in silence until the elevator doors dinged open. The three of them walked inside, then turned and faced the door as it closed. As the elevator rose upwards, Dr. Marie coughed. The elevator slowed to a stop and the doors opened. Dr. Marie, Harrack, Toaden, and Percy all stepped into the High Rise, where Alan Berkoff was waiting with a gigantic smile.

"Welcome!" Alan called cheerfully.

"Remove your officers that flooded into my house the moment I turned off the defense system. *Now*," Percy ordered, walking into the High Rise. Toaden followed close behind and pushed his glasses along his nose. Dr. Marie glanced nervously at Harrack as the two slowly stepped out. Harrack seemed wary.

"I am sorry for your discomfort, but"

"Just stop embarrassing yourself," Toaden said, cutting off Alan.

"Let's get this over with," Percy said, and cleared his throat. "Alan Berkoff. As owner of this bunker, I hereby strip you of- why am I being so formal? You're fucking fired. Now pack up whatever shit you have and *get the fuck out*," Percy said. Alan let out a disappointed sigh.

"Can I have one last request?" Alan said.

"No!" Percy and Dr. Marie yelled together. Then they both turned and looked at each other with surprise. Toaden sighed.

"I guess one last favor can't hurt," Toaden said. Alan smiled and pulled a security force radio out of his pocket, turning it on.

"Robbie!" Alan shouted loudly into it.

"What? Who are you talking to? Who's Robbie?" Toaden asked in confusion. As he and Dr. Marie looked around the room, a door in the wood paneling of the wall on the far end of the room opened up. Dr. Marie noticed and fixated on it as Toaden stared in the opposite direction. A woman with golden hair silently emerged from the darkness within the secret room. She held a silenced pistol in her left hand. Toaden finally looked in the right direction, then quickly turned to Alan. Percy also noticed the woman.

"How did you find out about the secret compartments?!" Toaden asked furiously.

"Secret compartments? Why the hell are there secret compartments up here?! I didn't say any could be-"

"Despite what you think, Winkle, you don't own this bunker. It's government property," Toaden said, interrupting Percy. Percy started fuming.

"I paid for almost all of this fucking bunker, and this is the thanks I get!? Some disrespect from a Danny DeVito look alike?!" Percy shouted.

"Can we do this *after* we remove Berkoff from office?" Toaden asked. Percy sighed in frustration.

"Fine," Percy begrudgingly agreed.

"Sorry to interrupt, but have either of you boys noticed *that woman is holding a fucking gun?!*" Dr. Marie shouted.

"I imagined this going very differently," Alan said with a look of blank confusion. Angel lowered her weapon and let her arms drop to her side. Toaden turned to Alan.

"What the hell is this? Civilians aren't allowed in here! And... why do I bother? It's not like you've followed any *other* rules," Toaden said.

"Fucking *gun!*" Dr. Marie reminded everyone. Toaden continued to stare at Alan.

"Like he'd actually hurt us," Toaden said and scoffed. The elevator dinged behind them, and the three turned around in surprise. After a moment of confused silence, the elevator opened and five security officers walked into the room. Four of them surrounded Dr. Marie, Toaden, Percy, and Harrack. The fifth walked over to Alan. As she stopped next to him and turned around, Jane McVellion smiled nastily. Toaden curled his lip up in anger.

"This is absurd. I'm ending this. *Now*," Toaden said, then shoved his way past an officer and marched purposefully over to the wall right next to the elevator. He pressed his hand against the wall, depressing the area slightly. In another second, the keypad popped out of the wall.

"Wait... what does that do?" Alan said nervously. Everyone stared at Toaden, and no one noticed Alan slowly slide Jane's pistol out of its holster.

"This will open up the vault door," Toaden explained, staring at the keypad.

"Why didn't I know about this? *How* didn't I know about this?" Alan asked anxiously. Toaden sighed.

"The only reason you're president is because of Winkle. Nobody else wanted you in charge, but we needed his funding.

Compromises were made, but there's one even Winkle didn't know about. They gave me and me alone the code to get out of here. I'm only supposed to use it if something goes horribly wrong. And I think *you've* gone horribly wrong," Toaden said, staring at the keypad the entire time. "Why are you doing this, anyways?"

Alan's entire demeanor suddenly changed. He suddenly seemed much more old. His lips drooped to create a sad smile. "You..." Alan choked, as if holding back tears. Then he continued, very slowly. "You couldn't even *begin* to imagine what I've been though." He said the words slowly, with a sober sadness. Then, just as quickly as he had sobered up, the smile reappeared on his face. He tightened his grip on the gun. Toaden hit the first number.

"Don't press another button," Alan warned, then raised his gun, pointing at the back of Toaden's head, while Toaden remained oblivious to the threat. Dr. Marie looked rapidly in between Alan and Toaden, but before she could say anything, Jane noticed and pointed her assault rifle right at Dr. Marie, smiling viciously. Toaden hit the second number. Alan's hands began shaking as he further tightened his grip on the gun. Toaden pressed the third button.

Alan pulled the trigger. Vice President Eustace Toaden's brain burst out of his skull, painting the wall a brain red. Toaden's body slumped forward, hitting the wall and slowly sliding down it, leaving a trail of smeared blood as his body fell. The entire room was frozen. Alan's hand continued shaking harder and harder. Suddenly he screamed in pain, dropping the gun and slowly bringing his hands to his head. As he continued screaming, the screams slowly morphed into laughter. Pure, insane, maniacal laughter.

"Well, it looks like the Toad has croaked!" he shouted loudly, his laughs taking over. Every other person in the room looked on with unadulterated terror. Even Jane seemed slightly unsettled. After over a minute, Alan's laughter finally started to fade. Still smiling, he turned to face Dr. Marie, Percy, and Harrack. "If it's okay with you guys, I'll just assume complete and total control of this bunker. Any objections?" he asked. Percy and Dr. Marie both still seemed to be in shock. Alan's eyes darted in between the two of them rapidly. "No? Great!" he said after a few seconds of silence. He turned to Jane.

"Right. Now for you," Alan said. Dr. Marie's lips twitched into a smile for a split second before returning to an expression of horror. Jane's face twisted into a scowl, and she reached for her sidearm. "I think it's time you got another promotion."

Jane froze. "Thank you very much," she said with satisfaction.

"No," the youngest of the four security officers in the room said. Another one of the officers turned and shushed him.

"Quiet, Dinlum!" Rick Farkass hissed. Johnny Dinlum ignored him and continued.

"This isn't right," Dinlum continued. Roy Bant turned to the fourth officer.

"Black, get your partner to quiet down!" Roy snapped under his breath. Joshua Black shrugged and shook his head in confusion.

"All of you shut up!" Jane yelled at the top of her lungs. Everyone's heads shot around to look at her.

"I won't stand for this anymore," Dinlum said, then raised his gun and fired without hesitation. Everyone in the room scattered as the bullets flew past Jane and Alan, smashing into the massive windows behind them. The bulletproof windows absorbed a few bullets before shattering. Roy raised his own gun, pointing it at Dinlum, but Rick panicked and ran straight into Roy, knocking both onto the ground. Joshua turned to Dinlum, but Dinlum quickly swung his arm around and pulled the trigger once more. The bullets hit Joshua in the side of his face. As Dinlum stepped further into the room, firing at the couch Alan and Jane were hiding behind, Dr. Marie, Percy, and Harrack cowered behind him. Percy frantically beat on the elevator button. Because the elevator hadn't gone back down yet, it opened instantly. The three flew into the elevator and threw themselves against the back wall. Dr. Marie sprung forward and began smashing the Close Doors button.

Angel, who had been standing in the far corner and likely unseen by any of the officers and had been watching all of this with a horrified expression of her own, snapped herself back into reality and raised her silencer. She fired once. Dinlum held the side of his throat as blood poured out from in between his fingers and he slowly collapsed to the floor. The elevator doors leisurely slid shut.

The three inside the elevator sat on the floor and panted heavily as the elevator began to slowly descend. All three slowly rose to their feet. Harrack began laughing.

"It was nice knowing you, *Doctor* Marie," he said with a sarcastic, yet still shaken, smirk. Without warning, Dr. Marie grabbed Harrack's arm and pinned it behind his back. Harrack yelled in pain as she forced him onto his knees. "Aren't you supposed to *help* people, not *hurt* them?!"

"Shut up, you little bitch. This won't leave any permanent damage. It'll just hurt like hell." She twisted his arm, and he screamed out even louder in pain. "And you're coming with us, or I'll make sure this is the most *pleasant* thing you ever experience again. Without being injured, of course."

"Fine, *fine!*" Harrack shouted. Dr. Marie held his arm for a moment longer, then released it. Harrack slowly got back up to his feet and rubbed his arm. Dr. Marie looked over at Percy. Percy, his expression still full of horror, looked back.

"You don't have to ask me twice," he said simply. Then the elevator slowed to a stop. Dr. Marie braced herself as the doors opened. There were no guards in the immediate area. Dr. Marie pushed Harrack out of the elevator.

"Move," she ordered. He obliged, and the party of three stepped out of the elevator. Dr. Marie grabbed Harrack's shirt collar and began running through the security station, with

Harrack struggling and tripping. Percy followed. She burst through the doors of the security station, still dragging Harrack, and forced open the chain link fence's door. She then began pushing her way through the group of stunned officers and civilians, with Harrack and Percy in tow. No one seemed to notice them as they all stared up at the High Rise. The group kept running into the residential area. They didn't get too far in when Dr. Marie slowed to a stop.

"Why the hell are we stopping?!" Percy yelled in a panic. Without answering, Dr. Marie quickly banged on the door to Daniel Butler's house. She banged on the door again, and Percy looked nervously over his shoulder.

"It's Dr. Marie!" Dr. Marie yelled at the door.

"We should keep moving. No one's here!" Percy said. As he said it, the door opened. Dr. Marie grabbed Harrack's shirt collar again, prompting a quick protest, before she threw him inside the building. Dr. Marie and Percy followed and shut the door. Captain Rex stood in the middle of the room, aiming a gun straight at Percy. Jaime Slewdjack was standing behind Rex, pointing his gun at Harrack. Toby Smalls was behind Jaime.

"What are they doing here?" Rex asked suspiciously.

"Winkle's in the same boat as us, now," Dr. Marie said, then looked at Harrack. "And I sort of just took Dr. Harrack hostage."

Rex pressed the barrel of his gun against Harrack's stomach. "You should hope you're not useless to us," Rex said. Harrack began sweating nervously.

"Let's worry about him, later," Dr. Marie said quickly. She paused for a moment. "Berkoff murdered Toaden." Rex, Jaime, and Toby all seemed caught off guard.

"What happened up there?" Toby asked.

"How did you get out?" Jaime added.

"One of the security officers just started shooting. At everyone but us, I mean," Percy explained.

"Nancy and Lucy are right. Not all of them are bad people!" Toby said, with a pinch of hope.

"Well, we know Berkoff is going to send people out to start looking for us. So what do we do, now?" Percy asked.

"We need to think about our next move carefully," Rex said.

"I'm more worried about their next move," Jaime said.

*   *   *

Rick Farkass and Roy Bant moved all three bodies along the wall on either side of the elevator. Alan was still shaking slightly. Rick and Roy stepped away from the bodies and stood in front of the elevator, looking at them. Alan slowly walked over to a nearby chair, the cushion of which had been destroyed by bullets. He reached behind the pile of stuffing and pulled out a small calibre pistol.

"Huh," he said. He looked at Jane McVellion. "We need to discuss our next move."

"Find them and kill them. Simple," Jane replied.

"Yes, but *how* are we going to find them?" Alan asked impatiently.

"Not my problem," Jane said, stomped to the elevator, pushing Roy and Rick out of the way. Jane hit the elevator door button.

"Send officers out to look for them," Alan ordered. Jane sighed.

"Fine," she said. Once the doors clicked open, she stepped inside. She turned to Roy and Rick. "Come with me," she ordered. Neither rushed, and slowly prodded over to the elevator. Alan looked over his shoulder at the broken window. He then looked at Angel Puer. He sighed and also walked to the elevator. Angel followed, and the five began descending.

"I guess I'll head to Percy's mansion," Alan said absent-mindedly. "Your officers are still there, right?"

"I don't know," Jane replied.

"Yes, they are," Roy answered.

"Good," Alan said. They reached the security station and stepped out of the elevator. The security station had refilled with almost all of the security officers. They all turned slowly to face the five occupants of the elevator as they stepped out. No one questioned why Angel was there, or why Alan was holding a gun.

"Listen up!" Jane said to the assembled security force.

"Percy Winkle, Dr. Linda Marie, and Dr. William Harrack are now all wanted fugitives," Alan announced. The entire security force began mumbling amongst itself.

"And what does Vice President Toaden think of this?" Aranai Fielding asked.

"And where is Vice President Toaden, anyways?" Joseph Nine added.

"Toaden is dead," Alan stated. The mumblings grew. "He, along with the other members of the Council, attempted a coup to take control of the bunker for themselves!" Alan continued. "We fought them off, killing Toaden and sending Winkle, Harrack, and Marie running. Unfortunately, two brave officers lost their lives trying to defeat the traitors." The mumblings grew to full blown conversations and soon began to drown out Alan. Aranai and Joseph exchanged a skeptical glance.

"Shut up!" Jane yelled. The crowd immediately silenced itself.

"Find these traitors and bring them in, dead or alive," Alan ordered. "Dismissed." The group of officers split up. Jane walked through the station and marched out the doors. Alan grabbed Roy's arm before he could walk away. Rick sat down on a bench, still with a look of shock and horror on his face. Roy looked at Alan.

"How long have you *actually* been leading the security force?" Alan asked.

"I wouldn't say I've been running it. I'm just better at organizing and leading than Chief McVellion. So I usually go and do that stuff while she's off killing people," Roy replied. Alan let out a "Hmm," then released Roy. He looked at Angel. She looked back without an expression.

A small crowd of confused citizens had gathered outside of the security station. Jane grunted as two of them approached her. The man and woman were holding each other tightly as they approached. The woman looked scared and confused, while the man looked concerned. The woman's stomach was protruding outwards slightly.

"What happened up there?" the man asked as he held the woman.

"Please, don't bother her," the woman whispered. Jane grunted and walked past Billy and Mary Lovell.

"You're lucky I don't kill you," Jane told the couple. The two stared at her back, holding each other tighter than before.

*   *   *

"Come in," Captain Rex said into the radio.

"What's happening?" Marta Girasol responded from the other side of the radio.

"Where's Zyz?" Rex asked.

"He went to the security station," Marta replied. "Hartford also left. Felt the house was too cramped."

"*He* thought the house was cramped?!" Nadia Schwartz said angrily in the background.

"Quiet," Marta said. "You still haven't said what's happening? And what's the next move?"

"We have Marie, and Winkle decided to join us. Harrack is also here, not that he wants to be," Jaime Slewdjack explained over Rex's shoulder. Rex glared at Jaime.

"Thanks, Jaime," Marta said. Rex sighed in defeat.

"Well, the security force is probably going to come looking for us," Dr. Marie said. "So we just have to keep our heads down and lay low."

"Easier done without this one," Percy Winkle said, pointing at Dr. William Harrack. Harrack frowned unhappily at Percy. Rex aimed his gun at Harrack again.

"Don't worry. He won't say a word. Right, *doctor?*" Rex said.

"Right," Harrack grunted.

"Good," Rex replied. He turned back to the radio. "Now is a good time to set a trap for some patrolling officers. That way we have less to deal with."

"We can't kill them!" Nancy House yelled from the background. Rex and the others in the house listened as random, muffled sounds came from the other end. They continued for a brief moment. At one point, a female voice yelled something. Then the door opened in the background and quickly shut again.

"What the hell just happened?" Jaime asked.

"Schwartz and House had a small fight. Sacks just walked out the door," Marta replied.

"Can you settle down?" Dash was heard saying in the background. Nadia then yelled something indistinguishable. The door then opened and closed again.

"And John just walked out," Marta reported. "*Mierda, esto es ridículo!*"

"Well, you *never* tell a girl to-"

"*Shut up!*" Marta yelled, cutting Nadia off. There was no response. "Anyways, what the hell do we do now?"

"Well, we set the trap. Who in the group knows how to fire guns?" Rex asked.

"Aside from you, Garrison, Zach, and I can all shoot," Jaime said.

"I'm not a crack shot, but I know my way around a trigger," Nadia said.

"I've never fired a gun, but I'll sure as hell learn," Marta added.

"Not exactly the best time to teach this sorta thing, but tough times, eh?" Jaime said.

"We also need someone to protect Marie, Winkle, and Harrack," Rex added.

"I can do that. I'm already here," Jaime volunteered.

"Alright. Just be ready to take care of our special guest if he causes any trouble," Rex said, looking at Harrack. Harrack turned to Dr. Marie.

"What was that you said about keeping me from being injured?" he asked. She shrugged.

"I think we'll take that on a case by case basis from this point forward," Dr. Marie responded casually. Rex turned back to the radio.

"Alright, so Girasol, Schwartz, and Hartford, will set up a trap for the security officers," Rex said into it.

"Shouldn't *we* get someone to protect *us?!*" Nancy said from the background.

"*Sácame de este agujero infernal.* I'll stay here, then," Marta said.

"But how are you going to protect us?" Nancy continued.

"Forget it, you're on your own," Marta said with a tired tone. "Please tell me we're doing this sooner rather than later."

"Yeah, we shouldn't waste time. I'll be over there shortly. Try to get Hartford and Schwartz ready," Rex said.

"What about Zyz? Should we wait for him to get back?" Marta asked.

"Where did he even go?" Rex asked.

"I think he said he was going to make sure that House, the officer, was going to use his radio," Marta said. Rex sighed.

"They couldn't have done that earlier?" Rex asked.

"It's not like *you* thought of it, either," Nancy said with a huff.

"Get ready to leave. I'll be right over," Rex said.

"*Gracias,*" Marta said. Rex clicked off the radio and handed it to Jaime.

"You know the frequency?" he asked.

"Yeah, this one, right?" Jaime asked, pointing at the radio dial.

"Yes," Rex said. He stayed motionless for a moment. "Good luck." Rex handed his gun to Jaime, stood up, and opened the door a crack. He peeked out, then nodded and disappeared out the door, silently shutting it behind him.

*   *   *

With Jane wandering around somewhere, Roy addressed the thirteen remaining security officers.

"They may not be armed, but still be careful, regardless. It's a small group, so you shouldn't need to go in groups larger than pairs," Roy said calmly. Aranai Fielding and Joseph Nine exchanged a glance.

"If they aren't armed, how did they manage to kill two officers?" Aranai asked. Roy sighed.

"As much as I'd love to answer that question, I won't. If you want the answer, ask Berkoff yourself," Roy said.

"What do we do if we find them?" Joseph asked.

"Try to bring them back here," Roy answered.

"Alive?" Joseph asked.

"Yes. Alive," Roy said flatly.

"To be fair, I'm more worried about McVellion getting her hands on them *alive*," Joseph snarked.

"I second that," Aranai agreed. There were scattered laughs among the crowd, however most stayed silent.

"You think I don't know that? Just do your job, even if your boss is a homicidal maniac," Roy ordered strictly. "Besides, this is President Berkoff's assignment, not Chief McVellion. So don't worry about her too much."

While there was still a medium sized crowd gathered under the High Rise, the majority of citizens had returned to their homes. A few pairs of officers went to guard Dr. Marie and Dr. Harrack's offices. A few other officers went to their houses.

Aranai Fielding and Joseph Nine casually wandered through the far end of the residential area.

"What do we do if we find any of them?" Joseph asked as they walked further into the area.

"Nothing," Aranai responded.

"So we're just gonna let them go?" Joseph asked.

"Yup," Aranai answered.

"Good," Joseph said with a smile. The two continued walking in silence. It wasn't long before they reached the very end of the residential area. They stopped just beyond the last row of houses. They stood there for a moment. Aranai sighed, and Joseph looked at his shoes. "Guess we should head back now, huh?" Joseph asked.

"Nah. I prefer the quiet out here. Plus I'd rather stay away from the others," Aranai responded.

"Ever think about standing up to McVellion?" Joseph asked.

"The thought has crossed my mind," Aranai replied.

"Should we?" Joseph asked. Aranai turned away from the back wall.

"Well-" he paused, suddenly squinting his eyes at the row of houses next to the one they came out of. He silently unholstered his weapon and began walking forward. Joseph followed nervously.

"What is it?" Joseph whispered anxiously.

"Glass," Aranai whispered back calmly. Joseph was confused for a moment until he saw the shattered glass laying in front of one of the houses, just below the window. The pair continued to slowly approach the alley. Aranai leaned against the side of the house opposite from the one with the shattered windows. Joseph pressed himself to the wall behind Aranai, nervously glancing over his shoulder. Aranai squinted his eyes and peered at the house intently. When nothing happened, he proceeded closer to the house, walking in between the two rows of houses. Joseph, still looking over his shoulder, didn't notice

Aranai advance. As Joseph looked forward, Aranai was almost halfway in between the houses.

"Wait!" Joseph whisper-yelled, and rushed to catch up with his partner. Aranai didn't hear him, and Joseph ended up running right into him. As Joseph bounced off the slightly larger man, Aranai spun around.

"Freeze!" Aranai yelled, pointing his gun directly at Joseph's chest. Joseph, slightly disoriented, froze. Aranai sighed and lowered the gun. Joseph relaxed and breathed a sigh of relief.

"You freeze!" a female voice suddenly yelled from a house behind Aranai. He spun around, raising his gun. Before he even had a chance to see who had yelled, a hail of bullets suddenly shot out from a second house across the street from the one Aranai had been trying to investigate. A bullet hit the side of Joseph's face, killing him before he even had time to react. Aranai covered his head as the bullets hit his kevlar vest and legs. As he began to fall, bullets started coming from the house he had tried to investigate. Within seconds, his bullet-riddled body was lying lifeless on the floor. Screaming could be heard in the distance.

The doors to four of the houses, including the two that had shot at the officers, opened, and one person from each house emerged. Nadia Schwartz exited the house that had drawn Aranai's attention, and Garrison Hartford exited from the house that had started shooting first. Captain Rex and Marta Girasol exited from the other two houses.

"What the hell are you doing?!" Rex yelled at the other two.

"I only fired because I heard shots!" Nadia said defensively. Rex turned to Garrison.

"They were onto us. And once pretty miss, here, blew our cover, I decided to fire before they could," Garrison explained with indifference.

"Aren't we trying *not* to kill the security officers?!" Marta said angrily.

"Hey, I'm just trying not to be gunned down like an animal," Garrison responded. "Besides, I never agreed to that."

"Let's just get out of here before any more officers show up," Rex said angrily. Marta sighed defeatedly.

"Yeah. Let's just... go," she said, looking sadly at the two bloody bodies in the middle of the street. Rex turned and trotted to an alley. The others quickly followed.

*   *   *

Shortly before dinner, the security officers began moving long, triangular devices out of one of the storerooms in the back of the station. Each edge of the triangle had been rounded off, and the top edge of each device had a large slit running all the way down it. Each device was about ten feet across, and about a foot wide. The security force placed them so that the end of each one was touching the end of the next one. The devices were placed in a wide circle around the back of the security station, and continuing around the dining area, surrounding it. Once all twenty or so devices had been placed, the security force returned to the security station. John Dash and DT Sacks stood watching this odd behavior.

"This can't be good," DT said.

"We should tell the others," Dash replied.

"What if they do something else, and we aren't here to see it?" DT asked.

"I'll go, then. You can stay here, if you want," Dash answered. He then turned around and began walking away before DT could say anything else. DT sighed. Zachary Zyz stood by the entrance to the security station, his arms crossed.

"Why are you still here? I already told you, active personnel only," Rick Farkass said with mild frustration.

"I left some things in there. I would like to get them," Zyz responded mechanically. Rick sighed with frustration.

"I already told you no! Like, twenty times!" Rick nearly shouted.

"I would like to get some things I left in my locker," Zyz said again. Rick groaned.

"Fine. Y'know what? I don't care," Rick stepped aside and began walking away. "Honestly." Zyz walked into the security station. He quickly marched to his locker, opening it up. He pulled out a couple personal items, which he put in his pockets, and a pair of binoculars with a strap. He draped the strap around his neck, looked into his locker for another moment, then closed it. He turned and walked over to the radio rack in the back of the room. He found his radio at the very end and pulled it off the wall.

"What do you need that for?" Roy Bant's voice asked from behind Zyz. Zyz turned around with a straight face.

"Things are getting tense. I might not have gotten cleared to be back on the force, but I should be on call if you need an extra officer," Zyz explained.

"Sounds good to me," Roy said. "Glad to know you're on our side." Roy offered a small half-smile. Zyz's expression remained unchanged. "Carry on, then." With that, Roy walked away. Zyz pocketed his radio, and headed back out the door.

Dinner came and the dining area slowly filled up. As the citizens began eating, the security force emerged from the station. As all remaining officers, excluding Jane McVellion, slowly dripped out from the station, DT quickly turned around and began heading away from the dining area.

"Go find Chief McVellion and bring her back here. Then round up all the citizens who aren't here, yet," Roy said.

"What are we doing?" John House asked. Roy looked over at him.

"It's become apparent that the fugitive Council members are not acting alone. Until we can determine the threat, we'll contain it," Roy responded. John House's expression grew both concerned and inquisitive.

"Okay, but *why* are we containing it?" he asked.

"I don't have time to explain. If you want answers, go ask President Berkoff. It was his idea," Roy said. "Now start getting the back walls up. Make sure they're set to thirty feet. Once you're fifty percent done, come back for your next assignment." The security force split off, going around the back of the building to the long devices. An officer stepped to one end of each device. They bent down to adjust a small dial built into the side with varying measurements in feet. Once the dial was set to thirty feet, they pressed a small button right next to the dial. Upon pressing it a second time, a thin, blue wall of polymer shot out of the slit on the top of each device. It had WINKLE ENTERPRISES written in large letters close to the top.

As it got closer to thirty feet, the ascend of the wall slowed to a stop. Once the wall had come to a complete stop, it began to emit a blue foam substance that quickly covered the entire wall, substantially increasing the thickness of the wall. As more walls went up directly next to each other, the foam coating of each wall mixed with the coating from the adjacent wall. John House stared up at the tall structure. Peter Corrad stepped over to him. John House didn't react to Peter's presence, and Peter turned to look at the wall. Peter reached forward and knocked on a clump of foam. The substance, now completely hardened, produced a small sound but retained its exact shape. Peter turned back to John House.

"Pretty cool, huh?" he asked. "I've never seen one of these in use before. They said it's supposed to be indestructible."

"I'd be more worried about it getting knocked down than destroyed," John House replied. Peter laughed.

"Well, I'm sure Winkle put in something to prevent that. Otherwise, you wouldn't see these things being used all over the Middle East," Peter responded.

"Well, let's just hope," John House said, then turned and walked away, without ever looking at Peter once. The more curious citizens who were eating dinner stepped away from their food to investigate the activities of the security force.

"Everyone, go back to your food!" Roy ordered loudly. Most of the group continued to stare. "Go back to your food, *now!*" Roy ordered louder and with a gun in his hand. The group begrudgingly returned to the tables and sat back down, still staring at the walls and watching the security force. As the security force gathered back at the entrance to the security station, Roy looked over at Percy Winkle's mansion. He looked down at the instant wall device directly in between the station and the mansion, which had not yet been activated. "Go bring that one back in the station," he ordered, pointing at the device. The other officers looked at it. A pair of officers quickly obliged, leaving the ten foot area open.

"Now what?" Rick asked impatiently, crossing his arms.

"If Winkle hasn't invented something helpful, we improvise," Roy said. He turned to Rick. "Take some other officers into the back and see if you can't find anything useful." Rick sighed but obliged. Roy began walking towards Percy's mansion.

*   *   *

DT Sacks stood in Tony Weitson's house with Captain Rex, Jaime Slewdjack, Percy Winkle, Dr. William Harrack, and Dr. Linda Marie. Rex turned to Percy.

"Care to enlighten us about this invention of yours?" Rex asked.

"Yes. It's most likely the Winkle Enterprises patented Insta-Wall. We usually use them as blockades. Or temporary walls in destroyed buildings. The Israeli and Palestinian governments buy a lot of them for all the bombed buildings that they still have to use," Percy explained.

"Can we destroy them?" Garrison asked.

"No, they're designed to be resistant to most types of damage. The only thing that would come close is heat, which would melt the solidifying foam, but it cools rapidly, so it would still be very difficult to effectively heat up enough of it on both sides to even think about breaking through," Percy continued.

"What if we just tried knocking it over?" Rex asked after a moment of thought.

"It super glues itself to the ground before shooting up the wall. Even with this rocky ground, it should still be rather effective. I doubt you could push it over. Maybe if you drive a car or something into it. But that's still a strong *maybe*," Percy said.

"So nothing we have would be even close to enough to take down one of those walls," Dr. Marie said.

"I'm sure you could find something in the security station," Harrack muttered mockingly. Garrison smacked his leg with his assault rifle. Harrack took a step away and looked down at the small man.

"Yes, but that's nothing *we* have," Dr. Marie snapped back.

"This could lead to serious trouble. We should plan our next move now, but without any idea what the security force is up to, it will be hard," Rex said thoughtfully.

"I hate to say it, but is there anything we can do besides waiting to see what they do next?" DT asked.

"I'm afraid not," Rex said.

"Then I guess we'll just wait and see," Dr. Marie said, frowning.

*   *   *

Roy Bant walked into Percy Winkle's mansion. The front hall was styled like many mansions, including a gigantic, crystal chandelier above a large hall that extended up to the third floor. In front of him were two elaborate staircases leading up to the second floor, from which one could see the entire hall from a balcony. Roy stopped for a moment to admire the ornate marble floors. After a brief moment of admiration, he stepped further into the mansion.

Walking up the flight of stairs, he heard noise coming from his left. He turned and began walking down the hallway. There were almost a dozen rooms on either side of the hall, and priceless, famous paintings were hung in between almost every door. Some sculptures were even interlaced along the walls. Once he was about halfway to the noise, Roy suddenly felt the barrel of a gun pressed against the back of his neck. He raised his hands slightly, but the gun went down after only a few seconds.

"Bant," Jane McVellion's voice acknowledged him. Roy turned around.

"Chief McVellion," he replied. She didn't respond, and after a moment, Roy turned back around and continued walking down the hall. He arrived at the end of it and opened the door the noise was coming from. He saw Alan Berkoff playing a video game on a television, yelling loudly at it. "President Berkoff," Roy said formally. Alan didn't hear him over the loud game and his own yelling.

"Berkoff!" Jane shouted in Roy's ear, causing him to jump slightly. Alan paused his game and turned to Roy and Jane, both still standing in the doorway. Alan smiled.

"Ah, Officer Bant. Come in. Chief McVellion, you're excused," Alan said. Jane let out a grunt and disappeared back down the hall. Roy stepped into the room.

"We've set up half the walls and will begin gathering the citizens soon. Just wanted to check in with you first," Roy reported. Alan smiled wider.

"Well, I'm glad you did. You'd be surprised how some people forget to do that," Alan said, standing up from the couch he had been laying on. "You could've done it over the radio, though. Just wanted to admire the scenery?" Alan asked with a laugh.

"I prefer to discuss these sorts of things in person," Roy replied.

"Excellent," Alan said, clapping his hands together. He then let out a slight wince of pain and slowly peeled his hands off of each other, both slightly shaking. His smile shrank, but remained on his face as he looked back at Roy. "Y'know, once this project is done, you should really hang out here, with us. You don't want to be in that hot, crowded place once everyone's shoved into it," Alan continued.

"Someone has to run it. And it shouldn't be done over radio," Roy replied.

"Oh, you can always check in. Or send McVellion to check in. Or I have someone upstairs who has a clear view of things," Alan said with a chuckle.

"I'm not going to ask," Roy said. "But I'll consider your offer."

"Good," Alan said with a nod.

"Should I begin to gather up the citizens?" Roy asked.

"Yes, go ahead," Alan said, turning around. He plopped himself back onto the couch and resumed his video game. Roy turned and walked out of the room. As he walked down the hall, he could hear Alan resume his yelling. As Roy reached the top of the second floor staircase, he noticed a small woman with golden hair leaning on the edge of the balcony.

"Hello," Roy said as he began to trot down the stairs. Angel Puer looked at him briefly, then went back to looking down at the marble floor below.

*   *   *

As dinner was beginning to wrap up, the security force, armed with assault rifles and full riot armor, prevented anyone from leaving. While some people did yell and try to force their way past, most quieted down and backed off as the officers raised their weapons. While four officers kept the lunch crowd at bay, the remaining officers stormed into the residential area. They began knocking on doors. If people opened up their doors, the officers would force their way in and shove the citizen out, then order them to go to the dining area. John Dash, Toby Smalls, Jaime Slewdjack, Marta Girasol, Nancy House, Nadia Schwartz, and Zachary Zyz were all cramped in Daniel Butler's house, the blind over the window drawn closed. They all froze and tensed up as a pounding knock came at the door.

"Open up!" a voice ordered from the other side.

"I think this guy is dead," another voice said, softer.

"Wait, really?" the first voice asked.

"Yeah, let's keep going," the second voice said. When no more sounds were heard on the other side of the door, the group collectively relaxed.

"*Que demonios esta pasando ahora?*" Marta asked.

"I hope Captain and the others are going to be okay," Nadia said with worry. The security force continued down the rows of houses.

"Open up!" an officer yelled as he smashed on Bill House's door. He continued banging for almost a minute before the door finally opened up.

"What the hell do you want?" Bill asked drunkenly. The officer grabbed his shirt and pulled him out of the house. "Hey, what the fuck?!"

"Go to the dining area," the officer ordered.

"I didn't do anything. I *support* you guys!" Bill yelled.

"Don't care. Just get to the dining area," the officer replied.

"Ugh, *fine*," Bill said, then turned and began to stumble down the street. All the officers passed by Tony Weitson's house without stopping, as his name had already been removed from the house's front. As a pair of officers knocked on Zachary Zyz's door without getting a response, they turned to each other.

"Wasn't he in the station earlier?" one asked.

"I thought so," the other said.

"Well, if he's not here, he's probably in the dining area," the first said. The two agreed on this conclusion and began heading back to the station.

*　　*　　*

"Officer Zyz, if you do not report to the dining area immediately, you *will* be killed on sight," Roy Bant's voice said ominously from the radio. The small crowd all looked anxiously at Zyz, who didn't reply. "Officer Zyz, this is your last warning." Zyz was silent. "Fine. You better hope you were captured by the fugitives instead of part of their group." The radio signal went silent.

"Why didn't you go back?" Nancy House asked.

"I'm not spending another moment with any of those murderers," Zyz snarled.

"Oh," Nancy said.

*　　*　　*

With almost all the citizens gathered up in the dining hall, the security officers who weren't guarding them were quickly raising the unraised walls. A ten foot polymer wall with a door and keypad built into it stood in between two of the Insta-Walls, directly in between the station and the mansion. John House stood in front of the last Insta-Wall. Peter Corrad walked over to him.

"What's wrong? You've been acting weird since that shootout," Peter said. John House stared down at the Insta-Wall base without responding. Peter sighed. "Fine, I'll get it for you." Peter bent down and adjusted the dial. As he hit the button the first time, John House hopped over the base, and landed outside of the pen. Peter looked up before pressing the button a second time. "What the hell are you doing?!" Peter said with alarm. John House pulled his sidearm and pointed it down at Peter's head.

"Press the button," John House demanded.

"You're a fucking psycho," Peter said with disgust as he pressed the button again. The wall went up and the two were separated. John House sighed, then holstered his weapon. Turning, he ran into the residential area.

October 14, 2031

"Here," Marta Girasol said, holding out a third of a sandwich towards Toby Smalls.

"I'll take it," Dr. William Harrack said. Garrison Hartford smacked him with the butt of his assault rifle. Harrack grumbled angrily.

"No, thank you," Toby responded before his stomach loudly protested.

"Please," Marta begged. Toby sighed and took the sandwich. He took a single bite and wrapped the rest of the sandwich up. Nancy House picked up a fourth of an apple wrapped in saran wrap. It was mostly brown and wrinkly.

"You've already had your rations for now," Captain Rex said commandingly, though also tired.

"It's going bad. It won't last much longer," Nancy argued. Rex sighed.

"If House and Schwartz return with more food, then we'll divide it up," Rex said. With a weak sigh, he slowly lowered himself onto a bar stool. The twelve members of the resistance were all sitting around various parts of the building. Toby stood up and walked away from the bar, sitting down at a table with Jaime Slewdjack. Nancy, placing the apple on the bar next to half a dozen, mostly-eaten food items and sat down at a table by herself. Zachary Zyz took a seat next to Rex.

"I might've underestimated the security force," Captain Rex said. "Their plan to starve us out is certainly effective."

"At least we're getting food. Even if it isn't much," Zyz replied.

"True," Rex agreed.

"So what do we do next?" John Dash asked, sitting down on the other side of Rex. "We haven't talked about a plan in days, and we need one sooner rather than later."

"I don't know," Rex admitted. "What can we do? The security station and dining area are a fortress, and so is Winkle's mansion."

Dash turned around to look at Percy Winkle, who was sitting at a table with Dr. Linda Marie. Percy looked up. "What?" The others didn't respond. "Don't tell me you're talking about trying to break into my mansion, *again*. I already told you it can't be done." Percy said grumpily, crossing his arms. Dash turned back to the others.

"There's only one thing we can really do," Marta said. The others turned to look at her. "Attack the security station." Everyone then stared at her in disbelief.

"You can't be serious," Harrack retorted skeptically.

"What's the alternative? Slowly starving to death?" Marta retorted. Everyone looked at each other, but no one said a word.

"If anyone else can't think of a better idea, then we'll start forming a plan," Rex announced.

"It's about damn time," Garrison said frustratedly.

"We should see if John and Nadia have learned anything useful about the station and the officers," Nancy suggested.

"They couldn't see over the walls if they tried," Harrack said.

"It's not like we have much of a choice. And if we are going to do something, we should do it before we don't have enough energy to do anything," Rex said.

"A human can survive going over three weeks without eating," Dash added.

"Not the time," Marta said.

"Damn. So there really is no other option?" Jaime asked.

"I don't think so," Dr. Marie said.

"Well, then let's all hope for a miracle," DT Sacks responded. Everyone silently nodded in agreement.

*　　*　　*

John House stood roughly a dozen houses into the residential area, staring through the binoculars at the ground in front of the Insta-Wall. It was bare. He looked up to the top of the wall. He waited for a few minutes. As he watched a small item suddenly flew over the top of the wall. He followed it down and saw it land on the ground. He lowered the binoculars and turned to Nadia Schwartz, who was standing next to him. He nodded once. She returned the nod and stepped out of the alley. Sneaking along the edge of the houses, she made her way cautiously but quickly to the area where the small object had landed.

Reaching the first row of houses, she ducked into an alley. She glanced towards the side of the encampment that held the only door in and out of the area. It was barren. She jogged to the other end of the alley and peered out. The other side of the encampment was equally empty. She trotted back to the first side and leaned around the corner once more, spotting the saran wrapped sandwich slightly squashed against the ground. Taking one last cautionary glance around, she quickly darted out. Running as fast as she could, she skidded past the sandwich. Without fully stopping, she bent down and grabbed the sandwich. Turning on her heels, she quickly sped back into the residential area.

Angel Puer watched all of this through the scope of her sniper rifle from the third floor of the mansion. The crosshairs on her rifle followed Nadia as she ran to the sandwich and back again. As she disappeared into the rows of houses, Angel opened her other eye and slowly moved her head away from the long gun. She pulled the gun back in through the open window and closed it. She began to dismantle the rifle. As she removed them, she placed the parts back into the case next to the chair she was sitting in. Standing up, she walked out of the room, leaving the case behind. As she walked down a dark stairwell in the back of the mansion, she could hear yelling below.

"I just hate it," Roy Bant said angrily.

"How could you hate this place?" Alan Berkoff asked.

"I don't hate this *place*, I hate not being able to see what's happening with my officers in person!" Roy replied.

"It's not like anything is really happening," Alan said. "The rebels will starve off soon enough. Even with the food the citizens are throwing them, they don't have enough for all of them. You did see who was missing, right?"

"Of course. And now I know exactly who is responsible for this mess," Roy responded. As Alan opened his mouth to say something, a door behind him opened and closed. He turned and saw Angel walking closer to them.

"Ah. Any sign of the rebels?" he asked. She shook her head slowly. "Darn." He turned back to Roy. "You really take it personally, huh?"

"Yes," Roy answered with aggravation. "Of course, they aren't the *only* ones responsible." Roy glared angrily at Alan. Alan raised his arms defensively. Angel placed her hand on the hidden holster on her hip.

"Hey, now. I want things to go back to normal just as much as you do. Once all this gets settled, we can work out some sort of deal that makes us both happy," Alan said with a smile. Roy sighed and backed off.

"I suppose. At least you didn't murder two of my fellow officers in cold blood," Roy replied. Angel also relaxed.

"If it makes you feel better, I can send Jane to go check on how things are going," Alan said.

"I'd prefer to go myself," Roy replied.

"But I'd rather have you here. Especially since I'm sure those rebels would be less likely to mess with Jane than with you," Alan said.

"Don't be so sure about that. But I won't stop either of you," Roy said. Alan's smile widened slightly. Roy turned and walked away, taking his radio off of his belt. He flicked it on. "Officer Castor, come in."

Winston Castor removed his radio from his belt and switched the input on. "Officer Castor here. What do you need?"

"Just checking in," Roy's voice emanated from the radio. Winston looked across the encampment, where the citizens milled about idly. There was a general sluggishness to the entire crowd. Only a handful of citizens moved with any energy or purpose. "We had another thrower earlier," Winston continued.

"How do you plan on punishing it?" Roy's voice asked.

"It was just a single sandwich. I decided to just let it go," Winston replied.

"We can't let these things go unpunished. Otherwise, more citizens might-" Roy suddenly stopped mid sentence. Winston waited a minute before saying something.

"Officer Bant?"

"Chief McVellion is going to check up on you in person soon. Just fill her in, and she'll take care of the punishment. We can't let these *rebels* get anything. The more they get, the longer everything stays like this. You don't want it to stay like this, do you?" Alan Berkoff's voice responded from the otherwise of the radio.

"N-no, Mr. President, sir!" Winston stammered.

"Good. Chief McVellion will help you out this time, but next time you should be willing to take care of it yourself," Alan said.

"Understood, sir," Winston said. The radio went dead, and Winston clicked his own radio off, releasing an exhausted sigh.

*   *   *

"Only a single sandwich?" Garrison Hartford asked with frustration.

"It's all they threw over," Nadia Schwartz responded weakly. Garrison sighed angrily.

"Your appetite seems pretty big for-" Garrison suddenly interrupted Dr. William Harrack by shoving the barrel of his gun in Harrack's face. Harrack's smug grin was immediately wiped off his face.

"For what?! Go on, finish that sentence!" Garrison threatened. Harrack opted to stay silent.

"Hey, don't rough him up too much!" Captain Rex called from the bar. "He could still be useful to us," Rex added under his breath. Garrison stared down Harrack for another moment before slowly backing off, while still keeping his gun trained on Harrack. Rex stared at the sandwich, counting his fingers and softly mumbling math to himself. Toby Smalls, John Dash, Jaime Slewdjack, and DT Sacks all sat together in silence at a table. Marta Girasol walked over and joined them, pulling a metal chair from a nearby table.

"Hey," DT said.

"Hi," Marta replied.

"How are you holding up?" Dash asked her.

"I'm... alive," she said, offered a small smile. Toby also smiled

"Well, as long as we're still going..." Toby trailed off, his smile replaced by a thoughtful expression.

"As long as we're still going, we ain't quitting," Jaime finished with a triumphant smile. Toby's smiled returned.

"Yeah, exactly!" he agreed with decent enthusiasm.

"And we're not giving up!" Marta said, her smile growing larger and more genuine.

"The odds may be against us, but we can still manage to pull through and beat them," Dash said with a shrug. As the others at the table, minus DT, let out a small cheer, Dash smiled.

"It's probably not a good idea to get our hopes up," DT said as they settled down. He was staring down at the table.

"Aw, come on! What good is giving up gonna do?!" Jaime asked loudly.

"It'll save us from the disappointed of losing," DT said, then stood up and walked away from the table. The others watched him walk to an isolated table in the corner of the room, their smiles slowly fading.

"Just give him time," Toby said, his smile once again small and sad. "He'll come back around."

"You can't expect everyone to stay hopeful. Everyone has a breaking point," Dash said.

"Well, we'll just have to fix him, then!" Toby said. "Right?" Dash smiled and let out a short laugh.

"Yes. We just have to fix him," Dash replied. "But let's try to fix our situation, first."

*   *   *

Jane McVellion entered the code onto the keypad on the door surrounding the encampment. Opening it, she stepped inside, quickly shutting the door behind her. The officer standing at the door slowly lowered her gun as Jane glared at her. Jane continued glaring as she walked further into the encampment. She marched through the crowd, pushing aside any citizen who was in her way. It didn't take her long to reach the security station fence. There was a knife jammed in between the pad and the base it was attached to, and multiple keys were missing. She gently pushed on the door, which swung open.

"Some citizens got a little... creative," Winston Castor said from behind her. Jane slowly turned around and looked at the man. He was five foot eleven inch, only three inches shorter than Jane, meaning she didn't have to look too far down to glare at him. Her shoulders were still significantly broader than his, however.

"Where are they?" she growled.

"We don't know. One of the officers chased them off without identifying them," Winston said. Jane sighed with frustration. "Anyways, at breakfast this morning, we had another thrower." Without a verbal response, Jane pushed Winston to the side. She stomped to the nearest table and quickly climbed on top of it.

"Everybody, shut up!" she boomed across the encampment. All activity immediately ceased and the entire area was silent and motionless. "Who threw food over the wall?!" she demanded. No one said a word. Jane looked down. She unholstered her sidearm and quickly shot the citizen standing closest to the table.

"Billy!" Mary Lovell screamed as her husband collapsed to the ground, a bullet hole in his head. She held his body close to her own and began crying profusely.

"Who threw food over the wall!?" Jane repeated.

"It was me!" someone in the back yelled.

"Come here. *Now!*" Jane ordered. The citizen slowly made his way through the crowd. "Faster!" Jane ordered, pointing the gun down at the hysterical Mary Lovell. The citizen quickly picked up her pace and was soon running straight at Jane. As she neared the table, she slowed to a stop. Jane turned to the rest of the crowd. "Time for an example to be made!" The woman who had confessed to throwing the food tried and failed to hold back tears. Jane grabbed her arm and dragged her back towards the security station's fence, where Winston Castor was waiting with crossed arms.

"What are you going to do with her?" Winston asked.

"Bring me a knife," Jane ordered. Winston turned and walked into the station, without uttering a single word. Jane picked up her radio and turned it on. "Got the bitch."

"Good," Roy Bant said from the other end.

"I think I have an idea that will help us with our little rebel problem," Alan Berkoff's voice butted into the conversation. Jane grinned nastily.

*   *   *

Lunch rolled around, and John House and Nadia Schwartz once again returned to the residential area, the pair hidden in the alleyways. John House peered through his binoculars at the area in front of the encampment. It was empty. He quickly panned up to the top of the wall. The two switched places once more. As John House raised the binoculars once again and looked above the body of the woman, a small object suddenly flew over the wall.

"We got something," he said as he lowered the optical device.

"Sweet!" Nadia said with a small fist pump.

"Something doesn't feel right," John House said. "I have a bad feeling."

"It's probably just hunger. You'll feel better after you get something in your stomach." Nadia paused. "If you don't tell the others, I won't either."

John House glared viciously at her. "No. We all need to eat. Including them."

"Alright, fine. Suit yourself, boy scout," Nadia said, then exited the alleyway and began her stealth mission down the rows of houses. Darting in and out, she soon found herself behind the first row of houses. She glanced at either side of the encampment. Both sides were clear. She dodged out, leaving the residential area.

The two officers hidden behind the two corner houses spotted her before she even knew they were there. As she skidded past the food item, one officer stepped out from behind the house and raised his gun. Aiming down the sight, the officer fired.

Nadia was completely caught off guard as the bullets flew past her, none actually hitting their target.

The other officer also stepped out and fired. As Nadia tried to reorientate herself, the shots fired from the second officer managed to strike her leg. Nadia cried out and collapsed to the ground. As the two officers approached, the encampment door opened up and another two officers came running out. John House, watching all of this through his binoculars, shakily raised his radio.

The group back at the bar all slowly got to their feet and approached the glass doors as the gunshot rang throughout the bunker. "Come in." Rex sprinted back to the bar and picked up the radio.

"What is it?" Rex asked.

"They got Nadia," John House said through the radio. The other occupants of the bar stood up and walked over.

"What do you mean they 'got' her?" Rex asked with urgency.

"They shot at her. I think they hit her leg. She's still alive, but she's surrounded by four officers. I don't think I can engage them," John House said. Rex thought for only a second before sighing.

"No, don't engage them. It's too risky," he said.

"Understood," John House replied bitterly. No one said anything as they all gathered around the bar with bated breath. A second gunshot suddenly rang out, as loud over the radio as it was outside the doors. The radio suddenly cut off for a second. Rex held the radio closer to his face.

"House, respond. House, what's going on?!" Rex practically yelled into the radio.

"She's dead. She tried to attack one of them. They killed her," John House said numbly. The crowd around the bar slowly broke away, most just returning to their seats in silence. Rex clenched the radio.

"Get back here when it's safe. We'll plan out our next move," Rex said.

"Understood. See you soon," John House said, before the radio went silent. Rex slammed his fist on the table. A third of the bar's inhabitants jumped.

"Damnit!" Rex yelled. He dropped the radio on the bar and marched straight out the door. Toby Smalls looked at the other three sitting at the same table as him.

"Should we try to do something?" Toby asked.

"I don't think we can right now," John Dash responded. The bar remained silent.

*   *   *

Both the bodies of Nadia Schwartz and the woman who threw the sandwich over the wall at lunch were hung up on the chain link fence surrounding the station. They were suspended by zip ties. The woman who had thrown the sandwich was covered in deep slashes across her face and arms, with the biggest one being across her entire throat and neck. Nadia also had a similar stab wound on the side of her neck, as well as a gunshot in her shoulder. Jane McVellion stood in the fence's door, which rested in between the two bodies. She quickly called for the attention of everyone, and the entire encampment silenced themselves and turned to face her.

"This is what happens when you don't listen to us!" she shouted, pointing at the bodies behind her. The crowd waited uneasily for her to continue. She never did, and instead turned away after her brief speech. She walked through the fence and proceeded into the security station.

Winston Castor stared at the building. Jane did not emerge for a few minutes, by which point the citizens were beginning to slowly return to their own business. Winston entered the station, but could find no trace of Jane. As he wandered around, the elevator leading up to the High Rise suddenly opened, surprising Winston. He turned and looked at it as Jane stepped out.

"What did you do up there?" Winston asked suspiciously as she walked past.

"Shut it," she replied. Winston had no reply. As Jane reached the door she stopped. After a moment, she turned around. "I cancelled dinner."

"What?! Why!? That's only going to make them *more* resistant to us!" Winston yelled.

"They need to learn a lesson," Jane said, then walked out the door before Winston could think of another response. She marched through the camp, the crowd of citizens parting to let her pass. She entered a combination into the keypad on the blue door and exited the encampment.

*   *   *

"Is anyone here a good runner?" Captain Rex asked. None of the other twelve occupants of the building responded, despite all of them eagerly looking at Rex. "Come on, Schwartz couldn't have been the only runner in this room!" No response. "Fine," Rex snapped. He once again walked to the front of the glass doors and exited the building. The others in the room all looked around at each other.

"What are we going to do now?" Nancy House asked.

"We need to attack soon," Garrison Hartford said firmly.

"We don't have a plan yet, though!" Marta Girasol replied, equally firm.

"Screw planning! When have our plans ever worked?" Garrison spat back.

"We can't just go in shooting!" Marta almost yelled.

"She's right. We might as well shoot ourselves if we're going to go in guns blazing," Jaime Slewdjack added.

"Then we'll simply starve here like cowards," Garrison said, crossing his arms.

"The first thing we should do is recon and intelligence," Zachary Zyz said. The others looked at him.

"Go on," Marta said.

"We watch their movements. Look for patterns. See when any of them move in between the mansion and the camp," Zyz elaborated.

"That's... not the worst idea," Garrison said, turning away.

"I've already got into the habit of watching them. I'd be willing to spend more time out there. Whatever brings these bastards down," John House said with conviction.

"Good. You shouldn't go out alone, though," Zyz said.

"I'll go with him," Toby Smalls said, stepping further towards the center of the group.

"How is he going to help?" DT Sacks asked.

"We just need someone to watch House's back," Zyz said.

"Please, John," Nancy House said, stepping closer to her brother. "Stop going out on all these dangerous missions." He smiled at her.

"I'll be fine. I know what I'm doing," he replied warmly. Nancy hugged him.

"I know. But this is serious," she said.

"You're damn right it's serious," Garrison snapped.

"Do you want to go help House and Smalls, then?" Zyz asked.

"*What did you just say?!*" Garrison yelled, attempting to stick his finger in Zyz's face.

"My last name is Smalls," Toby said.

"Oh," Garrison said, relaxing slightly. He frowned. "Fine. I'll go watch their asses."

"Good. Let's get Rex back in here and tell him the plan. I'm sure he won't object to it," Zyz said.

*　　*　　*

For the two years in between when Percy Winkle made the deal with the US government to the time the bunker became populated, Winkle Enterprises was on overdrive. While almost every person at Winkle Enterprises was entering their third day straight, a low level employee was working furiously, despite not getting any sleep for almost two days.

As this particular employee organized and transferred shipping orders, he accidentally switched the paperwork for two packages. One was for a standard shipment of semi-automatic pistols. The other order was for the prototype of an experimental and untested rocket launcher being developed by the company. While the testing facility received the shipment of standard pistols, the launcher ended up in the bunker's storage room. Rick Farkass now held this weapon in his hands. Next to him was the WINKLE ENTERPRISES PROJECTILE EXPLOSIVES box, it's lid pried off and discarded on the floor. Rick had spent most of his free time in this large storeroom, investigating the contents of each box carefully.

Meanwhile, outside in the encampment, it was almost time for dinner. As the citizens waited eagerly at the food dispensers, they were dry. A few banged on the dispensers, more yelled. Winston Castor stood by the chain link fence's entrance and the citizens become more unrestful. The citizens turned to the security force, who were beginning to converge around Winston at the fence. Many officers drew their batons or raised their rifles as more and more of the crowd began aiming their yelling towards the security force.

"Please, calm yourselves!" Winston yelled. The yelling only increased as the crowd began advancing. The officers with their batons drawn also stepped forward, and the crowd stopped. "I'm sorry about this, but Chief McVellion has turned off dinner for today, and I don't know how to turn it back on!" Winston continued.

"Why?!" one voice yelled.

"This isn't fair!" a second one shouted out.

"Please!" Winston urged again. The crowd started to settle down slightly. Then a small object flew from the back of the crowd. The metal spoon bounced harmlessly off of the helmet of one of the officers. The officer didn't react. Soon another utensil was flying through the air, this time a fork. It struck the arm of an officer who was holding a baton. The officer stepped forward and swung his baton into the crowd.

The crowd backed up and avoided the blow. The officer stared angrily at the large crowd. The front of the crowd had become silent. As the silence soon overtook the entire encampment, the angry officer slowly started to back away. All at once, without warning, a sudden storm of utensils flew upwards from much of the crowd. The officers stared up in disbelief as the dozens of metal objects came closer and closer to them. They were snapped back into reality as the spoons, knives, and forks rained down upon them.

As they ducked down and shielded themselves from the falling metal, the crowd rushed forward. The officer who had swung his baton was grabbed and pulled screaming into the crowd. The other officers barely had any time to react as the crowd smashed into them. Immediately, heavy gunfire ensued as the officers who had readied their assault rifles fired into the crowd. People fell in large numbers as more officers were grabbed. The remaining officers ducked through the fence and tried to hold the crowd back as they poured through the single entrance.

As three of the four remaining officers were able to use the bottleneck to their advantage, Winston was frantically pressing buttons on the keypad to the security station. As one citizen was quickly shot repeatedly, their body was suddenly grabbed by the person behind them. The body was pushed forward, absorbing the bullets and providing cover for other citizens to get out from behind them.

The officers began readjusting their aim as they were once again being flanked from multiple directions. Despite the officers continuing to cut down the citizens running at them, the crowd was quickly advancing closer and closer. Winston finally managed to enter the correct key combo as the door unlocked before he was grabbed and pulled back.

Rick clicked the rocket, which itself was also experimental and untested, into the launcher. Just as he did this, he heard the gunfire outside. He gripped the rocket launcher tightly, his finger off the trigger. Shaking slightly, he began creeping through the station. As the gunfire continued and got closer to the station he stopped at the far end of the locker room. He stood there, trembling, and watching the door. As he watched, the gunfire continued for another few minutes. The door suddenly burst open, and a few people poured in. A few scattered bullets followed them in, ricocheting around the room.

Rick jumped back and ran into one of the storerooms. He stood shaking in the back, hiding behind a box as he heard the door slam shut. As he cowered in his hiding place, he heard two pairs of footsteps rustle around outside the storeroom. As one appeared to stop altogether, the other continued further and further away. When the footsteps entered a different storeroom, Rick shakily stood up. Still gripping the launcher, he stepped out of the storeroom. As he cautiously looked around the corner, he saw Casey Goodwill standing right next to the entrance, only inches away from his face. Casey had a crooked and broken smile, her eyes held an empty insanity behind them. Rick's eyes went wide in terror.

"Remember me?" she asked, her voice low and hoarse. Her smile dropped into a frown. Rick stared into her eyes, frozen in fear. He didn't notice the standard dining area knife that that was clenched in her fist. "Remember Rose?" she asked, tilting her head to the side. Her voice had almost taken on a normal tone and her eyes suddenly filled with sadness, replacing the emptiness.

Rick didn't even have time to stammer an answer before Casey thrusted the knife into the side of his neck. The sadness drained out of Casey's eyes and the empty insanity returned once more, as did the crooked and broken grin. Rick fixated on her face as she slowly twisted the blade, tearing his flesh. His blood poured out and flowed down Casey's arm. His eyes began flitting and closed slightly, and the strength went out of his limbs. The loaded rocket launcher slipped from his fingers, falling to the ground.

Had the testing facility ever received the weapon, they would have immediately discontinued production. Between issues of the rocket being far too sensitive and powerful and a complete lack of safety features, the device should never have even gotten past the design phase. However, the weapon was built, regardless.

The rocket had significant weight, and the loaded launcher turned to face down as it fell. The active explosive impacted the ground, instantly setting it off. In a fraction of a second, the entire security station exploded outwards, incinerating the building and almost half of the encampment completely. In the next fraction of a second, the explosion detonated the multiple crates of grenades and projectile explosives in the station's storeroom. The resulting explosion devoured the entire encampment, the walls surrounding it holding back the flames for only another fraction of a second before becoming vaporized, themselves. The inferno reached outwards, flooding the start of the residential area with fire and surrounding Dr. Linda Marie and Dr. William Harrack's offices. At the same time it shot upwards, consuming the High Rise.

Alarms sounded and the massive bunker door began the process of unlocking. As Toby Smalls, John House, and Garrison Hartford began running from the approaching flames, the entire bunker started shaking. Above, the rock coating the ceiling began cracking and collapsing. As the small debris began raining down, a thick plate of the steel that formed the true bunker broke free, sliding past the neighboring reinforcement. It impacted the ground in five seconds, crushing over half a dozen houses in the residential area without any resistance at all.

As the walls and ceiling continued shedding their rock coating, the gigantic steel masses shifted and became unstable. As the vault door had just begun to move, the plate in the ceiling above it swung down, smashing the door with tremendous force, dislocating it from its tracks and causing the door to immediately cease opening. The plate that had crashed into it slid free of the neighboring plates that had been pinching it in place and it fell to the ground, landing in such a way that it appeared to be standing up. The fire still raged, but the force of the explosion had dissipated. The plate slowly toppled forward, landing just short of the smouldering remains of the security station. The only structures in the area that had survived were the two doctors' offices.

Inside the bar, the liquor bottles all began falling off of the shelves, while the ceiling of the building began fracturing and falling inwards. The rebels who hadn't gone outside in response to the explosion quickly evacuated the building. As the last person escaped from the bar, the structure collapsed. In Percy Winkle's mansion, the paintings that were hung up began falling off of the walls. Many of the statues lining the walls also toppled over. Angel Puer darted down to the first floor as the steel plate above the building fell down. She barely made it to the foyer as the plate decimated the left third of the mansion. Alan Berkoff, Roy Bant, and Jane McVellion came running and met up with her from the right wing of the mansion.

Despite the advice and warnings of multiple government employees, including a young architect by the name of Ms. Marta Girasol, the bunker lacked support beams throughout. However, all of them were eventually replaced by private contractors from Winkle Enterprises who had no such concerns. The only support beam in the entire structure was meant to support the entire ceiling. The massive pole ended up backing the elevator shaft, connecting the security station and High Rise. This support beam and the entire structures surrounding it no longer existed, and the bunker destabilized. However, despite the multiple ceiling plates that had fallen and the massive force of the explosion, most of the bunker eventually stabilized itself, uneasily settling back into an equilibrium. Many of the lights had shattered out of existence, but just under a third still remained active.

The rebels stood staring at the destruction as John House, Toby, and Garrison ran to them. The first one of the stunned rebels to move was Nancy House, who immediately ran towards her brother. The two collided into an embrace, both falling to their knees. Nancy began sobbing furiously.

"B-B-" She stopped to cry even more. "Bill!" she finally managed to yell out. John House held his sister tighter as she cried out. As tears began to roll down his cheeks, he collapsed into his own crying fit and the two remaining House siblings gripped each other. All the others were too shocked to move and just stared, open-mouthed, at the faint glow of the fire that still burned intensely.

October 15, ERROR
ERROR Log-ERROR
Doctor Linda Marie
Subject: ERROR

"I think this will be my last journal. Yesterday, there was a massive explosion. We have no idea why or how, just that only a few of us have managed to survive. Somehow, both my office and Dr. Harrack's offices have managed to remain standing in face of the blast. The only survivors, aside from the group I'm with, appear to be President Berkoff, Interim Chief McVellion, Officer Bant, and a third citizen I have managed to identify as Angel Puer, who we spotted earlier today. I think it's safe to assume that 'Angel Puer' isn't a real name. If someone ever finds these journals, I just want everyone to know the bastard responsible for all of this. Former Secretary of State, Alan Berkoff. We shouldn't stick around here for much longer. They could be back any moment. This is Dr. Linda Marie. Goodbye."

End of ERROR.

President Alan Berkoff

Vice President ~~Eustace Toaden~~ [DECEASED]

Chief Researcher Dr. William Harrack

Chief Physician Dr. Linda Marie

Head of Security ~~James House~~ [DECEASED]

Security Force (20):

Roy Bant - ~~Joshua Black~~ [DECEASED] - ~~Robert Cansky~~ [DECEASED] - ~~Winston Castor~~ [DECEASED] - ~~Peter Corrad~~ [DECEASED] - ~~Lucille Desin~~ [DECEASED] - ~~Jonathan Dinlum~~ [DECEASED] - ~~Richard Farkass~~ [DECEASED] - ~~Jacob Faunt~~ [DECEASED] - ~~Aranai Fielding~~ [DECEASED] - ~~Kate Finn~~ [DECEASED] - John House - ~~Barney Keeling~~ [DECEASED] - ~~Roberta Kisk~~ [DECEASED] - Jane McVellion - ~~Joseph Nine~~ [DECEASED] - ~~Scott Samona~~ [DECEASED] - ~~Catherine Vilner~~ [DECEASED] - ~~Gordon Yackit~~ [DECEASED] - Zachary Zyz

Citizens (90):

Bing Abbot [DECEASED] - Ann Akai [DECEASED] - Rose Anderson [DECEASED] - Jacob Ardune [DECEASED] - Robert Beaner [DECEASED] - Sarah Barnes [DECEASED] - Cherry Beau [DECEASED] - Dylan Beecut [DECEASED] - Margaret Belcher [DECEASED] - Andrew Bigelow [DECEASED] - Alfonzo Bogardanzi [DECEASED] - Daniel Butler [DECEASED] - Marino Cantopus [DECEASED] - Booker Cooper [DECEASED] - John Dash - Jet Dashel [DECEASED] - Mark DeFrana [DECEASED] - Samuel Dunkard [DECEASED] - Barry Eldren [DECEASED] - Jeremy Finickle [DECEASED] - Candice Finnell [DECEASED] - Haiten Fish [DECEASED] - Henry Flagelmeier [DECEASED] - Maxwell Geck [DECEASED] - Dr. Phillip Genson [DECEASED] - Marta Girasol - Casey Goodwill [DECEASED] - Chandler Haal [DECEASED] - Ernest Handler [DECEASED] - Garrison Hartford - Alfred Hatton [DECEASED] - John Heegan [DECEASED] - Mario Henderson [DECEASED] - Nancy House - William House [DECEASED] - Conrad Jackman [DECEASED] - Vincent Jax [DECEASED] - Harry Jenkins [DECEASED] - Leyna Kase [DECEASED] - Martin Kievan [DECEASED] - Wanda Lamon [DECEASED] - King Liardi [DECEASED] - William Lovell [DECEASED] - Mary Lovell [DECEASED] - Geoffrey Lowell [DECEASED] - River Maple [DECEASED] - Oliver Markus [DECEASED] - Delegan McHarvan [DECEASED] - Diana Mint [DECEASED] - Gilbert Nose [DECEASED] - Mickey November [DECEASED] - Conor O'Reilly [DECEASED] - Patrick Peaskill [DECEASED] - Jim Penn [DECEASED] - Jonathan Peterson [DECEASED] - Angel Puer - Richard Reel [DECEASED] - Captain Rex - Doug Roberts [DECEASED] - Hank Rockell

[DECEASED] - Dishtowel Sacks - ~~Jillian Sampson~~ [DECEASED] - ~~Nadia Schwartz~~ [DECEASED] - ~~Argus Scott~~ [DECEASED] - ~~Jeremiah Shoostand~~ [DECEASED] - ~~Robert Simpson~~ [DECEASED] - ~~Howard Skittering~~ [DECEASED] - Jaime Slewdjack - Toby Smalls - ~~Harold Smidt~~ [DECEASED] - ~~Janet Smith~~ [DECEASED] - ~~Nicolas Smithson~~ [DECEASED] - ~~Meegan Spoon~~ [DECEASED] - ~~Sean Tilling~~ [DECEASED] - ~~Gary Tills~~ [DECEASED] - ~~Barnaby Tob~~ [DECEASED] - ~~Colin Vacett~~ [DECEASED] - ~~Tia Valentine~~ [DECEASED] - ~~Amelia Vanisha~~ [DECEASED] - ~~Anthony Weitson~~ [DECEASED] - ~~Hannah Welt~~ [DECEASED] - ~~Dean Wentell~~ [DECEASED] - ~~Theodore Weston~~ [DECEASED] - ~~Andrew Wicker~~ [DECEASED] - ~~Peach Williamson~~ [DECEASED] - ~~Dell Willis~~ [DECEASED] - Percy Winkle - ~~Denger Woof~~ [DECEASED] - ~~Laney Youth~~ [DECEASED] - ~~Johnson Zip~~ [DECEASED]

October 16, 2031

At dawn, the seventeen survivors of the bunker slept uneasily. While the rebels had found a relatively untouched area in the back of the residential to move to, the president and his associates remained in the parts of the mansion that still stood. Although the bunker had stabilized, the loose plates above them all groaned and creaked.

Dr. Linda Marie stirred slightly, awoken by the sound of faint crying. She sat up, rubbing the sleep out of her eyes. Looking around, she noticed the people around her were all still sleeping. As Dr. Marie's awareness increased, she scanned her surroundings.

Jaime Slewdjack was sitting up in a nearby alley, pressed against a house, hugging his legs. As he sobbed quietly, Dr. Marie silently stood up and walked into the alley. With his face buried in his knees, he didn't notice Dr. Marie at first. He slowly looked up as she sat down beside him.

"I'm sorry," he whispered. "I didn't mean to wake you up."

"It's okay. I haven't been sleeping much, anyways," she said softly. "Need to talk?"

"It's just... it's my nineteenth birthday," Jaime said.

"Oh," Dr. Marie replied. She paused, thinking. "Happy birthday."

Jaime sighed and buried his face in his knees again. Dr. Marie sat there silently. After a moment, he looked up at her again.

"I miss my parents," he said in a small voice.

"Once we get out, you'll see them again," Dr. Marie said, offering a small smile. He let out a small laugh and his face settled into a sad smile.

"I wish I could give them a hug right now," Jaime said.

"You really miss them," Dr. Marie said absentmindedly. Jaime nodded.

"We were always really close. Sure, we would argue sometimes, like every family. But we always made up by the end of the day," Jaime responded. Dr. Marie let out a single laugh.

"Guess you never went through your rebellious phase, huh?" Dr. Marie asked. Before Jaime could reply, a shuffling from outside the alley drew their attention. As they exited the narrow passage, the others were beginning to wake up. Captain Rex was already standing. He turned to look at Jaime and Dr. Marie, but remained silent. Soon, the entire group was conscious. As the others picked themselves off the ground, Dr. William Harrack marched up to Rex.

"I need to return to my lab," Harrack demanded.

"Will you shut up about that?" Percy Winkle snapped tiredly.

"I already told you, you're not leaving our sight," Rex said, staring down Harrack.

"I have multiple bacteria and viruses in my lab. I have to make sure that none of them have escaped or gotten into the air. Marie has said that my lab is still standing, so these diseases could not have been sterilized. They could be a serious threat if let unchecked," Harrack stated. Rex, listening silently, nodded.

"Fine. But you sure as hell aren't going alone," Rex said.

"I'll chaperone him," John House volunteered as he stood up. Nancy House's eyes immediately went wide, filling with tears.

"Please don't go," she begged, wrapping her arms around him. "I... I can't lose you. You're all I have left."

"I'll do it," Garrison Hartford interjected.

"Fine. Hartford goes." Rex turned to Garrison. "If something seems fishy, don't hesitate."

"Trust me, I won't," Garrison assured him. Harrack grunted.

"Not everything is a plot against you. If any of the diseases escaped, I would die, too," Harrack said.

"That's assuming you're even being honest," Jaime said accusatory, crossing his arms.

"Fine. Let's just all die together, then!" Harrack said futilely.

"Just go and get back here as quick as you can," Rex ordered tiredly. No one intervened, and soon Harrack and Garrison were on their way out of the group.

*   *   *

Roy Bant kicked the wall violently. With a gasp, his eyes flew open. He quickly sat up, panting heavily. His head rapidly darted from one location to another. As his panic subsided and his breathing returned to a normal, steady pace, he pushed himself to his feet. Dazed, he walked out of the large bathroom into the main hall. In another moment, he was walking towards the main foyer. Reaching it, Roy found Alan Berkoff leaning on the railing, staring down at the shattered crystal chandelier. A path had been swept from the stairs to the main door. Alan looked up as Roy approached.

"Officer Bant," Alan said formally.

"Berkoff," Roy grunted. Before he had a chance to say anything else, Angel Puer appeared from a door opposite the railing. Alan stood up straight and turned around.

"Did the gardens survive?" he asked quickly. Angel nodded. "Well, we won't starve to death, at least."

"So we just spend the rest of our lives rotting away down here?" Roy snapped. Alan opened his mouth to answer, but Angel stepped forward, in between the two men. She looked and pointed straight up at the ceiling. The two men followed her gaze. Large cracks spread throughout the entirety of the roof. "So we'll just be crushed to death when the ceiling finally gives?" Roy asked unsurely. Both men looked back down at Angel. She gave a single nod. Alan began laughing. His laughs increased in pitch and tone. Both Roy and Angel took a few steps away from him. As his laughing slowly faded down, he retained the semblance of sanity.

"If I'm going to die here, I'm going to make sure those fucking rebels go down, myself," Alan growled, a vicious smile growing larger on his face. Roy sighed.

"I can get on board with that," Roy said, frowning angrily. Angel took another step away from the two men. Roy suddenly began looking around. "Where's Chief McVellion?"

"Oh, she went out. Didn't say where or why, though," Alan replied. Roy nodded, absorbing the information.

*　　*　　*

"What's that smell?" Garrison Hartford asked as he and Dr. William Harrack cautiously entered Harrack's office.

"The ventilation system must be damaged," Harrack said to himself, ignoring Garrison and stepping further into the lab. Garrison glared angrily at Harrack's back. Harrack quickly checked one of the terminals. "At least the oxygen supply is still functional."

"Well, just check your shit so we can get out of here," Garrison ordered. "And *don't* try anything." Harrack paid Garrison no attention as he walked into the backroom. Garrison sighed and began poking around the front office.

Harrack investigated each glass container carefully. As he moved from shelf to shelf, he muttered softly to himself. He walked up to the shelf containing the dozens of jars of white powder, his back to the door. He raised his eyebrows slightly as he noticed not a single jar had fallen off of the shaky rack.

As he stared at the shelf, the gentle chime of the door opening sounded. Harrack had only enough time to turn around before a series of gunshots erupted in the front room. Harrack jumped back, knocking into the shelf, causing it to jerk back and all the jars to shift. One jar above his right shoulder didn't move with the shelf and slid off, falling towards the ground. Harrack spotted the falling jar and shot his arm out to grab it. His fingers closed around the tightly packed jar as it was centimeters above the ground. He straightened his back and looked down at the jar in his hand.

The door to the front room opened, and Harrack immediately looked up. Jane McVellion emerged, half of her jaw blown off. The door closed behind her. Harrack let out a slight sigh of relief. Jane, gun still in hand, raised it and pointed it right at him. Harrack had just enough time to realize what was happening as she pulled the trigger.

The bullet hit Harrack squarely in the chest, sending his body flying backwards. He crashed into the shelf, tipping it over. As the dozens of tightly packed glass jars of white phosphorus smashed into the floor, they shattered. A thick cloud of white powder soon filled the small, closed, unventilated room. Jane wildly swung her arms around as the cloud enveloped her. The pyrophoric compound quickly ignited, and the whole room transformed into a massive fireball. A low, animalistic scream emanated from Jane, undeniably one of pain as the allotrope was absorbed deeper and deeper into her skin. She was covered completely, not a single inch of skin left untouched by the blistering chemical. What was left of Jane collapsed against a wall, as the fire raged on.

*　　*　　*

"Should we go look for them?" Toby Smalls asked.

"It's been almost an hour," Zachary Zyz added.

"We shouldn't risk anymore people," Captain Rex answered.

"But what if something happened to them?" Toby asked, worried.

"Well, if something happened, I think it's safe to assume we won't be seeing Hartford again," Dr. Marie said. "I just hope that bastard Harrack gets what's coming to him."

"What if President Berkoff managed to kidnap Dr. Harrack back from us? We shouldn't stay here," Jaime Slewdjack said.

"He's right," Marta Girasol agreed.

"We should be looking for a way out of this bunker," John Dash said. "It's the only thing we can do that doesn't involve a one hundred percent chance of dying here."

"But *how* are we going to get out of here?! In case you haven't noticed, we're just a little bit trapped," DT Sacks snapped.

"Dash is right," Rex concurred. "And if there's even a chance Slewdjack is also right, then we can't stay here. Harrack knows where we are. And you can never underestimate a surprise attack."

"He has a point," John House said, pointing at DT. "How *do* we get out?"

"We could try the door," Marta suggested. There were a few sighs among the group.

"You really think we can move it?" Jaime asked honestly.

"We might not need to," Marta said. Eyes turned to her curiously. "The door is supposed to happen in the event of... well, what happened should have set it off." Marta turned to Dr. Linda Marie. "Did the door look like it had moved when you went to your office?"

"Aside from being pushed outwards, not really," Dr. Marie answered.

"Are you sure about this system?" John House asked.

"Yes," Percy Winkle said. The eyes shifted to him. "The government insisted on it. An emergency protocol. Special sensors were put in place to insure that in the event of a massive shift inside the bunker, the door would open up."

"Massive shift?" John House asked.

"Like an earthquake, I guess. But inside the bunker, not outside of it," Percy continued.

"How can it tell the difference between whether it happens inside or outside?" Nancy House asked.

"Is that really an issue right now?" Jaime asked.

"The explosion may have been big, but it didn't really shake up the place," DT said.

"No, but the falling radiation plates certainly were," Dash replied.

"It's also possible that when the High Rise went up in flames, some of the programming was tripped," Percy added.

"Yeah, because your *idiots* had no idea what the hell they were doing!" Marta yelled. "*En serio, look at this place!*"

"Like you could do any better," Percy scoffed, crossing his arms.

"I *could!*" Marta shouted. "This stuff was my fucking *job!*"

"Calm down!" Rex shouted. The crowd settled into uneasy quiet for a moment. "It doesn't matter how this happened. It doesn't appear the door moved, so we should start thinking of a backup plan."

"We need to at least *check* the door," Zyz said. "Every other options leads to us dying in days. Maybe weeks, at the most."

"I second that," Dash added. "It's our best chance."

"We can't just sit here and die," Dr. Marie said firmly.

"Then what do we do if we really are trapped in here?" DT asked skeptically.

"This does seem like a long shot. We should worry about Berkoff and his allies, first," John House said.

"If we can get out, we might not have to deal with them at all," Jaime said.

"What if they had the same idea as us?" Nancy asked nervously. Rex pulled a handgun out of the single duffle bag. He grabbed Nancy's hands and put the gun in them.

"Then you shoot," Rex said simply. Nancy stared up at him.

"Maybe they already got out!" Toby said hopefully, before Nancy had a chance to refuse the weapon.

"I doubt it, but it's certainly a possibility," Dash replied. Before another person could say something, a large rumbling caused the entire bunker to vibrate. The rebels looked up to see the steel plates shifting again.

"Run!" Rex yelled. There was no hesitation in the group. They took off through the residential area, heading for the large vault door barely visible beyond the rows of houses. They made it over halfway there before the next plate fell. It was followed by more, and soon the entire back of the residential area ceased to exist. The plates in the walls buckled, and the ceiling sank further. The bunker was collapsing again.

Alan Berkoff, Roy Bant, and Angel Puer stepped outside of the mansion and all looked up at the shifting ceiling. "Run!" Roy yelled. The three began sprinting towards the bunker vault.

The survivors barely outran the collapsing ceiling. Bursting out of the residential area, they raced toward the remains of the dining area. They jumped over rubble and debris, dashing through piles of soot and ash. Most of them feinted to the sides of the jagged shrapnel that used to be the security station, but a few jumped over it, running through the bones of the building.

Ceiling plates had stopped falling for the moment, however the tremors continued. The group followed the lead of Zyz and Percy around the left side of the plate that had swung into the door. They ran along the side of it, the vault door looming above them. As Zyz and Percy cleared the metal slab, Percy raised his finger while still running, pointing ahead. The vault door had been shoved a great distance from its track, leaving enough space in between where the vault would have opened from, and the metal plate it slid into.

Rays of sunshine shone through the crack. Percy and Zyz shouted an excited whoop. As they closed the distance, a large chunk of rock coating fell from above the entrance, crashing in front of it. The rock only raised up about three feet, and there was still plenty of sunshine still shining through above it. As the rest of the group cleared the plate, Zyz looked up, and saw more rocks slowly sliding downwards. Enough rocks to close of the entrance. As Zyz quickened his pace, a small figure jetted out from the other side of the fallen plate, almost immediately surpassing their speed. The long, golden hair fluttered behind her as she expertly dove through the shrinking escape.

Before Zyz even had time to think about what had just happened, Roy Bant stepped out from behind the other edge of the plate. Raising his assault rifle, he open fired into the group trailing Zyz and Percy. The bullets tore into John House. His body pitched forward, landing hard and sprawling out on the ground. Nancy stopped and screamed, raising the handgun Rex had given her. She aimed it at Roy and squeezed off a few shots, screaming constantly. None of the bullets landed anywhere near their mark, but Roy stepped behind the cover of the plate.

Zyz and Percy reached the exit, which was now less than six feet tall and shrinking. Zyz immediately climbed up on the fallen rock and wedged his body in between it and the rocks below. They stopped sliding, but Zyz's face contorted under the extreme strain. Percy quickly pulled himself onto the rock and hopped through.

"Help... me!" Zyz begged hoarsely as he struggled under the weight.

"Nothing personal!" Percy shouted as he disappeared from sight. Zyz let out a pained yell. Rex had slowed to a stop, wielding an assault rifle, as was Marta and Jaime. Rex raised his rifle and stared at the edge of the plate. Roy leaned around the corner, and Rex didn't hesitate to pull the trigger. Roy disappeared again, and Rex stopped. Marta also slowed to a stop about ten feet past Rex. Dash stopped and stood by her side. Toby, DT, and Jaime kept running for the exit. Dr. Marie skidded to a halt and ran back to Nancy, who was still standing where she had stopped and was now hysterically crying. Dr. Marie grabbed her arm and began dragging her to the exit. Nancy verbally protested, but her legs moved, regardless.

"Come on!" Zyz yelled painfully as Toby, DT, and Jaime slowed to a stop under the rock he was standing on.

"I'll cover you!" Jaime said, turning around and raising his gun.

"You first!" Toby yelled to DT, offering a smile. DT quickly crawled up on the rock and made his way through.

"Your turn!" Jaime shouted over his shoulder at Toby.

"Not until everyone else-" Before Toby could finish the thought, Jaime turned around and grabbed him, pushing him up onto the rock and shoving him through the exit. Zyz let out another yell as Dr. Marie dragged Nancy to the door. She still gripped the handgun, pointing it at the edge of the plate. With a grunt, Dr. Marie pushed Nancy through the exit.

Roy leaned out from cover again and fired. Rex and Marta returned fire, with Dash tugging on Marta's arm. The two began to strafe towards the exit and Marta continued firing. Roy disappeared again and Rex stared at the spot. After a moment, he began to also trot after Marta and Dash. But Roy leaned over again and fired. Rex stopped to return fire. Marta slowed down and fired her rifle, as well. Rex hit Roy's leg and he stumbled out of cover. Rex aimed at him and pulled the trigger, however the clip was empty. Before he had a chance to reload, Roy fired again. The bullets slammed into Rex's chest and he staggered back, dropped the gun. Despite the wounds, Captain Rex was still standing. Roy fired again, this time toppling Rex.

Dr. Marie stared at the battle for a moment longer, then turned and pulled herself through the exit. Jaime raised his gun and squeezed off a few shots. "Kid!" Zyz called out. Jaime turned around to look at him. Jaime dropped the gun and dragged himself onto the rock and jumped through, into the sunlight.

Roy watched Rex fall for only a moment, before shifting his attention to Marta. He raised his gun. Before he could fire, a bullet impacted his shoulder. He jerked back as more bullets flew into him. Marta lowered the gun as Roy fell forward, his rifle skittering away. With Roy dead, Marta and Dash turned and sprinted at full speed to the exit.

"Look out!" Before Zyz had barely even finished saying the words, a low gunshot rang out. A bullet whizzed past Marta and Dash. It slammed into Zyz's side, who let out one final yell before his strength gave out. The rocks he had been holding up swiftly crushed him completely. Marta and Dash slowly turned around. Alan Berkoff stood at the edge of the plate, a smoking gun in his hand and a smile on his face. He began to slowly approach them, gun still held in front of him.

Marta raised her rifle again, but Alan was quicker. The bullet hit Marta in the center of her chest. She dropped the gun and Dash quickly wrapped his arms around her, tears forming in his eyes. She turned to him, then smiled and wrapped her arms around him. Dash stared helplessly into her eyes as his own filled with tears. Marta smiled at him.

"It's okay," she said as they slowly sunk to the ground together, holding each other tight. "It doesn't even hurt." The two laid down on the ground together. She widened her smile and closed her eyes. *"Ustedes fueron los mejores amigos he tenido."* The tears flowed down his cheeks and Dash choked and cried audibly. As the crying intensified, he grabbed Marta's assault rifle. Before he had time to lift it, he felt a gun barrel pressed against the back of his head. He tightened his grip on the weapon, but made no further action.

"You're him, aren't you?" Alan asked. Dash didn't respond. "The psychologist's son?" Alan continued.

"How do you know about my mother?" Dash asked, his body going rigid as chills ran up his spine.

"You *are* him. I found your file, but there were no pictures. No information at all, aside from who your mother was," Alan said. "How old are you?" Dash refused to answer. "You're probably too young to remember." Alan said. His tone was serious, almost sad. Tears continued across Dash's face. "You've at least *heard* of the Dash-Fickward experiment of 2004. When the government declassified it. You *have* to remember Albert Fickward."

"My mother's old partner?" Dash choked out. "He's dead. Stabbed to death years back. What does he have to do with this?" Dash suddenly whipped around, the assault rifle held firmly in his hands. He pressed the barrel against Alan's chest. "No. I should kill you right now," Dash said, barely above a whisper. Alan showed no reaction, his face blank yet sad. Alan didn't readjust his pistol.

"I was only nine at the time," Alan continued softly, seemingly oblivious of Dash. "The experiment was torture. It was supposed to test what happens when people have their freedoms taken away over a long period of time. But it was just an excuse to torture children."

"I don't believe you," Dash said through gritted teeth. His hands shook slightly, but he kept his gun trained on Alan.

"It was torture!" Alan yelled, as tears started to roll down his own face. "We were just kids, the five of us. At first, they let us do whatever we wanted. No rules. Then Dash and Fickward started putting limits in place. It started small; we had to eat our vegetables, couldn't jump on the beds, etcetera. But as long as we followed those rules, we could do anything else that we wanted. It wasn't anything too bad. We managed for a while. But things got worse. Much worse," Alan said, tears streaking further down his face. "The rules became so much stricter. And the punishments..."

"You're lying!" Dash screamed. "This is a trick!" As soon as the words escaped his mouth his expression changed.

"Why would I lie to you at this point?" Alan said feebly. Dash looked at the blocked off exit.

"I don't know," he admitted weakly. He returned his attention to Alan. "Maybe this is all just a game to you." The tears on his face slowed down, but were still present.

"I have nothing to gain from doing this. We've never even met before," Alan said plainly. "But you should know what kind of person your mother is. The rules became stricter, the punishments got worse. One of the others kids, she was only two when the experiment started. But she was a fighter. No matter what, she always fought back. I remember they studied her heavily. Apparently, they had never seen someone so young be so resistant. But they still tortured her anyways. She always talked back, though. One day, they got tired of her mouthing off, so they just... *cut* out her tongue. In front of the rest of us. They didn't even make a big deal about it. They did it so *casually*." Alan paused before letting out a small, sad laugh. "She ended up killing Fickward. By then, I already had some political power, so I pulled strings and managed to get her out of trouble. Even got her into a CIA training program. She took to it immediately. She was a natural assassin. She was so good, I pulled even more strings to make sure she got into the bunker."

"The woman that escaped?" Dash asked. His hands shook harder and the tears were still present, but diminishing. More steel plates slipped out of the ceiling, and the last of the residential area was expunged from existence.

"I'm getting ahead of myself. One day, Dr. Dash... your mother, told us it was the last day of the experiment. But it wasn't. We were taken back to our houses. All of us were so happy to finally be getting away. I think it was the first time we had smiled in years. But our parents were gone. Dr. Dash and Dr. Fickward were waiting in my house. The other kids said the same thing. I guess they took us home one at a time. Fickward told me that my parents thought I was dead. Then your mother..." Alan paused. He was beginning to hurt again. But he continued on, nevertheless.

"Yeah, I get the idea. She did something bad," Dash said, his face contorting angrily. "I know you hate my mother, and I'm sorry she did this, but this doesn't involve me." Dash glanced briefly down at Marta, still and smiling. Dash let out an angry yell and turned back to Alan. "And it doesn't excuse what you've done!" Dash yelled. Alan ignored him.

"That night was the first time we were sent to isolation. No matter what had happened in the years before, we always had each other. After this, they just started putting us in complete isolation for weeks at a time. We were eventually allowed to see each other again after more than a month, but the punishments only got worse from there. We had started planning an escape for years, but we could never get far with the plans. Turns out one of us was telling the scientists. We stopped talking about our plans around him. Heh, we basically isolated him, ourselves. I was eighteen when we finally had our chance. It started out with four of us. One of the girls backed out at the last minute. The rest of us managed to escape, though not without killing a few of the scientists. After we escaped, we split up but tried to keep in touch. The day after we escaped, the other man we escaped with committed suicide.

"It took a few years before she hunted down Dr. Fickward and killed him outside the building he and your mother kept us captive for so many years. I already told you what happened after that. The two we had left down I never heard from again. After I got out, I wanted answers. I wanted to know why this had been done to us. Once I found out it was a government operation, I got into politics. I couldn't access those restricted files at first. So I kept moving up the ladder, getting higher and higher positions. Finally, I managed to access the files. I discovered that the experiment was to see if it was possible to make someone completely submissive. But by then, the reasons why hardly mattered anymore.

"Once I entered politics, I realized what it felt like to hold all of the power. I thought I knew why your mother had done what she had. Why they had wanted complete control over us. So I *kept* climbing the political ladder, gaining more and more power for myself, more and more control. And it felt *so good*. I couldn't stop. I had to get more power, more control. Then everything went wrong, and I was *disgraced*. When I heard about Winkle Enterprises buying the bunker project from the government, I knew it was my best bet to get the power back. The control back. To have that feeling again. It took some begging I'm not proud of, but he agreed. But now the power is gone again. All gone. And there's nothing left for me. In here or out there."

Alan let go of his gun, the tiny weapon dropping to the floor. He collapsed to his knees in front of Dash and looked up at him. "I failed!" he cried out. His tears were replaced for a second by fury. "Despite everything, my biggest regret is not killing your bitch of a mother! I can only hope that Roberta finds her and finishes this for us." The tears quickly began pouring from his eyes. "But at least I'm taking *you* with me! My torturer's son..." Dash, his own face twisted with anger and sorrow, pressing the assault rifle against Alan's forehead. Alan stared into Dash's face. "Go on. Finish what your mother started all those years ago." Alan growled.

As the two men stared at each other, tears flowing freely from their eyes, filled with anger, the last lights popped out of existence as the last of the bunker's ceiling gave out. The remaining steel plates fell to the ground, as did the mountain above it. With that, the bunker ceased to exist.

*   *   *

DT Sacks, Toby Smalls, Dr. Linda Maria, and Jaime Slewdjack slowly walked down the path leading up to what had once been the bunker. Nancy House knelt down in front of the now-closed off exit, both of her hands wrapped tightly around the handgun Captain Rex had given her. The wind produced by the Winkle Enterprises helicopter as it flew away from the bunker had just died down. Angel Puer and Percy Winkle were nowhere to be seen. The small group of four took a few steps down the dirt path leading to the bunker. They held up their hands to shield their eyes from the low evening sun. Jaime pointed at something in the distance. The others squinted, looking just to the right of the sun. A distant city was on the horizon.

"Well, I guess we better start walking," Toby added, with only a small hint of optimism. Before anyone had a chance to say something else, they all heard a gunshot behind them. The group jumped and snapped around. They had just enough time to see Nancy's body tumble backwards. Dr. Marie and Jaime rushed over to her. Dr. Marie and Jaime knelt down next to Nancy. Dr. Marie sighed in disappointment and stood up. Her hand still loosely held the gun.

"Let's hope that's the last life the bunker claims," Jaime said sadly. DT and Toby slowly approached from behind.

"She just..." DT froze. "We made it out. After all that, why would she... she just..."

"I guess she just couldn't handle losing all of her brothers so close together," Dr. Marie said faintly. A strong wind suddenly blew against their backs, whipping their clothes around. The small group slowly turned around. In the far distance, where the city had once stood, a small but unmistakably shaped cloud now climbed higher into the sky. The four stood frozen, staring silently. DT closed one eye and held his thumb up in front of the explosion. Dr. Marie was the first to speak. "I forgot about that."